BULLY

BULLY

Does Anyone Deserve to Die?

A True Story of
High School Revenge

JIM SCHUTZE

WILLIAM MORROW AND COMPANY, INC.
NEW YORK

It is the policy of William Morrow and Company, Inc., and its imprints and affiliates, recognizing the importance of preserving what has been written, to print the books we publish on acid-free paper, and we exert our best efforts to that end.

Library of Congress Cataloging-in-Publication Data

Schutze, Jim.
    Bully : does anyone deserve to die?   a true story of high school revenge / Jim Schutze.
        p.   cm.
    ISBN 0-688-13517-X
    1. Juvenile homicide—Florida—Fort Lauderdale—Case studies.
2. Murder—Florida—Fort Lauderdale. I. Title.
HV9067.H6S38   1997
364.1'523'0975935—dc20   96-9060
                                                                    CIP

Printed in the United States of America

First Edition

1   2   3   4   5   6   7   8   9   10

BOOK DESIGN BY ROGER GREINER

FOR MY NEPHEW, CHRIS RYAN, WHO HAS MADE HIS OWN WAY

WITHOUT THE WORK AND ADVICE OF Doris Cooper, my editor at William Morrow, this would have been a different book (not as good). Tom Colgan, my editor at Avon Books, was quick and on the money as ever. Janet Manus, literary agent, and Justin Manus, attorney, are among the smartest, best, most enjoyable people on the planet. My wife, Mariana, and my son, Will, have learned to live with my absences. I don't know how they stand it.

THIS IS A TRUE STORY.

BULLY

CHAPTER ONE

THE WALL ABOVE LISA'S BED WAS A SHRINE TO YEARNING. PICTURES OF fantastic studs in G-strings with their chests and haunches greased and flexed languished next to glossy photographs of gorgeous, wet-lipped women in everything from fashion magazine poses to soft-porn stretches. These Olympian men and women steamed up the wall above her bed in a crazy jumble, and above them she had taped a headline cut from a newspaper that said, WHAT WOMEN WANT.

Lisa spent hours here, naked on this bed, alone in the muggy little townhome across the street from the Embassy Lakes Mall in the new community of Pembroke Pines. Her father was long gone. Her mother came home tired every day.

In the quiet house Lisa's yearning was pure. She lay on her bed looking up, and her heart burned.

The thing she wanted was a boy. She had never had a boyfriend, never a date, never a boy who even teased her at school. She felt fat and ugly. When she lay on the bed and looked up at her pictures, she imagined what it would be like to have a boy love her and make her completely happy all the time. Once in a while she shyly told her mother how she felt, but mainly she kept it all to herself. It was her secret religion, lying here and looking up, dreaming and wanting, waiting for something to come true.

As Lisa saw it, and as she told her mother, the story of the last few months had been the story of a miracle. In the back of her mind she had made a deal with her desires: If the boy turned out to be less than handsome, less than perfect, she would accept him and cherish him with all her heart and body. The men on the wall were gods to worship, but she would settle for a regular guy to love.

Then when her dreams finally came true, when her boy did finally appear, he was not a regular guy at all but a statue, a hunk, a man more beautiful and sexy and perfect than even the pictures above her bed.

She had to pinch herself to make sure she was not just crazy with lonely wanting. Her heart raced every waking moment. When she was with her mother she talked a mile a minute and every word was about him. It was as if she could not get her breath.

Years of wanting and worshiping had been answered. Her savior and prince had stepped down off the wall of her dreams and into her waking life. He was nineteen years old. His name was Marty Puccio. And he wanted her.

LISA'S NEIGHBORHOOD LAY A BLOCK OFF SHERIDAN STREET, JUST ON the border between the part of Broward County that is no longer really new and the part that still is.

Sheridan Street, a major thoroughfare, runs east and west across Broward County, from the coast to the Everglades, much of it through the city of Hollywood, just south of Fort Lauderdale proper.

Everything old in Broward—Fort Lauderdale itself and Hollywood—is jammed up against the beaches. Everything new is west, inland.

The western end of Sheridan Street is far inland, in the area the suburban kids call "Out West." It's an undeveloped expanse of sawgrass marsh, where alligators roar in the dark of night and roosting egrets sleep with one eye open. It's so far west that it's out beyond the newest developments, in a rural area of fish camps and shanties—still the old Florida. Caravans of eighteen-wheelers loaded with sugar beets come rumbling up Highway 27 from Homestead, and at a cross-roads kiosk truck drivers sit on stools at ten P.M. swilling presweet-ened iced tea and eating crispy deep-fried catfish beneath a Seminole thatched roof.

When you go east, Sheridan Street quickly becomes multilaned and passes through the expensive new suburbs. Developers here have choked the marshes dry by dredging out little lakes and piling up the muck. Brand-new communities have golf courses at their hearts and moats and gated walls all around them.

The street, loud with night traffic, moves on through the older sub-divisions—yesterday's dreams of the good life, where the houses are much smaller and already down-at-the-heels. As it passes through the community of Hollywood, Sheridan Street brushes against seedy apartment buildings and neon-lighted commercial strips, then bursts out over a causeway carrying it above the Intracoastal Waterway—a gray brackish canal behind the long barrier island that shields the mainland from the sea.

At North Beach Park, where Sheridan Street ends, a narrow board-walk meanders off from the parking area to a dark grove of sea-grape shrubs, with fat earlike leaves that rise up from the sand on thick undulating stems. In the night breeze, the sea grapes weave and whis-per like gentle dinosaurs, careful not to step on the sea oats and sea lavender and prickly pear cactus at their feet.

In the ocean moonlight, the beach is a glowing limb of sand writh-ing off into distant constellations of hotel lights. Palm leaves clatter, and out in the deep lie anchored ships whose bobbing cabin lights wait for cargoes to arrive and for berths to open the next day in Port Everglades.

A young couple are surfing on the night waves. They are long and thin, almost naked, glowing in the moonlight. Their wet bodies are as smooth and sinuous, as perfect and pearly as the beach itself. They never laugh, only smile, lighted from within by the pleasure of this place and their own bodies.

3

It is as if Sheridan Street has risen in the swamps of The Beginning, passed through a time of gated communities and shopping malls, of pawnshops and table dancing, and now, separated from the Earth by the Intracoastal Waterway, it has arrived in God's Very Heaven.

JUST BEFORE CHRISTMAS, 1992, LISA AND HER BEST FRIEND, ALI, went to a little swim shop at the back of a new mall on Sheridan just inland from the causeway. Ali knew how badly Lisa wanted a boy, and she kept telling her she would have to get out on the beach and work for it. But Lisa, who was always overweight, was self-conscious.

It was easy for Ali. She was small, had perfect legs, and an ass and breasts straight from a fashion magazine. Her very cute face was set off by twinkling blue-green eyes. She had an ideal beach body. On top of that, her hair was great. Lisa's dull red mane always felt lumpy and oily, no matter what she did with it.

But Ali insisted it was all a question of ''attitude.'' She took Lisa by the hand and dragged her to a shop behind the Publix grocery store in the old beach community of Dania. She made her try on swimsuit after swimsuit until finally, to Lisa's amazement, they came up with a one-piece number in which Lisa actually felt almost good.

When they left the shop with the suit in hand, Lisa was optimistic. Ali always had that effect on her, on everybody. At seventeen, Ali was a year younger than Lisa, but she seemed much older. She was tough and crazy. She cared about her friends. And she had money. The suit cost almost one hundred dollars, but Ali paid for it as if it were a burger and fries.

They walked past the mail store and the video store, to the Publix at other end of the mall. Brand-new and salmon-tinted, the mall was a southwestern-style stucco structure with a roof of orange plastic tile. They went inside the Publix and walked to the back to the deli department to order submarine sandwiches.

What they saw behind the counter made Lisa suddenly feel so awkward she couldn't even order. Standing there in form-fitting polo shirts and shiny black shorts were two of the most perfect hunks Lisa had ever seen in her life. They were the kind of boys who usually didn't act as if girls like Lisa were even alive.

Neither one was tall. Bobby Kent was five feet eight inches, and Marty Puccio was five feet seven. But they were built. Their necks were thick and ropy, biceps massive, forearms slablike; and their pecs poked out from beneath their shirts. Both had pretty eyes—Marty's hazel-brown and Bobby's darker—and lovely faces. They were perfect, in a rippling, video-game, Stallone sort of way. They were male sex partners beyond all imagining. Lisa was afraid to look at them or open her mouth.

Ali dissed them, daring them to get mad. She ordered a sub, and when they started making up her sandwich, she said, "Hey, aren't you supposed to put on those cellophane gloves? I don't know where those hands have been."

They took the bait and made a lot of sex jokes about where their hands might have been. Bobby looked at the swim-shop bag Lisa was holding and said, "Got a new swimsuit?"

Lisa turned slowly and looked at him, as if to say, "Who, me?" She looked at Ali. Ali gave her shoulders a jerky, impatient little shrug, telling Lisa to talk.

"Yeah," Lisa said woodenly.

Bobby, the darker one, put his hand on Marty's shoulder and shoved him hard, so that Marty stumbled. "Hey asshole," Bobby said. "Ask the bitches to meet us at North Beach. We'll party."

Marty smirked and shrugged. He proposed that they meet across the causeway at North Beach Park in three hours when the boys would get off work. Ali shrugged nonchalantly and said, "Maybe."

"Great, babe," Bobby said. "You can be my date. My friend here is into the full-figured gals."

"Hey, fuck you, Bobby," Marty said.

Ali said, "How about my sub, asshole?"

Lisa and Ali rode around in Ali's bright-red Mustang "five-point-o" all afternoon, cruising from mall to mall, buying CDs, a dress, some tennis shoes.

"Those guys are fine," Ali said.

"He was making fun of me," Lisa said.

"No shit, Lisa. He was just being an asshole. Guys are all like that. The other guy, the smaller one . . ."

"The cute blond one . . ."

"Yeah. Marty. He still acted like he wanted to meet you tonight at North Beach."

"Meet you, you mean."

"No, his buddy's already got dibs on me. His buddy's the boss. Bobby. Hey, you heard what Bobby said. His friend likes big girls. So. You're big. So good."

"I've never been around a boy who was that much of a hunk," Lisa said.

"So cool. So we'll meet them, we'll check 'em out."

At the hour set for their rendezvous at North Beach Park, the sun was just beginning to dip down behind the city. Beyond the beach, the ocean moved up and down in deep swells beneath a blue-gray shadow, crashing white against the sand. Even though the sun was dying, the air was still hot from the day.

Lisa was wearing her new swimsuit and a new pair of slaps on her feet. She was almost numb with apprehension about what they would think of her or say when they saw her in a swimsuit, especially the mean one, Bobby.

But when the boys arrived in the parking area, they seemed barely to notice the girls. They nodded hello. They were wearing baggy surfer-style swimsuits. They unloaded short-boards from the top of Bobby's car and hurried straight into the water. Lisa and Ali followed them.

Bobby threw his board to the sand and ripped his T-shirt from his torso, revealing a hard quivering webwork of muscle and sinew. He turned toward the girls, did a fist in palm, chest-flexing pose for them, grinning maniacally. Then he snatched up the board and surged into the sea with it under one arm, smashing into the whitecaps with his shins, chin thrust forward. A few yards into the surf, he opened his mouth and emitted a long, high-pitched, thrilling scream.

Marty took off his own T-shirt. His body was even more dramatically defined and developed than Bobby's, but Marty did not perform any flexing poses for the girls. Instead he left his board on the sand and went down to the water to check the temperature with his arm. Then he reached into the hip pocket of his swim trunks, extricated a stick of board wax, and gave his short-board a light going-over.

Marty slipped out into the water quietly and in moments was paddling out. The waves were good only close to the beach, where long powerful swells humped up and broke on the shallow sand. Farther out at the sandbars, where the really good waves sometimes broke, the seas were slow and smooth.

Bobby was up first, sliding across the front of a halfway decent wave, wobbly on one leg, shrieking, then falling backward as the board shot out from under him. For an instant all the girls could see was his right foot sticking straight up out of the water, tethered to the board. Then his head popped up, shaking right to left to snap away the salt water. He honked his nose with both hands and let out a loud "OOooo-ee!"

Then the girls looked up and saw Marty. He was upright on his board on a strong wave, hands barely out from his sides. The board was screaming in toward the beach beneath him, but Marty looked almost as if he were standing still—floating, a hawk at the edge of the wind. He rode the wave in almost to the beach and then stepped off running. He trotted up gracefully onto the sand and came to a stop a few feet in front of Lisa.

"You guys want to go to a party?" he asked her.

Lisa started to look around for Ali, but Ali had turned her back and was watching Bobby swim out again.

"Sure," Lisa said, her face and voice devoid of expression.

"Great," Marty said. He smiled. "Let me see if there's one more wave out there for me. Then we'll go have some fun."

Lisa watched him as he strode back out gracefully into the blue-green surf. The falling sun behind her lighted his back and made it glow. Her heart was churning, full and racing. She wanted to run after him and ask, "Did you smile at me? Did you mean to smile at me? Do you know how beautiful you are?"

Ali nudged her from behind.

"Cute butt," she said. "He's sweet. The other one's an asshole."

Lisa said nothing for a long time, while she watched Marty paddle out to where Bobby was waiting.

"So what do you want to do?" Ali asked. "Go party with them?"

"What?" Lisa said. She turned and grinned at Ali. "Fucking right."

The girls hid behind a parked van and changed back into street clothes while the boys rode the last waves of the evening. Bobby suggested they move Ali's Mustang to the street outside the park so it wouldn't get locked in when the gates were closed. He said they would drive to the party in Bobby's car. Lisa said quickly that it would be okay to do it that way.

Ali didn't think much of Bobby's car—a ten-year-old black Camaro with heavily tinted windows. She wondered why he was so proud of it.

Bobby and Marty sat in front. Bobby turned south on A1A, the beach road, and drove through a mile or more of low-rise hotels, condos, and strip shopping centers. As soon as they were under way, Marty rolled an enormous "fatty"—a marijuana cigar of the Jamaican proportions preferred by surfers—and passed the dope to the girls, both of whom sucked eagerly on it and passed it back to the front seat.

Bobby pulled into a seedy shopping strip and told Marty to go into the liquor store and buy tequila. When Marty balked at spending his own money, Bobby snatched his ear in a fist and twisted it hard.

"What's that, boy? What did you say, boy? Did you say, 'Yessir, boss, I sure will buy that booze for you now, boss'?"

Marty tried to laugh, then shouted with pain. The moment Bobby released him, he exploded from the car and went to buy the liquor.

Ali looked at Bobby in the rearview mirror.

"You're an asshole," she said.

"Ohhh baby!" Bobby said. "You KNOW what I like!"

Ali snickered.

"C'mon up here, babe," Bobby said. "I'm startin' to dig you a little bit."

Ali got out and joined him in the front. When Marty came out with the booze, he got in back with Lisa.

They drove farther south on the beach road, swigging tequila from the bottle on empty stomachs, sucking down deep drafts of marijuana. Bobby put a rap tape in the stereo, and suddenly Ali realized what it was about his car that Bobby thought was so hot. The snarling, scraping, thumping sound of the Geto Boys exploded from several thousand dollars' worth of amplifier and speakers, including a bass speaker behind the backseat that made the whole car vibrate.

It was dark now. They passed the Hollywood Beach Resort, a huge, deep-pink, Moroccan wedding cake of a place, built in the twenties when the Hollywood beach was a scene from an F. Scott Fitzgerald story. Bobby's Camaro rocked and humped along down A1A, past boarded-up marinas and convenience stores, jumping in and out of lanes, leaping and bumping to the screaming lyrics of the Geto Boys.

The drunker and higher Lisa got, the more exquisite Marty appeared, as if he were not real—a fantasy partner from the wall of photos above her bed.

Bobby turned left off A1A on Azalea, a narrow street leading to the Harry Berry Memorial Park. He stopped near a parking lot next to another stretch of beautiful public beach like North Beach Park.

Bobby reached over, grabbed Ali by the shoulders, and pulled her head toward his lap. "Welcome to the party, bitch!" he shouted.

She pushed him back sharply, then moved toward him and started to have sex with him at her own pace.

At the moment Bobby first touched Lisa, she froze, unable to breathe. She had tried a million times before to imagine what it would feel like for a boy to put his hands on her, but she had never once imagined it would be like this, his fingertips hot and tingling on her skin. He slipped both hands up under her T-shirt and caressed her breasts, then pushed a hand down deep inside the elastic waistband of her pants, reaching so quickly for her crotch that he made her jump, and caught her in his fist as she jerked toward him. He lowered his face to hers and shoved his rigid tongue through her lips.

She moaned, reached up with her hands and took his shoulders, pulling him to her. Only when he fell against her did she realize he had already squirmed out of his shorts and was pulling down on hers, ready to enter her. She gave herself to him in joy and ecstasy, all to the shattering rhythm of the rap tape.

When she was back at home on her bed, staring up at the pictures on the wall above her, Lisa knew that her life had changed forever. He was too wonderful. It was all too romantic.

Once having tasted Marty, Lisa knew she would have to die before she could give him up, before she ever could allow him to leave her bed. Losing him, returning to the realm of unrequited longing would be far worse than death itself. Her love for him was instant and savage. It was life and death. He was her hunk. She was his bitch.

FOR A BOAT CAPTAIN WITH NO BOAT, TOM HILDEBRAND HAD STRUCK it rich. Most of the men who called in response to his ads in the Fort Lauderdale *Sun-Sentinel* were over forty years old—lawyers, doctors, air-traffic controllers, men of position and income. His clients lived in the posh new golf-course subdivisions popping up all over South Florida, where once there had been only sawgrass and alligators.

Tom Hildebrand's customers didn't just want sex, like drunken suburban johns cruising for street hookers in family cars. Tom, an unemployed charter captain with a certain savoir faire, had staked out a much more specialized, hotter, more intense territory for himself than that. A boat captain in Florida sees rich men when they don't care, knows about their dreams of heaven.

His market was accessible only to men with a serious amount of money, men who wanted to make a very nice present to themselves. The men who called Tom Hildebrand knew exactly what they wanted. They wanted it very badly.

Girls. Not women. Girls. Very young girls. The upper limit was sixteen or seventeen. Some of them asked for fourteen-year-olds, and one even asked for a nine-year-old.

And they didn't want slum girls. They wanted nice girls, pretty girls from good neighborhoods—girls who could have been their own daughters.

Tom Hildebrand gave them what they wanted.

It was cheap, only $150 for an hour. Not bad, when you considered that businessmen in the expensive hotels up and down the Florida coast might be paying $2,000 and up for sex with a woman in her upper twenties or even in her thirties.

He didn't have a problem getting the kind of girl his clients demanded. Some girls were passed on to him by another pimp in the Fort Lauderdale/Miami area—a man who rode his girls harder, shoved crack cocaine down them, and put them in dangerous situations. Sometimes that pimp got tired of a whiny kid who wasn't up to speed, so he gave her to Tom, whose business ran to a softer trade. After a girl had been around the block a few times with the tough pimp, she was glad to get to Tom.

But most of Tom's girls just showed up on their own, fresh as daisies, brought to him by other girls. He normally ran a stable of a dozen or so really young ones.

At fifty-nine, he was tall, slender, with piercing blue eyes, an aquiline nose, and hair just beginning to thin. He wasn't bad-looking. The girls trusted him. He took 40 percent of their money. He kept his own money in a cabinet in his house trailer, and he often stored their money for them there, too. Some of the girls earned as much as $3,000 a week.

He kept marijuana for them in a Healthy Choice frozen dinner box in his freezer, but he did not force crack or LSD on the girls. When he recruited a new girl, he took Polaroid pictures of her naked, performing different sex acts, in order to have something to show the clients.

He said to the girls, "I do not force you to see these guys. If you want to work, you have to call me, because, otherwise, I am not going to budge to come after you."

The girls came to him from the best high schools, out in the new subdivision areas where most of his clients lived. One girl, Morgan, fourteen years old, had been made a "peer counselor" to Caitlin, an even younger girl in her middle school. Morgan had mentioned to Caitlin one day that she was having trouble making enough money as a baby-sitter to keep up with things—the clothes, the CDs, the bathing suits and sunglasses you need for the beach. She told Caitlin she wished she could find baby-sitting clients who would pay more. Caitlin sent her to Tom.

Later that same week, Tom called the principal's office at Cooper City High School where Morgan was a student and said he was a member of her family and needed her to come home. Tom had given her a pager, which he beeped with a prearranged code. Following his instructions, she left school and went to wait for him at the Embassy Lakes Mall. When she got to the appointed place, another girl was also waiting there—a girl named Alysson, whom she knew from Cooper City High.

Tom picked them up and drove them west on Sheridan Street to the Weston area, an expanse of brand-new subdivisions. He dropped the girls off at a huge new house. A man in his early thirties answered the doorbell and ushered them into an enormous living room. He stripped, and so did both girls. They both kissed him and allowed him to fondle them, and then Alysson performed fellatio on him.

He paid them $100 each. They paged Tom and punched in all zeros—the signal that they were done. He showed up minutes later and picked them up. After paying Tom his $40, each girl had $60. They felt rich.

Morgan became one of Tom's hardest-working whores. As he did with all of his girls, Tom supplied her with condoms and gave her instructions on how to deal with unusual requests. Because she was so young, this involved actually telling her how to do certain things.

Tom's ads ran in the *Sun-Sentinel* for about two years before the police had time to get to him. He had been using the Holiday Inn in Oakland Park for a lot of his assignations. Oakland Park is an aging community just north of Fort Lauderdale, squeezed between the U.S.

95 Expressway and Highway 1. It's a place to go to find mid-priced tourist hotels and motels.

Sergeant Glenn Osani, forty, a thirteen-year veteran of the Oakland Park police force, set up the sting. The two officers assigned to carry it out were Detective Brian Rupp, twenty-six, who had been on the force six years, and Detective Forrest "Jay" Santalucia, who had been with the department five years.

Rupp and Santalucia both had received many official commendations, and there were letters and memos in their files showing that the department believed they were fine officers. But Rupp had been in trouble a year earlier for allowing a prostitute to go too far in performing fellatio on him before he made an arrest.

It's a difficult area, especially when officers are left on the vice squad for years at a time. The policy is always that they must not complete a sex act with a prostitute they are about to arrest—that is, they must not allow themselves to reach orgasm. But they do have to go down the road a certain distance, so that a defense attorney will not be able to argue that the whole thing was a misunderstanding. Experienced hookers who suspect anything will try to get a police officer to climax quickly in order to spoil the arrest.

The police setting up the Hildebrand sting worked with an "informant"—a civilian who made the original call on the ad in the *Sun-Sentinel*—in order to have an official citizen complaint in the file.

Tom Hildebrand drove to meet his new "client" and allowed him to sort through the hundreds of photographs of naked girls in the trunk. The man chose two students at Cooper City High.

On the afternoon of May 25, 1993, with the cooperation of the Oakland Park Holiday Inn, Sergeant Osani took over two adjoining rooms at the hotel and set up a video camera in one, so that the camera would be able to shoot and record sound through a hole in the wall.

Tom Hildebrand picked the girls up at the mall. He was driving a rented green Toyota. He drove them to the Holiday Inn, gave them the room number, and dropped them off.

One was a beautiful Asian-American girl, sixteen. The other was a gorgeous Italian American, seventeen, with flowing red hair to her shoulders, exquisite features at the very moment of ripeness, and a throaty laugh beyond her years. Both were expensively dressed.

The informant and Detective Santalucia greeted them inside the room. The girls asked the two men for $300 in advance, and the men handed it to them in $50 bills. Then the girls stripped off their clothes and led the men to the two beds. In one bed, one of the girls performed fellatio on the informant. In the other, the other girl fondled Detective Santalucia's penis with her hands.

When the fondling had gone on for several minutes, Detective Santalucia began to grow anxious—worried it was going too far. In the next room, Sergeant Osani and Detective Rupp were watching through the lens of the video camera.

Santalucia turned to the camera hole and gave the prearranged signal that he wanted Osani to send in Rupp for the arrest. But the seconds continued to tick by, and Santalucia became even more agitated. He gave the signal again. He finally muttered out loud, "Come in."

But instead of arriving to make the arrest, Brian Rupp came to the door posing as a friend of the men inside. He asked the girls if they would perform fellatio on him, too. The girls agreed. He didn't have enough cash to pay the $150 fee, but the girls agreed to take $102— all he had.

While the camera hummed in the next room, one of the girls performed fellatio on Rupp. She stayed with it for thirty-six seconds— the amount of time it took him to climax in her mouth.

Then Rupp and Santalucia arrested the girls.

While the girls were being secured, two other members of the five-man vice team closed in on Tom Hildebrand, who was lurking in the parking lot in his green rental car. Hildebrand admitted immediately that he was waiting for two girls to come down from a room in the hotel where he had sent them. He opened the trunk of his car, allowing the officers access to the hundreds of Polaroid snapshots inside.

The story made headlines for a few days after the arrests. Hildebrand was touted as the Fagin of a child-prostitution ring. Television made a great deal of the fact the girls were from middle- and upper-middle-class backgrounds. Within a week, the story had faded from the local news.

There were no stories in the newspaper asking, "How Could This Happen?" There was no profile of the lives of the middle- and upper-middle-class kids in Cooper City High School. This story of arrests in a teenage prostitution story passed in and out of local consciousness as if it were a story about a routine drug bust or a bad accident on the freeway.

It was not until some weeks later, when a young assistant state attorney for Broward County was viewing the evidence tape, that a fist slammed down on a jumbled desk sending coffee slopping and papers flying, and an angry shout of "Shit!" brought silence to a crowded office on the fourth floor of the Broward County Courthouse in downtown Fort Lauderdale.

"He came in her mouth!"

Others hurried to the desk and shouldered their way in to view the tape as it scrolled back and forth over the pertinent moment. "Look at this shit! Right here. The dumb son of a bitch comes!"

The young prosecutor decided to call for an investigation of the conduct of the arresting officers, especially in light of the age of the girls.

Word of the investigation and the tape leaked out. WSVN Channel 7 and WPLG Channel 10 went to court to demand copies of the tape for their evening newscasts. Suddenly the Hildebrand story, which had been routine almost to the point of tedium, became the day's titillating topic of conversation on every morning-drive talk show and around every office coffee klatch in Fort Lauderdale.

Earlier that year, Fort Lauderdale Vice-Mayor Doug Danziger had been videotaped by a surveillance team while having sex with a prostitute named Kathy Willets. That tape had been shown over and over again on Fort Lauderdale television stations. It was explicit and constituted a socially acceptable form of public pornography. The tape created a tremendous buzz in the community.

Now there was a palpable shiver of excitement at the prospect of a new tape, one that would show beautiful teenage girls from new suburban neighborhoods performing fellatio on young cops.

In the political background, Oakland Park Mayor Raymond Finn was just in the process of winding down a long personal battle with the Oakland Park Police Department, in which he had succeeded in getting former police chief William Strachan to resign. When word leaked to the press that the State Attorney's Office was investigating the conduct of the arresting officers in the teenage hooker case, Finn told reporters he was pleased that the investigation was taking place.

The other story getting a lot of mention on the radio call-in shows was the existence of a little black book seized from the trunk of Hildebrand's car. The book was said to contain the names and phone numbers of hundreds of male clients, and as is common in such cases, there was excited speculation about just whose name might be found in the book.

In the end, Rupp and Santalucia were fired, and Osani, their supervisor, was demoted to patrolman. (Rupp and Santalucia appealed their firings through an administrative process. They came to a settlement with the city, and after a year off the force, they were both restored to the Oakland Park Police Department as ''road officers'' on regular patrol.)

A judge ruled that the TV stations could have the portions of the videotape in which the officers and the girls, all fully clothed, were exchanging money for sex, but the stations could not have or show the portions where everyone was naked and having sex. The names in the little black book were never divulged.

Hildebrand, who was facing a life sentence, struck a deal with the state and pleaded guilty in exchange for a twenty-year sentence. The girls were not charged. Instead, they were allowed to cooperate with the police in an investigation of the teenage hooker ring, aimed mainly at finding out what other girls were involved so that parents could be notified.

One of the girls whose naked photographs were found in Tom Hildebrand's trunk—a girl who eventually developed a friendship with

Brian Rupp—was Ali Willis. She was a friend of Eileen Traynor, the Asian-American girl Rupp arrested at the Oakland Park Holiday Inn.

TWELVE YEARS EARLIER, WHEN ALICE JEAN SLAY AND LISA CONNELLY were five, their families sent them to St. Bernadette Catholic School in Davie, a fairly new suburban community built around the Rolling Hills Golf Club southwest of Fort Lauderdale.

The girls were darling in checked dresses, matching hair bows, and patent leather pumps, squeezing each other's hands and squinting up with fake smiles for a family Polaroid. Their parents were still together. In her second-grade workbook, Lisa drew a crayon picture of herself, her mother, and her father, all with upturned smiling mouths, standing next to a little house. Next to it, probably copying a teacher's instructions, she wrote, "How good it is to belong to a family."

A short time later, Lisa's father left them, and by the time they were both twelve years old, Ali's father was gone, too. Lisa grew somber and stubborn; Ali was impulsive and wild.

Ali's mother, Virginia Slay, did what she could. Ali had begun having sexual intercourse at age twelve, at the very first inkling of her sexual development. She stayed out all night and came home stinking of spilled wine coolers and adolescent sex.

She ran away when she was fourteen. She was mad at her mother. On October 26, 1989, Ali and a girlfriend phoned Nigel Rambaran, eighteen, and Diego Molina, nineteen—boyfriends they had been forbidden to see again—and asked them to take them to Miami. There, in the craziness of the city, they could all be punks and live free forever.

Instead, the young men took the two fourteen-year-old girls out west to a place where a new freeway overpass was being built over an empty expanse of sawgrass. One young man was a member of a gang called the Zulus, and the other belonged to a gang called Foke Um. It was evening, and the site was abandoned. The men parked their 1984 Plymouth Duster on the shoulder, where it would be out of sight from the freeway.

Then they held knives to the girls' faces and told them they were going to play Truth or Dare. They would ask the questions. The girls would try to answer. Each time the men deemed that the girls had given the wrong answer, the girls would have to take off an item of clothing.

It ended with the men raping the girls many times in the backseat of the Duster and on a blanket thrown down on the bare dirt next to the shoulder.

When the men were sated, they allowed the girls to put their clothes back on. They pushed them into the back of the car. They were driving toward the sea when they stopped for gas in Hialeah, just north of Miami. Someone saw the two young girls, battered and frightened, cringing in the backseat of the Duster, and called the police.

The first police officer on the scene was sufficiently apprehensive of Rambaran and Molina that he called for backup before confronting them. Eventually the two men pleaded guilty to sexual battery with a deadly weapon, armed kidnapping, assault, and robbery. A judge gave an eighteen-year sentence to Rambaran and twelve years to Molina.

But even after they were sentenced, Ali's terror grew. She was afraid they would escape. She was afraid the Zulus or Foke Um would come after her seeking vengeance. She was afraid of things she could not express.

Her mother, Virginia Slay, then fifty-five, was remarried to a man fourteen years her senior, owner of a successful electrical contracting business for which she worked. She was concerned about Ali but could not stay at home with her.

When Ali told her she was afraid to go back to the ninth grade at South Broward High School, Virginia allowed her to transfer to Cooper City High. But when Virginia took her there to begin her first day of school, Ali became hysterical and refused to get out of the car. Virginia took her home.

The next morning Ali went back and managed to complete a day of classes at Cooper City High, but she showed up at school only infrequently in the weeks ahead, and a month later she dropped out, having completed her formal education.

Virginia and her husband, Albert, came home one night and heard hammering from Ali's bedroom. They found Ali feverishly nailing blankets over the windows.

"Ali, why are you doing that?" Virginia asked.

"I don't want anyone to know what bedroom I sleep in."

When Virginia and her husband tried to get Ali to stop nailing blankets to the wall, she began screaming at them that they did not realize the danger she was in, they were in. Albert approached her to take the hammer from her hand, and she threw it at him, then picked up chairs and tables and threw them at him and her mother, screaming hysterically until finally she collapsed into a trembling mass in the corner.

Her mother sent Ali to a therapist, but no one told the therapist Ali had been raped. Ali sat sullenly through the sessions and failed to mention the rape herself. She never discussed the rape with her mother, who decided that what her daughter really wanted to do was forget it.

It was a harsh way for a fourteen-year-old to learn a lesson. But the lesson was clear. Throw yourself sexually at violent older men, and eventually you will come to pain.

The way of the world around her was to forget pain by putting it out of sight and memory, by seeking comfort instead. Virginia and Albert did everything they knew how. There was nothing they were unwilling to do. They only wondered what it might be. But instead of being helped, Ali grew tougher and more careless with her life.

When Albert sold his business two years after the rape, the Slays also sold their home in Broward County and moved 150 miles up the Florida coast to Palm Bay, on the "space coast" near Cape Canaveral. They bought a large new home on a gently curving street in a "planned community"—all with the express intent of moving Ali away from her demons in Broward County.

But Ali kept going back. She was famous among her friends back in Broward for having a lot of cash and being willing to spend it freely. She loved going back and being the center of attention.

Her mother tried to compete with whatever it was that was tugging Ali away. Virginia gave Ali credit cards and paid the bills, even when Ali used them to hire stretch limousines and drive her friends up and down the Florida coast. She gave her the expensive Mustang 5.0, which only made it easier for her to get back to Broward.

Ali, who was unencumbered by school or job, found that her friends back in the Fort Lauderdale area were unable to break away quite as easily as she. They all still lived with their parents, even those who were working, and several of them were still in school.

One time in early 1993 when Ali showed up in Fort Lauderdale and began scouting around for a place to stay, she found that none of her friends' parents were willing to put her up. A girlfriend said, "Why don't you go stay with my friend Tom? He's old, but he's cool."

Tom Hildebrand was delighted with the blond gamine at his door. Before the night had passed, he had added pictures of her to the collection in his trunk, and he immediately began sending her out on tricks.

"Tell this man," he said, "that you are fourteen years old. See what he does."

Ali drove the red Mustang to a large home at the edge of the Cooper Colony Golf and Country Club in Cooper City. She walked into the open garage, as Tom had instructed her, and pushed a button next to the door inside. A bald pudgy man in his early fifties, in a rumpled open-collared white dress shirt, suit trousers, and stocking feet, opened the door, a glass of white wine in one hand. He peered at her through the tops of his bifocals, expressionless. He looked her up and down, appraisingly.

"How old are you?" he asked.

"I'm only fourteen," she said.

He turned and put the glass of wine on a shelf behind him. He turned back to face her, then solemnly took a half step backward, dropped to his knees, stretched his hands out before him, and pressed his forehead against the floor in a salaam.

He rose, took her by one hand, and ushered her down a long narrow corridor and through a series of rooms to a huge bedroom decorated in chintz and fluffy pillows. Ali saw silver-framed photos of his wife and children on the top of a small black-lacquered writing desk.

He took her shoulders in his hands, turned her so that her back was to the bed, and gave her a reverent peck on the cheek. Then, as he fumbled to remove her blouse, skirt, and underwear, he began repeating over and over again: "You are so beautiful. You are such a pretty little girl. So little. So pretty. So young. I like girls who are very young. How old are you?"

"I am fourteen."

"You are so pretty. Such a pretty little girl. Just fourteen. I like little girls. Young pretty little girls like you. I like them very much."

When she was naked, he fell to his knees again before her and began smothering her with kisses. When he was done with her, he paid her $150 and said that he would ask Tom for her again.

IN 1993, WHILE ALI WAS TURNING TRICKS FOR TOM HILDEBRAND, HER mother persuaded her to enroll in the Palm Bay Christian Academy to try to complete high school. There she met Michael Willis, nineteen, by whom she became pregnant. She married him and gave birth to their child, a girl whom they named Brandy.

For a short time, Michael Willis came to live with Ali in her parents' home, but he and Ali were divorced only a few months after their marriage. Ali gave the baby to her mother to care for, while she continued to prowl the Florida coast in her hot red car, turning tricks for Tom Hildebrand and charging clothes for her friends on her mother's credit cards.

The one thing Ali's mother could say in her defense: She never left home—not permanently. When she did disappear, it was only for a day or so, usually to visit Lisa.

*   *   *

THE MORNING AFTER SHE MET MARTY PUCCIO AND HAD SEX WITH him at the beach, Lisa told her mother about him. Maureen Connelly, a burly woman who didn't wear makeup, was hurrying to get ready for her job as a dispatcher for her brother's garbage-hauling business.

"I've got a new boyfriend, Ma," Lisa said in the kitchen of their townhome.

Maureen stopped moving, looked closely at her daughter, then said, "A new what?"

"A new boyfriend."

Lisa, still in robe and slippers, was getting herself a cup of coffee.

"A boyfriend! What kind?"

Lisa blushed, then shrugged and giggled. "A hunk."

"Really?"

"Yeah."

Lisa told her mother how they had met at the Publix, how the boys had asked them out, how they had rendezvoused at North Beach and then driven together in the car.

"You gotta meet him," Lisa said.

Maureen came over and gave Lisa a huge hug. When Maureen looked at Lisa, she always saw the irresistible, bubbly little hazel-eyed girl who had so delighted both parents by her arrival on Earth. Maureen had always called Lisa "my miracle baby," because she was born at the end of a long string of miscarriages and heartache.

When Lisa came, it seemed as if everything in life was going to be all right from that point forward. Nothing else mattered. At the urging of her husband, who was well paid as a steamfitter, Maureen left her job as a Green Stamps clerk and came home to be a full-time mother to this delightful little gift of God.

Maureen's family came down en masse to Florida from the Bronx in the 1940s, the way immigrant families used to come to New York and

Boston from Ireland. Florida was a land of unlimited opportunity and heavenly beauty, and all the many members of Maureen's extended Roman Catholic clan had come down to claim their place in it. Now that Maureen was a mother, at long last, her own place seemed secure.

But it was not. Maureen's husband left when their daughter was just approaching adolescence. Maureen went back to work, dispatching and sometimes driving trucks in the family business. Her husband stayed in close touch with Lisa for a few years after the split-up, but when he established his own new family, his contacts with Lisa grew less frequent. Maureen tried to explain to Lisa it didn't mean her father loved her less.

"Honey," she said, "it's just how things are sometimes."

Lisa had always done well in school—A's and B's without even trying hard. When she was in the eleventh grade, her father rewarded her by sending her money for a car. She bought a 1986 Firebird, a used car but in good shape and fast. Her mother paid for gas and insurance.

By this time many of her girlfriends in Cooper City High were skipping school to do things like turn tricks for Tom Hildebrand, including Ali, who had not yet moved to Palm Bay. Lisa was not a candidate for Hildebrand's troupe, but once she got the Firebird, she tried to keep up with the others by skipping school and running with them in her new car.

In a surprisingly short time after getting the car, Lisa had amassed enough unexcused absences to be suspended from school. Her mother was pained but not shocked when Lisa announced she was not going back. She had found a job as a counter clerk at DryClean USA in Embassy Lakes Mall, right across Sheridan Street. She didn't need school, she said. She was dropping out of the eleventh grade.

A short time later, Lisa wrecked the Firebird. The car was insured only for liability. Neither she nor her mother had remotely enough money to pay for the repairs. So now she was a high school dropout with a minimum-wage job at a dry-cleaning establishment, no car, and no one in the world to love her but her devoted mother.

The good-looking girls she had gone to high school with, many of whom were also dropping out, liked Lisa. She had a headstrong, daring streak that made her interesting. She was like her mother: Nobody pushed her around.

Sometimes Maureen looked at her darling girl, especially when Ali or some of the other cute girls were around, the ones the boys thought were hot, and she saw in her what the boys probably saw—not the delicious miracle-baby of her mother's eye, but a fat girl, grown sullen in her shyness and disappointment, sloppily dressed, round-shouldered, testy.

Sometimes when she was cleaning house, Maureen would pause at the foot of Lisa's bed and gaze up at her bizarre collection of sexy photos on the wall. Maureen could feel the yearning and the desperate teenage loneliness painted there, and it brought silent tears to her eyes. She yearned for a boyfriend for her daughter—just once. Just one boy. What could it hurt? Maureen decided privately she would wait and see whether this fair prince whom Lisa had met at the Publix in Dania was actually going to stick around.

Then, in the weeks after Lisa's announcement, Maureen saw that Lisa was spending a great deal of time with the boy. Lisa was alive, lit up from deep within. When she talked to her mother about this boy, her eyes gleamed like the most beautiful gems ever dug from the heart of the planet. In Maureen's ear, her daughter's wonderfully happy voice was a song, and her laugh was the thrill of life itself. Maureen prayed devoutly that the boy would be good.

Lisa brought him home finally, and Maureen was genuinely astonished. He really was a hunk, like the naked muscle-men on Lisa's wall. In the boy's physical presence, Maureen looked in her daughter's face and saw frantic, panting devotion.

Marty seemed a little sullen to Maureen. His eyes didn't meet hers when she spoke to him. He did not feel compelled to say hello or good-bye. She had determined, through questioning, that he came from a good Italian Catholic family. He certainly didn't have the good manners the nuns used to teach.

But Lisa was in a state of transport. She could speak and think of nothing but Marty. His looks, his likes, his skill as a surfer—"He was a sponsored surfer, Ma. He almost got sent to Cape Hatteras. For the championships."

Lisa even acquired a pager so that Marty could reach her whenever he wished. Maureen paid for it.

One night, when she could get a word in edgewise, Maureen said, "Lisa, I never knew it was possible to be so much in love."

Lisa looked up at her mother, drew in a long aching breath, and hunched her shoulders, rocking. Maureen bit her tongue and hoped for the best.

Then, about a month into the relationship, Maureen was pulling things from a hall closet and overheard Lisa in her room talking to Marty on the telephone. She heard Lisa say, "Don't ever hit me again."

As if an alarm bell had gone off over her head, Maureen stood up straight, threw down her armload of linens, pushed into Lisa's room, took her by the shoulder, and whirled her around. Lisa's face was black-and-blue and swollen from one side of her nose to her cheekbone.

Maureen snatched the phone from Lisa.

"Did you hit my daughter?" she shouted into the receiver.

There was no answer.

"Did you hit my daughter, yes or no? Is that a hard question for you, Marty?"

A cold angry voice on the other end said: "The only thing I can say to you lady is, you're a pig and so is your daughter."

When Maureen slammed down the phone, she whirled and saw Lisa throwing clothes into a carry-on bag.

"What are you doing, Lisa?"

"I'm going to stay with him. His parents are away for a week."

"Lisa!"

"He wants me."

Lisa bulled her way past her mother and walked out through the front door. Maureen ran to the door and saw Lisa climbing into a girlfriend's car.

"What about your job?" she shouted as the car pulled away.

"I'm going to quit!" Lisa shouted back. "I just want to be with Marty, Ma."

CHAPTER TWO

THE HOLLYWOOD HILLS SUBDIVISION, FOUR MILES IN FROM THE COAST, was still fairly new in the mid-1970s when the Puccios moved there. The terrain is perfectly flat. The place names in the area date from an era when Florida was seriously competing with Southern California to become home to the film industry.

The houses in Hollywood Hills are one-story stucco structures with two or three bedrooms, a "Florida room" or screened porch on the back, and a small swimming pool in a small backyard. In the seventies, South Broward High School in Hollywood and Hollywood Hills Elementary School, just a few blocks from the Puccio home, had reputations as the best schools in Broward County. Owning a home in Hollywood Hills, Florida, at that time, was about as good as it got for a middle-income American family. Some would have said, then, that it was as good as it got for a middle-class family anywhere in the world.

It seems unlikely anyone would say that now about any part of Broward County. Fort Lauderdale police say the average price of a handgun among middle-school students in Broward County, ages thirteen to fifteen, is the same as the price of a cocaine rock—about ten dollars. A fourteen-year-old middle-school student in Oakland Park told a reporter for the Fort Lauderdale *Sun-Sentinel* that you don't even have to pay for a gun if you join a gang—you get one free with your membership.

IN 1993, BROWARD SCHOOL OFFICIALS SEIZED EIGHTY-EIGHT WEAPONS from middle-school students, including eight guns. An eighth-grade student shot and killed a friend in his bedroom. A fourteen-year-old Lauderhill boy shot and killed his mother and aunt with a Colt .45 he had taken from his cousin. School officials seized a gun from one boy when his panicked mother called the school to report her own pistol was missing.

But then again, if places like Lauderhill and Hollywood Hills have gone sour since the seventies, the question remains, what other American middle-class havens have not? In 1994 Harvard University's School of Public Health published figures showing that 60 percent of students nationwide in grades six through twelve knew where they could go to get a gun quickly, and 39 percent knew or were close to someone who had been killed or wounded by gunfire.

Two decades before, when the Puccio family moved into Hollywood Hills, none of that—not the guns, not the gangs, not the violence, not any of it—was remotely a part of middle-class reality, there or anywhere. Veronica and Martin Puccio, Sr., were confident they were doing the very best they knew how for their three sons, of whom Martin junior was the middle child.

Martin senior was a long-time salesman for a film production company in Miami, a "post-production" house that provided studio facilities to moviemakers, where they could put the polishing touches on their work. A tall slender man with a mustache and a distinguished bearing, he was good at what he did.

His wife, Veronica, a tall stunning blonde with a penchant for pink, worked part-time as a receptionist for a doctor, but her main occupation in life was motherhood. Someone once asked her what she hoped for, what she wanted in life.

"Babies," she said quickly. "Family."

She put in long hours and logged miles beyond counting hauling her boys to all of the activities, lessons, and avenues of improvement Broward County could offer—church, karate, music, soccer, baseball, swim team, theater group. Whatever was there, whatever the other kids were doing, she saw to it that her boys did all of it, too.

The family attended church and Sunday school regularly. Religion, worship, prayer, moral instruction were important parts of life in the Puccio household.

Veronica took Marty with her to her charismatic Catholic singing group, and he often walked around the house afterward singing the up-beat Christian songs to himself.

Veronica felt music should be an important part of her children's lives. She bought them plastic toy instruments to play each Christmas, but none of them ever took formal lessons.

The Puccios were gardeners, and they exulted in South Florida's long tropical growing season. The circular driveway in front of their house on West 42nd Avenue was obscured from the street by lush exotic plants and shrubs.

Martin and Veronica Puccio did not separate or get divorced or abandon each other or their children. They stayed together, loved each other, supported their children, and made their home the center of their lives. Marty was a special part of the family. They called him ''Loverbug.''

Five years after the Puccios moved in at the south end of the block, a family of Iranian immigrants, the Kents, moved in at the north end. Fred and Farah Kent (originally Khayam) had come to America and Florida in search of freedom and economic opportunity. Educated people, they did well quickly. Fred put himself through the rigorous training and licensing procedure required of stockbrokers and was soon doing good business in his field.

The Kents quickly shed all but the faintest trace of their accents—they could have been taken for immigrants from Michigan or Pennsylvania as easily as from Iran—and adopted the dress, social style, and social ambition of Americans.

Like the Puccios down the block, the Kents ferried their son,

Bobby, and his older sister, Laila, to piano lessons, dance, karate—the rituals of a middle-class childhood. They insisted that Bobby address adults as "sir" and "ma'am"; that he speak when spoken to and always defer to his elders. Fred and Farah Kent talked to their children often about the importance of education, hard work, and commerce—how any kid who was willing to work and willing to take risks in business could become whatever he dreamed of being. This was America.

The Kent children were exuberant, buoyant. Two years after he joined the same class Marty Puccio attended at Hollywood Hills Elementary, Bobby was voted "king" of his class in a mock election. As he would be for the rest of his brief life, Bobby was already a leader—a kid whom other kids liked and looked up to.

Far from being jealous of the new kid on the block, Marty was drawn to him. They seemed almost instantly bonded at the hip—two little boys, one blond, one dark, both handsome and healthy, running and playing together so inseparably on the block that the neighbors began calling them the "Siamese twins."

They rode bikes and skateboards, played ball, teased girls. They explored vacant lots, brought home frogs and snakes, and took a huge, rollicking, little-boy delight in scaring girls and grown-ups with their finds.

Bobby was the hearty one—the instigator. As they matured and entered middle school together, Bobby was growing into the larger of the pair. Neither was tall, but Bobby was naturally muscular, while Marty was thin as a rail.

Marty enjoyed Superman capes, hats, and plastic swords long after Bobby had become too cool for dress-up. In all of their activities, the preparing of a proper costume beforehand was almost more important to Marty than the activity itself. He stopped wearing capes only when Bobby began to call him "queer" and even beat him up for wearing them.

And yet it was Marty who became the champion of their pursuits. His slight, wiry build allowed him a balance, grace, and quickness that Bobby did not possess.

Marty was so good on a skateboard that older boys used to invite him to come skateboarding with them at the malls, in downtown Fort Lauderdale, and at the beach—a thing almost unheard-of in the age-stratified world of suburban boy culture. Both Marty and Bobby were quick to get involved in surfing.

Surfing is in some ways a natural out-growth of skateboarding for preadolescent boys growing up near the sea. But there is a difference. If skateboarding is a pastime, surfing is a way of life.

Innovation and style in the sport of surfing still come from Southern California, where the waves are bigger, the season longer, the traditions deeper. By the time surfer culture gets to Florida, it is sometimes a bit of a jumble. The kids on the beach in Florida tend to embrace all of the anti-establishment elements of surfing enthusiastically, but the culture of surfing itself is, for them, derivative—a thing they get from ads, magazines, TV and movies, rather than inventing it themselves.

The end result, socially at least, is pretty much the same. They skip school whenever the waves are good. Many ardent surfers wind up dropping out entirely.

By the seventh grade, Marty was already a very accomplished surfer, accepted by older surfers at the beach as the ''grommet''—the little kid who gets to join the older surfing gang.

His father spoke proudly to friends and associates of Marty's accomplishments as a surfer. So did all of his uncles. For the adoring middle-aged adults watching Marty from the beach, this was the fruition of the dreams that had drawn them all down here in the first place.

In the north, in the world they had left behind, this business of beautiful sun-burnished young people riding on roaring waves like gods on chariots was something you saw in Elvis movies. Now, here, this boy, their own flesh and blood, was actually living the dream. Marty's skill was a point of family pride in the extended Puccio clan.

*   *   *

THERE WAS NOTHING ROMANTIC OR EXCITING ABOUT SURFING FOR Fred Kent. It was a game for children to play at the beach. Riding a board on top of the waves? What was that? Fun? Perhaps. But so what? The most complicated thought process it involved was "Wheee!"

In Fred's view, there was something irritatingly passive and flat about Marty Puccio. There was no fire, no ambition eating his gut. Not even nibbling.

Fred Kent lived and died on the stock market every day. He made cold calls. He took risks. He fought hard for his money. Life was good, but life was serious. He knew he was not going to leave his son enough money to make a difference. All he could leave him was what he could teach him. He wanted to be sure Bobby knew how important it was to have ambition and guts, to be brave and indomitable.

Marty was a polite boy, but in a rote, trained, almost sullen way that one assumed lasted only as long as it took for the nearest adult to turn his back. By teaching Bobby manners—real manners—Fred hoped to teach him to engage adults, take a position, have presence, a part to play in the real world.

Clearly the place where Marty lived—really lived, in his own heart and soul—was entirely within the world of kids. Only among other kids did Marty show any real animation. The only time he ever seemed excited about accomplishing anything was when he was engaged in childish pursuits—skateboarding, surfing, fiddling with new computer games.

Fred Kent didn't trust Marty. He didn't want him to be his only son's closest friend on Earth.

THE PUCCIOS, MEANWHILE, WERE HEARING THEIR OWN VERSION OF things at the other end of the block. They were treated to none of the quiet passivity that Fred Kent found so irritating in their son. Instead, behind closed doors and in his own home, Marty grew nervous and dissatisfied as he approached adolescence.

He wouldn't tell his family what was upsetting him. He began saying that he wanted to move away, that he wished the family could find a house in another neighborhood. But he never said why, and the Puccios never pressed hard enough to find out.

Marty's surfer friends knew right away. Bobby showed up at the beach with Marty, dressed identically, a matching short-board under his arm. Bobby expected to surf with the same group of older boys who surfed with Marty. Many of them were already school dropouts who had acquired full-time sponsors among the shops or businesses in the Lauderdale area.

From his very earliest days on a board, Marty was a thing of wonder. As in gymnastics, there is a moment in surfing life when a very young quick body may be ideally married to the sport. Marty didn't simply ride waves—he soared.

In the seventh grade, Marty Puccio weighed 90 pounds, while the average competitive surfer weighed at least 150. His weight allowed him to stay up longer on the waves. At only five feet six inches tall, he had a lower center of gravity than many of the older boys. Years of skateboarding had given him great legs, able to kick and nudge the board wherever he wanted it to go or move.

Bobby, however, was clunky on a board—a little too heavy, a little too slow. The older boys at the beach put up with Bobby because he was Marty's best friend and Marty obviously couldn't keep him away. But they only put up with him. They didn't respect him as a surfer, and that translated to disliking him.

Bobby sensed it, and he resented it. In the *neighborhood,* he was the boss. Marty was his sidekick. That was how it had always been.

One day at the beach, in view of the older boys, Bobby told Marty to go back to a concession stand and buy him something to eat. When Marty asked for money, Bobby told him to pay for it himself. Marty refused, and Bobby hit him in the face, hard enough to send blood sheeting down from his nose. The other boys intervened, ready to beat Bobby to a pulp, but Marty waved them away.

Marty stripped off his shirt, wadded it up, and pressed it to his nose. Then he trotted off to buy Bobby his food.

But while Marty was at the concession stand, one of the older surfers started in on Bobby: "Hey, Kent. You're a total asshole."

Bobby stiffened and said, "What are you gonna do about it?"

"How about I kick a new hole in your butt?"

Now all of the older surfers had gathered around Bobby.

Another surfer said, "Just leave, Kent. Go home. Get off the beach."

By the time Marty got back with the food, Bobby was gone. Most of the older boys had returned to the surf, but one of them had stayed behind.

"Why do you hang with Kent?" he asked. "Nobody likes him. He drags you down. You don't need that asshole."

"I know," Marty said. "But he and I have been best friends since we were real little kids."

It was dark outside on the block when his surfing friends dropped Marty off in front of his house. Marty retrieved his board, said good-bye, and watched the car pull away. He turned slowly, looked up and down the block warily, and then started up the circular driveway toward the front door. The surfers stopped their car at the corner and watched.

Bobby stepped out from behind a tall flowering shrub at the other end of the driveway.

"Hey, man," Bobby said.

"Hey."

"I need to talk to you."

"Leave me alone, Bobby. I'm wiped. All I want is to go in and . . ."

Bobby stepped up to him quickly and grabbed him by an elbow. "I need to talk to you, I said."

Marty dropped his board on the driveway and allowed Bobby to steer him out to the sidewalk, where they would be obscured from the windows of the house by the garden plantings.

"I just wanted to say I'm sorry, man," Bobby said.

"O.K. I know it, man."

Bobby slipped his arm up around Marty's neck and looked deeply into his eyes. "We're best friends, right?"

Marty was looking down at his feet. "Yeah. Of course."

Bobby pulled him closer, until their foreheads were touching. "I'm sorry," he murmured.

"O.K.," Marty whispered softly.

Marty went into the house and disappeared into his room without a word to his parents. Bobby walked down the block to his own house.

The older boys in the car pulled away and drove toward Sheridan Street.

"Hey, what are they, man, queers?" one said.

"Who the fuck knows?"

By the time the boys were ready for the eighth grade, both sets of parents were ready for them to attend separate schools, even though the two households had never discussed the issue with each other. The Kents were delighted when they learned that Marty was going to transfer to Nova Middle School in nearby Davie—a small town that had become an engulfed suburb during the seventies. The Kents kept their son in the middle school nearer home, and the boys seemed to go their separate ways.

Even though they saw each other in the neighborhood and still spent time at each other's house, the distance afforded by going to different schools seemed to help. Marty was less anxious and surly around the house. Bobby buckled down to his studies and began doing much better in school.

Advancement from middle school to high school presented Marty with a new dilemma, however. The high school associated with Nova Middle School, Nova High, did not begin classes until 10:00 A.M. That meant it was not possible to finish classes and get out of school before 3:30 or 4:00 P.M. The best waves at the beach were almost always dead that late in the afternoon. In order to go to school and still get in some good surfing every day, you needed to start your classes at least by 9:00 A.M., preferably by 8:00 A.M. It was possible to do that at South Broward, and South Broward was where Bobby Kent went to school.

The decision was easy for Marty. He had to surf. He joined a group of surfers who made the trek from Nova to South Broward, part of a migration of surfers to South Broward that took place every year from all over the city.

When he got to South Broward High, Marty found the tables had turned somewhat since the days when Bobby had tried to tag along with him to the beach. Bobby Kent was something of a figure in the hallways of South Broward High School.

He was good-looking. He had already started pumping himself up by lifting weights. He was a good student. And he was gregarious. Wherever Bobby Kent went in the hallways of South Broward High, a group of kids gathered around him, many of them good-looking girls, all having a great time.

Marty, on the other hand, was one of the surfers who had transferred into South Broward so they could get out of school early and hike to the beach. There was a tangible division between the serious students who wanted to go on to college and the surfers. What had been so cool in middle school was beginning to look like loser-city in high school.

But Bobby flew to Marty and took him under his wing. They were back together, thicker than ever, and now Bobby was more clearly than ever the one in charge.

It had been a long while since Marty and Bobby had kept really close and constant company. Both boys had changed.

For one thing, Bobby had developed an interest in pornography. Marty was taken aback the first time Bobby showed him his collection of magazines and books dealing with both heterosexual and homosexual sex. When the two of them looked at the pictures of gay men having sex, they made a great show of being disgusted, laughing hoarsely, and calling the pictures every kind of gross name they could think of.

Marty sometimes was revolted, not so much by the sexual aspect of what was going on in the pictures and videos as by the cruelty, the obvious overtones of brutality, torture, and compulsion—the fact that some of the people whose pictures had been taken, especially young children, looked as if they were being forced to perform at gunpoint.

But those were the ones Bobby loved. The more savage and raw, the louder his guffaws. If Marty complained that the fare was too grotesque to look at, Bobby would get behind him, throw one arm around his neck, grab a handful of hair in the other, and lie there on top of him, yanking his head back and forcing him to watch.

Marty, ever the surfer, had developed a major appetite for marijuana—the good, powerful stuff that could get you really whacked on a few drags. The money his parents gave him every week as an allowance was more than enough to keep him in dope.

When the two of them were waiting at the corner every morning for the bus to South Broward High, Marty fired up a big fat joint and insisted that Bobby join him. Bobby, who intended to get some learning done at school, resisted a little but usually gave in.

At school, they were joined at the hip, always together, but now with Bobby in the lead and Marty as the faithful and deferential sidekick. They still found great joy in scaring people and grossing them out, as they had when they were little boys, but now their glee derived from a postadolescent fascination with things sexual and eliminative.

At the end of the day, when they were back on the block where they had grown up together, Bobby usually wheedled Marty to come look at his pornography with him. Marty acted as if he didn't want to, but he almost always gave in.

Bobby encouraged Marty to join him at the YMCA, where he had been pumping iron and building up his body for the last couple of years. Marty had grown self-conscious about being slight. His build might have been great for surfing, and it might have been all right in middle school, but the look in high school was bulk—big muscles, big chest and neck, big arms, huge thighs, tight butt.

Marty said he wasn't sure he was up to doing the work.

"Marty, you just do what I do."

"What?"

"Steroids."

"Oh, shit, man, you do that stuff? I can't believe it, man. That shit'll mess you up."

"No way. Not if you do it right. You know why people say that shit? Because they're jealous. Steroids just make you more of a man. More macho. Bigger balls."

Marty started lifting weights with Bobby for two hours every day after school, and taking steroids. In the tenth grade, Marty was also still trying to keep up his surfing. On days when the waves were good his surfer friends waited in a pickup truck or van at the bus stop in front of South Broward High School.

"Hey, man," they called, "five-foot walls! Let's go be heroes!"

Bobby always spent the day in school, then drove to wherever they were surfing to pick Marty up and take him to the weight room at the Y. When he arrived at the beach, they were usually still out there.

The wild screams of the surfers exulting in the sheer power of the ride echoed against the surging walls of water behind them. Their cries hovered strangely over the beach, like bird sounds. It was a sight that made Bobby bitterly jealous.

At the gym, Bobby was a harsh taskmaster, always pushing Marty to pump more weight, do more repetitions, take more steroids. The effect on Marty's body was rapidly visible: He bulked up quickly, inflating his arms and legs, popping out his chest, and thickening his neck.

Marty liked it. His self-consciousness diminished. If anything, he began to enjoy showing himself at the beach, shedding his baggy surfers trunks and T-shirt for a bikini swimsuit and muscle shirt.

The effect of the new bulk on his surfing ability was not good, however. The litheness and quickness that had made him such a stunning rider disappeared. With every new ounce of bulk, he grew more like Bobby, clunky and slow, too heavy to ride far and too awkward to ride well.

The more time Marty spent with Bobby, the less use Marty's surfer friends had for him, anyway. Bobby was a bad surfer, and he was a good student, the two cardinal sins of Florida surfing culture. Marty was becoming too much like him.

Gradually, Marty stopped going to the beach so often. One by one, his surfer friends dropped him.

Bobby, meanwhile, was becoming decidedly stranger. For one thing, he had started washing his hands at least a hundred times a day, whenever he had a spare moment. Marty asked him about it, and Bobby said he just believed in good hygiene.

Bobby had a quicker temper, too. At unpredictable moments, he would explode into a dangerous rage, often with bad consequences for Marty.

One day a few weeks after Bobby had bought a Camaro, he persuaded Marty to go with him to a sex shop where he was going to buy pornography. On the way back from the shop, Bobby was so eager to look at his new pictures that he told Marty to drive.

Driving west in heavy evening traffic on Sheridan, Marty allowed himself to get squeezed out of his lane by a bus. In maneuvering away from the bus, he bounced the front wheel of the car sharply off the curb.

The next thing he knew, as he was still driving in traffic, Bobby had thrown down the magazine and was screaming at him, his face blood-red, veins bulging in his neck.

"You fuck! You stupid fuck! You messed up my car!"

"Hey, man, it's not hurt."

"Shut up! Shut up, you stupid piece of shit!"

The blow came so fast Marty had no time to recoil. Bobby smashed his fist directly into Marty's nose. A spike of pain shot up through his forehead, his eyes blurred, and he could taste blood on his lips.

"Christ, man, you want me to wreck the fuckin' car?"

"Shut up! Shut up!"

Bobby hit him again in the side of the head, again in the mouth.

Marty was able to get the car around a corner to a side street, where he pulled to the curb, threw open the door, and leaped out.

Bobby scrabbled over the seats and came out Marty's door.

"Get in the car," Bobby said, standing in front of the open door.

Marty screamed at him: "Hey, screw you, man!" He bolted toward Bobby and hit him as hard as he could in the gut. Bobby doubled over, groaned, and fell back against the car. He straightened, walked around the car, and got back into the passenger seat.

"Come on, man," he mumbled. "I'm sorry. Please. Come on. Let's go."

Marty wiped blood from his face and got back behind the wheel. Bobby grabbed him by the neck, as if to choke him, but pulled his head close to him and whispered, "I'm really sorry, man."

"Get your hands off me, Bobby."

"Yeah. Let's just go, O.K.?"

That was not the last time Marty came home with huge swollen bruises on his face and dried blood still caked in his nose. On some of those occasions, he begged his parents again, as he had as a little boy:

"Can't we move? Can't we just fuckin' move out of this dump neighborhood?"

But he always rushed to his room and slammed the door when his parents asked what had happened to his face. Afraid as he was of Bobby, he was more afraid to let his father know he was an eleventh grader who still got himself whipped by a bully and then came home to cry about it.

When the steroids were pumping through Marty's veins and he was alive with aggression, Bobby showed him ways to work it off without losing his temper and getting his face smashed: The two of them developed a shared taste for sadism.

At first, Bobby and Marty found that they enjoyed picking on retarded people. They even developed a characteristic way of doing it.

For some time, Bobby had made a practice of hanging around the special education wing of South Broward High School, where he was likely to find retarded kids in the hall. He made other kids laugh by baiting the retarded students until they got mad, then slapping at them until they broke down and rushed off sobbing.

He and Marty elaborated this ritual into a practice that became a sort of signature for them. After school, when the retarded kids were either waiting for buses or, if they were really luckless, trying to walk home, Marty and Bobby would close in on one of them. One carried the football.

"Hey, wanta play catch?" one of them would call.

Whether the retarded student said yes or no, Bobby and Marty would initiate their special brand of catch. Dancing in a circle around their victim, they would take turns throwing the football as hard as they could at his or her head. When one of them bounced the ball off the victim's head, the other would try to catch it.

Marty and Bobby laughed uproariously at the flailing and shrieking of their quarry, but even as they laughed they both also gave themselves over to rage—a kind of surging, roaring, delicious, almost sexual rage that made their eyes bug out and left white flecks of foam at the corners of their mouths.

On a few of these occasions, they were caught by school authorities and sent home for the day. Marty, who was always more out of control and more likely to get caught, was suspended for longer periods.

Troubled by what was going on with their son, the Puccios tried to talk to him. All he would say was that he wished they could all move away from Hollywood Hills.

Veronica said: "Marty, we can't just walk away from our jobs and move away because our son is having problems."

But Marty insisted almost hysterically that he needed to get away from something or someone in the neighborhood. Sensing it was Bobby, the Puccios did agree, finally, to allow Marty to go live with his aunt, Dottie Fische, in the community of Hudson Falls in upstate New York. The plan was for him to finish high school there.

After four months, it was clear that Marty Puccio, the pumped-up ex-surfer from Lauderdale, was not destined to fit in with either his aunt's life or the expectations of the Hudson Falls school district. He returned home, and midway through the eleventh grade, Marty dropped out of school entirely.

He seldom went to the beach. He spent most of his time sitting around his parents' home, watching daytime television and waiting for Bobby to get home from school so they could go to the Y and begin working out together.

When Marty dropped out of school, alarm bells went off in Fred Kent's mind. Now he saw Marty clearly as the enemy—a typical spoiled American, a wasted slug of a kid who would drag his own beloved son down with him.

Bobby was staying in school, but he was also squandering hours every day on weight lifting, which Fred considered a stupid waste of time.

Fred Kent announced that he was taking the family out of Hollywood Hills and maybe out of the Lauderdale area entirely. He could do what he did for a living anywhere. He even put the house on the market to show how sincere he was.

Bobby was abject.

"Please, Dad. Please don't make us move away. I promise, I'll stay away from Marty. Just please don't make us move away."

Fred Kent relented. But he insisted that Bobby get a job after school.

Bobby, articulate and mannerly when he wanted to be, had no trouble doing so. He quickly landed a job making submarine sandwiches behind the deli counter at the Publix on Sheridan Street in Dania. Within a week, Bobby had persuaded Marty to apply there, too. Then Bobby persuaded his manager to hire him.

They often worked shifts together so that they could leave together and go work out. One evening Bobby spied an elderly retarded man who regularly shopped at the store. The man lived in a cheap apartment complex a mile west on Sheridan and walked his groceries home in plastic bags. In the presence of his supervisor, Bobby asked the man if he would like help getting his groceries home. The man readily agreed, and the supervisor looked pleased.

Marty went to Bobby's car and got the football and some marijuana. When they were out of sight of the store, Marty and Bobby handed the man's groceries back to him, and then, when the man's hands were fully loaded, they asked him if he wanted to play catch.

"What?"

"Catch, asshole!"

"No."

There on the shoulder of Sheridan Street, in full view of traffic, they pounded the elderly retarded man's head with the football, laughing uproariously as the man darted in all directions, out into traffic and down into the ditch, scattering his groceries as he cried out for mercy.

Either no one called the police, or the police did not arrive in time. However, one of Marty's old surfing buddies from Nova Middle School did happen by in a car, on his way home from the beach, and witnessed the scene.

He looked at the beefy, crazy-eyed thug with foam at his lips, laughing as he attacked a defenseless old man, and he shuddered to think what had become of his skinny, happy-go-lucky surfing comrade—the grommet. But he knew better than to stop or interfere.

As their taste for trouble increased, Marty and Bobby were not always so lucky with the law. The money from their jobs making subs at the Publix wasn't enough to pay for the expensive running shoes, sunglasses, and other gear they felt they had to have. And Bobby had developed a passionate interest in improving the stereo system in his car—a hobby that required thousands of dollars.

The two had discovered they could supplement their wages severalfold by stealing things from cars. They picked up the tricks of the trade from friends: a quick tap with a crowbar was enough to quietly shatter some types of windows. For others, the best tool was a spark plug swinging at the end of an electrical extension cord.

In 1992, Hollywood police arrested them while the boys were prowling the streets of a retirement community near North Beach Park. Police officers found the crowbar and the spark plug on a cord, along with a quantity of marijuana.

Because of their ages, and in accordance with standard procedure in Florida courts, they were released without penalty. Because Marty had already incurred an earlier marijuana arrest, his parents were required to seek family counseling.

The Puccios joined a Tough Love parental encounter group, in which the lesson was that parents must build up their own resolve. They must be willing to make their children pay the costs of their

misdeeds and suffer the consequences. They must be able to insist
that their children shoulder responsibility or pay for their refusal with
a loss of privileges.

Veronica was the one who attended most of the meetings. Martin
was unable to take time away from work. In Marty's case, the group
decided Veronica should come down hard. The recommendation was
that she require her son to earn money and buy his own groceries or
not eat.

The relationship between Marty and Bobby was growing more intense and more densely tangled. Bobby's long-standing interest in pornography had developed from a passive desire to merely look at dirty
pictures to a more active, aggressive desire to make them himself. He
talked to Marty about the money they could make together by pro-
ducing their own pornographic videos and selling them. Bobby was
especially interested in homosexual pornography.

Bobby did not suggest that he or Marty appear in the films they
would make. Instead, he talked about recruiting gay men to perform
in front of the camera. Homosexual sex was still the ultimate gross-
out to them, but one they found enthralling.

Even before Marty dropped out of school, he and Bobby were
spending frequent evenings at the Copa, a gay cabaret and disco on
the border between Hollywood and Fort Lauderdale. While there looking for gay men with whom to make pornographic videos, Marty and
Bobby presented themselves as a gay couple.

One of the entertainments offered by the Copa was a kind of
amateur-hour strip show, in which men from the audience took the
stage and tried to impress fellow revelers. Bobby pressured Marty to
perform. Bobby argued that Marty's youthful and now very pumped-
up body would be a powerful draw for the kind of gay men they were
looking for.

Marty ultimately agreed. One night he went to the stage suffering
all kinds of stage fright, embarrassment, and fear. Once on, however,
with the shrill cheers and wolf whistles of the crowd in his ear, Marty
made a surprising discovery. He liked it.

It was fun. It was even a turn-on. The adrenaline of performance, the sensuous thrill of the motion—it wasn't terribly unlike surfing a five-foot wall at North Beach.

Bobby became more sadistic and domineering. Some of the worst beatings Marty had to endure from Bobby came when Bobby decided that Marty was actually enjoying the homosexual roles the two of them had adopted as their deep cover at the Copa.

Marty had stopped urging his parents to move, but he continued to come home covered with unexplained bruises and cuts. Whenever he and Bobby were in the company of other male friends, Bobby went to great lengths to show how mean he could be to Marty and how little regard he had for Marty's feelings.

One afternoon an old surfing friend from Nova, Craig Tolz, dropped by to see Marty. Marty said that he was just on his way up the block to see Bobby, and he asked Craig to come along.

Craig had never liked Bobby, but he hadn't seen Marty in a long time, so he agreed to accompany him. At Bobby's house, the three of them stood out on the front lawn. Bobby seldom invited anyone other than Marty into the house.

Bobby told a long story about the attack-trained Doberman his family kept penned in a run in the backyard. When he had finished telling the story, Bobby turned to Marty and said, "Go play with the dog."

Marty smiled weakly and said, "C'mon, man, don't start that shit."

Bobby said, "What, you don't like my dog, asshole? You think there's something wrong with my dog?"

"C'mon, man."

Bobby's face flushed a deep purple, his eyes began to bulge, and he walked up close to Marty, his face inches from Marty's.

"I said play with my fuckin' dog, man."

"Oh, God."

"Play with the goddamn dog, asshole!"

Tolz tried to intervene: "Listen, you guys, I'm not really up for this shit. . . ."

"Shut up!" Bobby roared. Wheeling back to face Marty, he hissed, "Go play with my goddamn dog, butt-fuck!"

Marty was defeated. He accepted it. He dropped his chin to his chest, like a child, then turned and walked around to the back of the house.

Tolz was horrified as he heard first the opening of a rusty gate, then the roaring growl and bark of the dog, then Marty squealing with pain. The metal gate rang out as it was slammed shut. A moment later Marty came limping around the corner of the house, his ankles and calves bloody and torn.

Tolz left hurriedly.

When Bobby and Marty weren't at each other's throats in a steroid-induced rage, they were inseparable buddies. They had a sort of act they did together, which was either very amusing or completely and instantly repulsive, depending on the audience. It was a suburban tough-guy schtick, their naughty-naughty-boy routine from childhood, but now with a darker and much more aggressively sexual edge.

One day they pulled up in Bobby's Camaro in the carry-out lane at a McDonald's in suburban Hallandale. Marty was driving. A pretty teenage girl served them at the window.

"Will that be all?" she asked, after she had handed Marty his French fries.

"No, baby," Marty said, smiling blandly. "There is one more thing. I wonder if you would mind sticking these fries under your skirt and pissing on them for me?"

The girl in the window hoped she had misunderstood the handsome young man, but in the very same instant she realized she had not.

"Pardon me?" she said.

"I like my fries after a good-looking babe like yourself has pissed on them," Marty said with a phony smile. "Do you mind?"

She shook her head and stared at him. He stared back, smiling and rolling his eyes.

She laughed. "You are a very perverted young man," she said.

Then, speaking with an affectedly effeminate lisp, Marty said, "Oh, yes, I am. Very, very perverted. Do you know any young men who might also be perverted, who might be interested in coming over to my house and playing perverted little games with me and my friend?"

"Hey, fuck you," Bobby growled from the passenger seat. "Speak for yourself."

The girl in the drive-through was suddenly aware that a fellow worker, a twenty-seven-year-old man who was openly homosexual, had come to her side and was looking down on the boys in the Camaro.

"I like to play," the man said to the boys. "What's your name?"

Marty eyed the man in the window. "My name's Frank," he said.

"Can I have your phone number, Frank?" the man asked.

"Sure."

Marty gave him his parents' home phone number. When the man had written it down, the boys peeled off in a roar of engine noise and wild hooping and jeering.

That night the man called. Marty answered and the man recognized his voice. But when the man asked for Frank, Marty said there was no one by that name at that number.

The man gave his name and suggested the person on the other end tell Frank he had called. Marty slammed the phone down on him.

A few days later, the man was surprised to see Marty come into McDonald's by himself. Marty came to the counter and asked for the man by name. When the man came forward, Marty asked if they could talk for a moment.

Sitting at a small table around the corner from the counter and out of the manager's view, Marty put on an engagingly flirtatious manner. He told the man his real name, and he suggested broadly that he might be available as a prostitute.

The man was polite but candid. He had been open about his sexuality for a long time; he was not a kid; and he thought prostitution and promiscuity were too risky.

Marty shifted tactics and told the man that he and his friend were looking for gay men to appear in pornographic videos they were going to produce and sell.

"Ah, yes," the man said. "Porno flicks. No, that's not for me, either."

"Do you know anybody who might be interested?"

The man laughed. "Yeah. There is a guy who comes to mind." He gave Marty the name of Larry Shafer, a forty-two-year-old unemployed computer programmer in Hollywood.

SHAFER, WHO HAD JUST BEEN ELECTED PRESIDENT OF THE HOLLYwood Beach Kiwanis Club, had only recently started experimenting with his own homosexuality.

Marty called Shafer, and they spoke for a long time on the telephone. Marty told Shafer that he spent a lot of time at the Hollywood YMCA, pumping iron with his friend Bobby. Shafer told Marty he, too, had joined the Y the year before, to build up his physique. He said he would look for Bobby in the weight room next time he was there.

At some point not too long after that, Larry Shafer found Marty and Bobby doing their daily two-hour workout. Marty was on his back on a weight bench, and Bobby was straddling him from above, spotting for him.

Bobby and Marty presented themselves as a gay couple. This time, instead of Marty coming on as a prostitute, Bobby said that he was the whore of the pair and earned $100 an hour for sex, $200 for an all-night stand. Marty came across as the less aggressive, sweeter partner.

Larry was not at all interested in Bobby, who seemed dark and dangerous. But he was instantly taken with Marty, whose smile melted his heart. Even though Marty and Bobby did a lot of kidding, Larry Shafer sensed something genuine and warm in Marty. He was also attracted to him.

Just before they left, Bobby suggested that Shafer meet them two nights later at exactly 10:30 P.M. at the Copa. Shafer said he would see what he could do.

On the agreed night, Larry Shafer waited at the bar for thirty minutes after the time of their appointment. He had been sitting with his back to the bar, watching the door. He was not surprised that neither of the young men had shown up. Behind him, an emcee was announcing the beginning of the amateur striptease competition, and Larry Shafer turned to watch.

He was astonished when a pair of dancers stepped up and one of them turned out to be Marty. Bobby was nowhere in sight.

Marty took the stage confidently and gave a mock bow in recognition of the wild applause and wolf whistles he was drawing. Obviously this crowd knew his act well.

The deejay played a record, and Marty began to strip. His moves were smooth, sinuous, and smoldering at first. He rode the wave of catcalls and laughter, stripping himself down to a pink G-string.

His dance partner, wearing a black G-string, was a bigger man who was even more pumped up and veiny than Marty. He moved in close and pulled Marty to him. As they danced skin-to-skin, the two of them simulated homosexual sex.

When the act reached its climactic moment, Marty exploded into a sexual frenzy that brought the men in the room to their feet, stamping, cheering, and whistling their delight.

Afterward, still wearing his pink G-string and glistening with sweat, Marty slipped onto a stool next to Larry. He accepted a drink. Breathing hard, he suggested that he and his friend Bobby would like to come visit Larry to talk some business. Larry agreed eagerly.

On their first visit to his small house in Hollywood, the boys were fairly well behaved. Bobby was quiet, Marty flirtatious and sweet. They mentioned their idea for pornographic videos, and Larry said that he would think about working with them.

Marty explained that he lived with his parents. He said that when his parents were away traveling, he often hosted homosexual orgies at the house. At the moment, unfortunately, the parents were in residence.

Marty explained that his mother had joined a group called Tough Love in an effort to make a better boy of him. As part of the Tough Love regimen, Marty said he was being required to buy all of his own groceries. He didn't mention his job at Publix. Instead, he said that he was low on funds and that, as a result, he was having to go hungry quite a bit.

Marty told Larry that he sometimes earned money for food by acting as a telephone prostitute—that is, he called men and spoke to them suggestively on the telephone while they masturbated. Marty said that he was also able to deliver very high-quality drugs for money. As a good-faith gesture, he and Bobby shared with Larry some of the potent marijuana they were carrying that night.

By the time they left, Marty and Bobby had taken $300 from Shafer in the form of an emergency loan and had come to an agreement that Marty would call him and give him phone sex three times a week, in exchange for a weekly payment of $25.

In the weeks following, Marty was faithful to his commitment. He called three times a week from his bedroom at home, while the other members of his family went about their business in the rest of the house. He talked to Larry Shafer until Shafer climaxed.

Even though Marty was prostituting himself, Larry nevertheless felt genuinely drawn to him by the things Marty said during phone sex. When Marty and Bobby showed up to collect the $25-a-week fee, however, there were problems.

After one visit, Larry discovered he was missing a pair of speakers from his stereo. On another occasion, tapes from a Blockbuster video store were gone. Another time a videotape rewinder, another a food blender. Each time the boys came calling, they stole something, and each time their technique was identical: Marty decoyed Larry in one room while Bobby searched the rest of the house, looking for loot.

But the stealing was less of a problem for Larry than what happened when he complained about it. On several occasions, Bobby exploded and unleashed a volley of punches on Larry's face, leaving him bruised and swollen for days. On a few of these occasions, Larry Shafer called the police, but in the end he always declined to sign a complaint.

He came back to the boys each time, or allowed them to come back to him, because he couldn't resist Marty. It was always Marty's smile that melted Larry's resolve. Until the last time.

*　　*　　*

DURING THIS PERIOD, MARTY AND BOBBY MAINTAINED TO EACH other that they were not homosexuals and that homosexuality disgusted them. Their activities with Larry and other gay men were, in their eyes, merely an extension of the sadistic kind of fun they had always enjoyed.

Bobby continued to explode at Marty, usually when he decided that Marty was actually enjoying homosexuality, and on those occasions Bobby gave Marty physical beatings, some severe.

But the redeeming theme in everything they did and in all that they were experiencing was, Bobby said, their plot to make pornographic gay videotapes. That was how they were going to strike it rich and never have to make another submarine sandwich at the Publix store. It was for this mission that they were subjecting themselves to the ultimate gross-out horror of proximity to gay men.

And finally Larry Shafer agreed to make a movie for them. He needed money badly. The boys had promised instant big bucks. Larry said he would star in their production, which was to be called *Rough Boys.*

It was a major moment for Marty and Bobby. The video would be a very high-quality production, of the same quality Marty's father was associated with at the postproduction house where he worked. They would film *Rough Boys* in a commercial studio, though obviously not the one operated by Marty's dad's company, and they would market it through the world of porno stores, about which Bobby knew so much.

When Larry showed up at the studio at the appointed hour, he learned that not only was he to be the star of the movie, he was the only actor. Another surprise was that, in all their eagerness to tend to the logistical details of the production—renting the studio, buying tape, finding a dildo and leather straps and so on—the boys had forgotten to write a script. In fact, they hadn't really even thought about what the story would be.

But they were unconcerned. The plan was for Larry to take off all of his clothes, stand in front of the camera with the straps and the dildo, and wing it. At appropriate moments, they would call stage directions to him from off camera. Marty knew from listening to his father that 99 percent of the work was done in the editing room afterward, anyway.

The musical backdrop for the drama had been prerecorded on another occasion. It was an array of gay reggae music—something Marty was developing as his own métier—which he performed with an ensemble of gay performers he had recruited.

While Marty's gay reggae music echoed from a boom box in the background, Larry walked naked to the center of the barren studio and stood disconsolately for a while in front of the gently whirring video camera. Then, at a hoarsely whispered suggestion from Marty offstage, Larry began attempting to masturbate for the camera.

When that enterprise seemed not destined for a dramatic conclusion, another stage whisper from behind the camera directed Larry to begin playing with the dildo. When he put it behind his buttocks and began sodomizing himself, Marty's excited voice off camera shouted, "Oh, yeah! Put that thing up there!"

For the next act, Marty ordered Shafer to put the soiled dildo in his mouth. Shafer said weakly that he could not do that. Marty told him he had to do it, nagged him and threatened him. Shafer looked off warily to the side, presumably to where Bobby was lurking. He resisted for a long while, as the camera clicked off and on again. Finally, looking frightened, he agreed and put the dildo in his mouth.

In the background and out of view, Marty and Bobby both crooned at the grossness of what they had accomplished.

The money they had promised to share with Shafer never materialized, because no porno stores were interested in buying *Rough Boys*. The video, even after editing, still contained all of Marty's loud stage directions from behind the camera, along with a lot of terrible camera work and bad sound, to say nothing of the fact there was no story, not even any lines, and the sex acts themselves were not well performed. It was, in short, worse than the scores of other badly video-taped home porno movies that kinky and would-be kinky couples brought to porn-shop owners every week, looking for a few quick bucks.

Even while Marty and Bobby stole from him, and while Marty took money from him as a prostitute, the boys continued to wheedle and beg loans, always in the form of emergency amounts needed to tide them over rough spots. The deeper Larry Shafer fell into their snare, the less able he was to fend them off.

At one point, in a move that had more to do with face-saving than need, Larry asked that the boys do some work for him in his backyard. They reluctantly agreed to erect a series of prefabricated fence sections across the back of the yard. It was hot on the day the boys showed up for work, and they had come well supplied with marijuana, a boom box, and Marty's gay reggae tapes.

The place where Shafer had instructed them to put up the fence, at his property line across the back, would have required a small amount of digging, clearing roots and removing small pieces of concrete. Rather than exert themselves, the boys merely moved back into the property where there were no obstructions and put Larry Shafer's fence up across the middle of his yard.

By this point, Shafer had been through a lot with them. Their youth and exaggerated good looks had exerted a powerful draw on him. But he was, after all, a man in his early forties who had some education and some accomplishments, who had earned the respect of the business community in his town. In spite of all the painful and difficult changes he had been experiencing in his sexuality, Larry Shafer was not a fool. He could tell idiots when he saw them.

He unloaded on them. How could they possibly not understand that a fence must go across the property line? How many years of school did it take to figure that out?

Bobby flew at him in a foaming rage, pushed him stumbling backward into his house, hit him hard in the head, smashed his nose and jaw, hit him hard in the stomach and ribs, blow after blow until Shafer was curled in a bloody ball on the floor, begging for mercy.

Bobby stormed off to his car. Marty stayed behind. He lifted Shafer gently to his feet, stroked his hair back, and tried to comfort him.

"I'm really sorry, man."

Shafer was barely able to speak or hold himself erect. He nodded to show that he appreciated Marty's concern. Marty turned and walked toward the door, then stopped. He turned back and gave Shafer that wonderful, radiant, little-boy smile—the one that always turned Larry Shafer's heart to Jell-O.

Marty stepped toward him, still smiling, holding his left hand toward him as if to take his hand. Just as Shafer was trying to force a smile in return, Marty uncoiled his right arm and hit Shafer in the gut with a blow so ferocious that it caused him to vomit.

Marty called him a few times after that, obviously angling for money, but Larry Shafer had learned his lesson. He never saw either one of them again.

BOBBY WAS THE ONE WHO HAD PUSHED IT. HE WAS THE ONE WHO shoved Marty forward to hustle gay men at the Copa, to seduce them by performing onstage in a pink G-string. Bobby was the one who lay on top of Marty and made him watch pornographic videos or look at gross pictures in books.

But Bobby was the one who went into a foaming steroidal fury whenever he decided that Marty was, in fact, acting gay. That was the whole secret, the scam, the plan, the game, the cool part: They did all this stuff to take advantage of gay men, but they were not themselves gay. They were studs—pumped up, pectoralized, muscle-butted beach heroes. They were the kind of men for whom the babes would give it up in a minute. The rest of it was all just a joke. Bobby wanted Marty to remember that. When he thought Marty had lost the thread, he beat the hell out of him. And Marty put up with it.

Amazingly, given all that was going on in his world, it was Bobby, however, who was able to stick to the main thread of his own life. Marty dropped out of school, but Bobby stayed in. Marty's academic record at South Broward had been a ludicrous string of D's, E's, Incompletes, and other expressions of dismay. But Bobby's record was respectable.

Not great, but adequate. He was on a path with a future. Not a stunning future, but a future. He was successfully completing a program that would put him in line for admission to South Broward Community College in a special curriculum for physical therapists. Bobby saw it as a way he could work and work out at the same time.

If anything, it was testimony to his sheer youthful resilience that Bobby was able to accomplish all that he did. He was able to stay in school and continue to meet the basic requirements in spite of the massive amount of dope he and Marty were now smoking every day, the considerable amount of drinking they did, the exhausting two-hour weight-lifting sessions every day at the Y, to say nothing of the hustling and porno-cruising in their spare time.

A major factor in his ability and will to keep it all together was his father, Fred Kent, who never let up, never stopped paying attention to his son, never stopped urging him to do the right thing.

Bobby's main interest in life, aside from sex and dope, was the sound system in his car. He lavished money and attention on it. The fact was, however, that Bobby was not gifted mechanically, especially not at the fine work involved in installing and wiring electrical components in a car. He was too clumsy and short-tempered. Marty was far better at that sort of thing.

Bobby was a senior in high school when he got the Camaro, with money he had earned and saved himself. He bought the basic stereo system for the car and then told Marty he wanted him to install it. The installation turned into a horrific ten-hour struggle outdoors in the brutal Florida summer.

Marty thrashed around under the hood and in the trunk of the car until he was bathed in sweat and his fingers were bloody. It took forever to get the system to work properly, but every time the system failed to work or Bobby thought Marty had somehow marred his new car, he exploded and beat Marty in the face and chest.

One day, Fred Kent sat down with his son to talk to him about the future. He was unhappy that Marty was back on the scene. Fred was struggling to find a way to lead his son toward a strong healthy future.

"The main thing you care about, it looks like to me, is your car stereo."

"Yeah. So what?"

"That's O.K. Whatever you're really interested in, that's what you're interested in. You just need to find a way to take that interest and turn it into an opportunity."

"Like?"

"Well, if car stereos are what you're interested in, you could go into the car-stereo business."

"How?"

"You just do it. I'll help you. I'll set you up, Bobby. You want to open a place, say, where you do car stereos and window tinting for people, stuff like that, I'll set you up. I'll put you in your own business. That's the greatest future you can have in this country, Bob— run your own business. Be your own master."

"If I do that for you, can we hire Marty?"

"Marty?"

"Yeah. I wouldn't want to, like, you know, have to work there all day long or something if Marty couldn't be there with me or something."

Fred decided to put the matter aside for the moment and bring it up at another time.

Bobby sought to ensure that Marty would not turn gay by insisting that Marty have sex with females. Marty was not especially averse. The only hitch was that Bobby was the one who decided which females Marty should have sex with. And they were always big.

Fat, as Bobby put it. Fat girls. Part of the routine was to start having sex with them and then make fun of them for being fat. The sex itself was often cruel and abusive.

*   *   *

LISA ARRIVED AT THE PUCCIO HOUSE WITH HER OVERNIGHT THINGS thrown hastily in a bag. Sharon, a friend from Cooper High who turned tricks for Tom Hildebrand, gave her a ride and accompanied her into Marty's house.

Bobby was there. Marty's parents were off on a trip for several days. The boys had the house to themselves, and what they had in mind was an orgy. They began by offering Lisa and Sharon marijuana and booze. Then they ushered them into Marty's bedroom for what they considered to be the seductive tour de force—a private screening of *Rough Boys*.

"Watch this shit," Bobby exulted. "We made this. We know the guy in it from the Y, he hangs there. You won't believe how gross this is."

Sharon agreed that it was very gross, too gross to watch. But Lisa barely noticed. She was so excited merely to be in Marty's company that she didn't care what else was going on.

During the next forty-eight hours, Lisa and Sharon tried to leave the house, but the boys refused to let them go. They plied them with more drink and dope and dragged them back to Marty's bedroom again.

Some of the play was between Marty and Bobby, always in the form of simulated but not actual sex. At one point, Sharon asked the boys if they were gay. They exploded in laughter, as if they had taken her in, and then proceeded to mime more sex acts between themselves.

The session ended when Bobby discovered that Marty had left a loaf of bread open on the counter in the kitchen. Bobby wanted to make a sandwich, but the bread was stale.

Bobby pushed Marty into his bedroom and slammed the door. The girls could hear Bobby beating Marty in the room—the loud whack of punches landing on flesh, Marty's pleas for mercy. Sharon wanted to flee, but Lisa couldn't leave while Marty was in danger.

Half an hour later the two young men emerged from the room. Marty's mouth was puffy and caked with blood, and his right eye was already closing around a nasty blue bruise. He had been crying.

Bobby announced that the party was over and the girls could go home.

It had been two days of nonstop sex, booze, drugs, and mayhem. When Lisa got home, she was exhausted and a wreck. She was in seventh heaven. She had a real boyfriend.

CHAPTER THREE

IN EARLY 1993, ALI WILLIS WAS LONELY IN PALM BAY, AWAY FROM HER friends in Broward County. She needed a sidekick. She found Heather Swallers.

Heather was seventeen, a little girl with a cute body, brown hair, thin lips, and a baby face. She fell short of being quite pretty only because her eyes were dull and mechanical.

Heather was poor. She had come to Palm Bay to live with Cindy Hanlon, her aunt, because she needed to be away from her mother, Jackie Callahan, who was living in a cheap hotel in Cocoa Beach.

The beginning of the story probably lay lost in the distant past, layered beneath wasted generations and ruined lives, but the only beginning Heather knew was the death of her grandmother.

For years her grandfather, a vicious drunk in Kankakee, Illinois, had beaten her grandmother senseless whenever his demons were upon him. His rages were bloody and sexual. He beat and raped whomever he could lock in the room with him.

Finally he killed his wife. In 1970 in a screaming rage, he took a claw hammer to her and caved in her face and skull. Then, locked in the room with her for the next two days, he continued to drink and have sex with the corpse. The story of the murder and subsequent trial was on the front page of the *Kankakee Daily Journal* for months. Heather's mother was fifteen when it happened. She was in the house the whole time.

She became the same sort of severe alcoholic her father had been. She was mesmerized by his memory and even took his name, Jack, as her own. She drifted from man to man until she found an older man who got drunk, flew into rages, and beat her as severely as Jack had beaten her mother. She stayed with that man longer than with any of the others.

Heather and her little brother, Shane, grew up as baggage, trailed behind by their mother as she wandered from motel to motel, man to man. Once in a while they went to live with relatives while their mother was in a detoxification center. Heather never was able to concentrate long enough to accomplish anything in school, and anyway, she was seldom in one place long enough to attend.

The children were spared nothing. They watched while men abused their mother. One time they stood by helpless while she lay on the floor, unconscious, and a man angrily poured booze down her gullet and stuffed pills in her mouth with his dirty fingers, trying to crank her up for more sex.

On occasions such as these, little Heather would wait until the coast was clear, then creep to her mother's side where she lay on the floor, pull off her shoes, lift her head gently, put a pillow under it, then cover her with a blanket.

In Jackie Callahan's waking moments, the horror of what had happened to her own mother was never far from her mind, like a creature wriggling across the surface of her brain. The worst times for Heather and Shane were the long nights when their mother, drunk and raving, would make them stay awake and listen to one of her readings.

Even before they were in kindergarten, she made them sit on the floor and listen until she passed out in the wee hours. A bottle of vodka in one hand and packs of cigarettes at the ready, she read aloud from her treasured copy of the transcript of her father's trial.

She searched for the most gruesome testimony—the screams, the wounds, the necrophilia—and read those passages to the bewildered, sleep-deprived infants who sat before her. She read the transcript to them over and over again, until she had sealed the words inside their souls.

Ali met Heather one evening at the mall and decided she was cool. There was something in Heather that was childlike and tractable, yet tough. Her clothes were cheap and dirty, so Ali decided to do something about it.

Two days later Ali borrowed her mother's credit card, took Heather to the mall, and bought her $500 worth of clothes. It was the most amazing thing that had ever happened to Heather Swallers in her entire life. She hadn't known before that such things could be done, that someone could appear in her life, a fairy godmother, wave a piece of plastic at clerks, and transform her into Cinderella at the ball.

At seventeen, Heather had done lots of dope, lots of booze, and lots of sex, but nothing had ever made her feel the way she felt when she walked out on the street that day wearing the new clothes Ali had bought for her.

Ali took Heather to Parsons Circle, to the spacious new home of her mother and stepfather, Virginia and Albert Slay. The two of them did what Ali herself did just about every day of her life when she was in Palm Bay. They walked into the house without speaking, walked past whatever adults or other human beings may have been around, went into Ali's room, and closed the door.

Later, when they came out for food, Ali introduced Heather to her mother. When Heather appeared again the next morning for breakfast, it was clear she was going to be living in the Slay residence for a while, even though it did not seem necessary for Ali to announce or explain that fact to anyone.

In general, the adults around eighteen-year-old Ali Willis walked on eggshells. In her wild fits of anger and her drug panics, to say nothing of her involvement with members of gangs like the Zulus and Foke Um, little Ali had demonstrated dramatically what could happen if people pushed her over the edge. The edge was always convenient.

She often kept an assortment of young people with her in her room. It was where the father of her child had lived during his brief sojourn away from the home of his own parents. Ali did not expect to be asked a lot of questions about who was staying with her or what they were doing.

THE OTHER PERSON SPENDING LONG HOURS BEHIND THE CLOSED DOOR to Ali's room was her new boyfriend, Donny Semenec, a rosy-cheeked seventeen-year-old high school dropout. Donny and his sixteen-year-old brother, Shawn, lived with their mother, Donna Ferreira, thirty-four, and her husband.

It had been five years since the boys had last seen their biological father. They heard from him by telephone once every few months.

Donna Ferreira had worked for the state of Massachusetts as a nurse. She had divorced the boys' father because of his severe drug problems. Donny was three at the time. She eventually married Anthony Ferreira, and in the summer of 1992 she and her husband moved to Florida from Taunton, Massachusetts, because they were seeking a healthier environment in which to raise the boys.

It was a little late for Donny. In his last year at Taunton High School, he had missed ninety-six days of school and had earned a grade point average of D.

He was not a mean kid. In fact, his demeanor was so sweetly passive that officials in Taunton suspected him of having undiagnosed learning disabilities and put him in a special-education section for slow and retarded students.

He was accident-prone, perhaps as a result of his drinking and drug use. Not long after moving to Palm Bay, he was severely injured while riding a bicycle in traffic and spent two and a half months in a hospital.

In addition to the excused absences related to his accident, he also managed to rack up twenty-four unexcused absences in his first semester in Palm Bay High School. School officials kicked him out for poor attendance and for being willfully disobedient.

His parents, both of whom worked hard and tried to set a good example for their sons, were strict with Donny. They set rules and expected both boys to honor them. They insisted Donny do something about his drug problems. At their urging, he cleaned up his act, re-enrolled in high school, and achieved a grade point average of C.

But then he just quit. He dropped out of school and joined a loose-knit cabal of boys who were not in school, had no jobs, lived with their parents, and drove around Palm Bay all day drinking beer, smoking powerful dope, and going to the beach. He attracted the eye of Ali Willis.

Ali took Donny to the mall and bought him expensive sunglasses, tennis shoes, shirts and pants. He was mesmerized by her use of credit cards, her ability to buy whatever she felt like buying.

She was also good-looking and sexy, and she wanted his body. For Donny Semenec, the slow pretty boy with a head full of marijuana fumes, Ali Willis was too good to be true. He became her slave.

Ali hexed the adults away from the door to her room with a constant unspoken threat of madness and chaos if they pushed her or made her angry. Behind the closed door, she arranged her own little family, entirely according to her own rules. At one side she had Heather, who worshiped the ground she walked on, and at the other she had Donny, who would do whatever she asked.

In late June 1993, Heather tracked down her mother, Jackie Callahan, and talked to her on the phone:

"I'm kind of messed up," she said. "I think I have a drug problem."

"What drug?" her mother asked.

"Crack."

Jackie, who knew the ropes, managed to get Heather admitted to a rehabilitation center in Melbourne, Florida. Heather had been there only three days when Ali reached her by phone.

"I'll come pick you up, babe," Ali said. "I'm going down to Lauderdale to see my old friend Lisa from Catholic school days. She's got this new boyfriend who's a stud. He has a buddy named Bobby, who's good-looking, too. I met him once down there last winter. She wants me to come down there and go out with him."

*   *   *

IT WAS LISA'S BIG PLAN. SHE FIGURED IT OUT OVER A PERIOD OF weeks, lying there on her bed in the back of the little town house in Pembroke Pines, staring up at the posters of men with huge muscles and women with bare breasts.

After that first night when Ali and Lisa met Marty and Bobby at the Publix and had sex in Bobby's car, Ali had returned to her parents' home in Palm Bay. Since then she had not been back to Lauderdale. As far as Ali and Bobby were concerned, their meeting had been a casual, meaningless passing of ships in the night.

But they did screw, Lisa remembered. And Ali had said she thought Bobby was cute-looking.

Early in the summer of 1993, after Lisa and Marty had been together for about five months, Marty began treating Lisa even more abusively than before. With Bobby egging him on, laughing in the background, Marty had pushed Lisa around in front of her friends, calling her "Fat-Ass" and "Shamu."

On one occasion, Marty invited Lisa to his house while his parents were away. He persuaded her to strip naked in front of Bobby; then Bobby and Marty had taken turns beating her with Marty's broad leather weight-lifting belt and having sex with her.

But Lisa wasn't the only one who sometimes wound up on the nasty end of the stick with Marty and Bobby. One night she was with them, cruising Embassy Lakes Mall in Bobby's car, when they saw two very pretty teenage girls whom Lisa knew from school, Susan, fifteen years old, and Claudia, seventeen. Lisa suggested they stop and pick the girls up, and Marty and Bobby agreed.

The five of them jammed themselves into Bobby's Camaro and decided to make a run down Sheridan to the beach for some moonlight skinny-dipping in the surf. Bobby cranked up his stereo full blast, until the car was literally throbbing with the beat of the Geto Boys.

Before joining the others, Susan and Claudia had been smoking marijuana behind the Pizza Hut where Claudia worked as a waitress. The motion of Bobby's car winding and careening wildly through traffic and the incredible brain-pounding din of the music made her feel sick.

"I'm think I'm gonna throw up," she moaned in the backseat, but no one heard her.

Finally she did vomit, pitching forward suddenly with a motion of the car so that a few flecks of her vomit spattered Bobby's face.

Bobby wheeled the car wildly around a corner and screeched to a halt at the curb in a residential neighborhood. He leaped out, eyes bulging, veins on his neck popping. He was bellowing at the top of his lungs:

"Goddamn it, you fuck!" he screamed at Marty. "That bitch hurled on me! It got in my mouth! It got in my mouth!"

More than angry, Bobby seemed to be genuinely panicked, as if he were about to come unglued.

Marty reached into the car, grabbed Susan by a shoulder, and dragged her roughly out onto the pavement. "Shit, bitch, you messed up his car! You piece of shit!"

Claudia came forward to intervene.

"Hey, chill, will you, asshole? She's sick, that's all. We've been blowing some dope, the music was too loud, your friend drives like shit, she got sick. So what?"

Claudia took Susan by the arm and led her to the front lawn of the house where they had parked—a typical middle-class one-story brick-fronted home on a canal with a screened Florida room in the back. Claudia found a garden hose and began using it to wash the vomit off Susan's front.

The boys, meanwhile, were back by the car, conferring in urgent whispers. Bobby kept jabbing Marty in the chest with one finger and pointing at Susan and Claudia. Marty was nodding his head, trying to calm Bobby down.

Lisa stood next to the boys, listening to what they were saying.

"O.K.," Marty said calmly after a while. He walked up the lawn toward the girls. "Get back in the car," he said to them.

Claudia, who had been around trouble before, said, "Get back in the car? Why?"

"Because it's O.K. It's cool. He's chilled. Everything is cool. We're going to take you home. We can't just leave you here."

Claudia surveyed the neighborhood. It looked harmless enough. "We'll stay here."

"No," Marty said sharply. "I said get back in the fucking car."

At this point, Lisa came up the lawn and took Claudia by an elbow.

"What are you doing, bitch?" Marty demanded.

"Nothing," Lisa said sullenly. "Talking to my friend."

Lisa led Claudia off a few yards, then whispered in her ear: "Don't get in the car."

"Why?"

"Bobby wants Marty to take you out somewhere so they can do something to you."

"Do something? Like what, Lisa?"

"Beat the fuck out of you. They'll do it bad. Believe me. And probably rape you."

Claudia looked at Lisa's face for a moment to appraise what Lisa was saying. "Shit," Claudia muttered.

She turned and walked quickly to the door of the house where they had parked.

"Hey!" Bobby shouted when he saw what Claudia was about to do. He started toward her, but by then the door was already open.

A middle-aged, middle-class, African-American man appeared. Behind him appeared his concerned wife, then two teenaged children.

"What's going on?" the man asked.

"My friend threw up in this guy's car," Claudia said. "Now him and his buddy are trying to make us get in their car, so they can rape us or beat us up or some shit like that."

The man quickly scanned the group—Claudia in front, Susan standing suddenly a few yards away, soaking wet, obviously stoned, Lisa with her, the two young muscle-shirted bodybuilders at the street.

He turned and said over his shoulder to his wife, "Call 911." Then he said to his own children, "Get away from the door."

He came out onto the lawn and walked down toward the street a few paces.

"Get out of here," he said to Bobby and Marty.

"Hey, fuck you, man!" Bobby screamed. He began dancing in rage at the side of his car, rolling his fists in the air. "Fuck you! Fuck you!"

The man, closer now, lifted his arm, pointed his finger straight into Bobby's face, and said in a thundering bass, "GET OUT OF HERE NOW!"

Bobby and Marty both deflated instantly, like popped balloons. They yanked open the car doors, jumped in, and raced off in a roaring cloud of smoke and gravel.

"Can we use your phone?" Claudia asked the man.

"No. Give me a phone number. I will call someone for you."

IN THE WEEKS AFTERWARD, LISA LAY IN HER BED REMEMBERING THIS and other incidents in which her beloved Marty turned into a Jekyll and Hyde monster. It seemed to Lisa that Marty behaved that way only when Bobby was around. The problem was that Bobby was always around.

She believed that Marty's feelings for her were tender and loving but that he pretended to be cruel and abusive in order to keep Bobby happy. If only Bobby weren't so close to Marty, if only Marty could find some way of achieving a little distance, then perhaps Lisa and Marty could be happier together.

And so there, lying on the bed and looking at the images above her, she had stumbled onto her plan—to introduce Bobby to Ali and engineer things so that Bobby and Ali would date, have sex and be together, thereby freeing Marty from bondage.

Ali had been experimenting with witchcraft—mainly sneaking out into cemeteries at night with Donny Semenec and Heather, doing drugs, having sex, swearing blood oaths, and muttering mumbo-jumbo incantations taken from comic books. Lisa told her Bobby was "into some really weird sex, like spooky shit that you wouldn't believe,'' which aroused Ali's curiosity.

Ali had sensed that night at South Beach that Bobby was strange, but she was excited by the possibility he might be even stranger than she had suspected.

Heather was waiting in a city park down the street from the rehab center in Melbourne, waiflike and wan in tight-fitting blue jeans and T-shirt, with her things in a pillowcase. When Ali rolled up in her red Mustang, engine snorting and roaring, stereo booming, clouds of dope smoke rolling out of the windows, Heather's face lighted up into the brilliant cherubic smile of a little girl who has just spotted her mother in the car line at school.

They barreled off down the coastal freeway for Lauderdale, both of them laughing with the sheer delight of being young and off on an adventure. A little later, when the high from the marijuana had settled and brought on a familiar dullness about the brain, Heather sat back against her seat and sighed. She reached up with one hand and ran it dreamily over Ali's shoulder.

"Thanks, Ali. For getting me."

"No shit," Ali said. "Got to stick with my homies."

Heather smiled. "How's that guy?"

"Donny?"

"Yeah. Is he still living with you?"

"Yeah."

"He's cute."

"Yeah. Donny's O.K. But wait till you see this friend of Lisa's boyfriend. Bobby. He has got a body! I mean, a body!"

"Does Lisa want you to fuck him?"

"Yeah."

They both laughed and then lapsed into silence for the rest of the long drive down.

Heather and Ali stayed with Lisa in her room that night. The next day, Heather stayed behind, sleeping in Lisa's bed and watching daytime television, while Lisa and Ali drove in Ali's car to Marty's house. Marty's parents were at work. Bobby was at school. Marty and Bobby were not due to start their next shift at the Publix until the following evening.

Marty, Lisa, and Ali sat around in Marty's bedroom, smoked some dope, drank a few beers, and talked.

"Is Bobby nice?" Ali asked. "I mean, can he be?"

Marty shrugged and looked embarrassed. "Well, you met him."

"He was an asshole when I met him."

"Well, we've been friends since we were born almost."

"So he must be nice."

"I guess."

When Bobby came home from school, his parents were not yet home. Marty called and told him he was coming over with the girls.

When they got there, Lisa explained that she had invited Ali down to go out with Bobby. She said she thought they would make a nice couple.

Bobby was flattered. He enjoyed being the center of other people's plans.

Lisa and Marty went into the family room at the far end of the house to watch television, allowing the other two some privacy.

Ali and Bobby found themselves in an unaccustomed position. Seated together at the kitchen table in Bobby's parents' home, with less than an hour to go before his parents would return, there was little they could do but talk.

Ali told Bobby a few things about herself—that she had been married and had a child, whom her mother was raising. She did not mention that she had once worked part-time for Tom Hildebrand as a whore.

Bobby told her that he intended to amount to something in the world.

"I'm gonna go to college," he said.

"Really?"

"Yeah. I'm only four credits away from graduating. I've got a B average."

"No shit!"

"Yeah."

"What are you going to do after college?"

"I don't know. Me and my dad are thinking about going into a business together, one of those window-tint and sound-system places, like."

"Oh, yeah. Those are cool. So you'd have your own one?"

"Yeah. My dad wants to set me up in one. He's always on me about it."

"Well, that's cool. I mean, like that he wants to help."

"Yeah. My dad's pretty cool."

That evening when the girls returned to Lisa's house, Ali called her mother in Palm Bay. "This guy I came down here to see is pretty neat, Ma."

"Is he?"

"Yeah. Like he's going to go to college, and then his dad is going to set him up in a business and everything like that."

"So you like him?"

"Yeah. I think maybe he's marriage material."

The next night Lisa took Ali to Bobby's house for the consummation. Bobby's parents were away. Bobby was wearing baggy khaki shorts and a crisp white T-shirt. With his dark hair slicked back crisply, his body tanned and fit, he looked preppy, clean, and scrumptious.

Lisa bumped her friend on the shoulder and shrugged to wish her luck. Marty snickered sheepishly when Bobby turned and did a quick biceps-flexing muscle pose for him. Then Bobby took Ali by the hand and led her back to his room.

Ali stood next to the bed, smiling demurely, and removed her own clothing.

Bobby lifted his T-shirt up with both hands and exploded out of it. He stripped off his shorts and underpants with a thumb, then grinned at Ali in obvious pleasure at his own physique. She nodded and smiled, showing her approval.

Bobby turned his back to her and fiddled with a videocassette recorder. She admired his body from behind. Then they both slipped into bed.

Just as they came to rest beside each other, their bodies stinging hot, the videocassette in the machine cranked to life. Ali looked up and was surprised to see on the television set above her head a scene in which two men were engaging in anal intercourse.

"Oh, man, that is gross," she said.

"Oh, c'mon, baby!" Bobby said. "You can tell your daddy. That shit turns you on."

"No, it doesn't," she said, turning away. "It's gross."

Ali was on her stomach on the bed, looking away from the television set. Bobby slipped up on her back, pinning her down.

"Get off me," she said.

He took her head in both of his hands, pressing hard against her temples, and forced her to look up at the television set, where the two men were engaging in homosexual sex.

"Watch it, baby," he crooned. "Watch it!"

"Get the fuck off me, asshole!"

But he didn't get off. When she resisted again, he slapped her in the face, forced her onto her back, and thrust into her. "Tell me I'm the best you ever had," he crooned.

"Fuck you."

He slapped her again, harder this time. "I said tell me I'm the best, baby! The best you ever had!"

He slapped her so hard that her head rang.

"You're the best I ever had," she said, crying.

He laughed exultantly, nearing climax. "Say it again, louder! Yell it!" He slapped her with one hand and then with the other.

"You're the best I ever had," she screamed.

Later, when Bobby and Ali rejoined Lisa and Marty at the front of the house, Lisa was eager to know how sex had gone between them. She had a lot riding on it.

Bobby went to the bathroom to wash his hands. Lisa led Ali into the kitchen.

"So?" Lisa said with a smirk, digging Ali in the ribs. "How was it? He's a stud, eh?"

"More like a goddamn queer," Ali muttered angrily. "What a total dick-head! The fucker raped me!"

Lisa shrugged, sullen and defensive. "Well, shit, Ali, I told you he was kinky. I thought you were into kinky now, with all your witch shit and so on."

Marty wanted to know what they were talking about. Lisa turned, angry now, and told him:

"Bobby must have played his goddamned queer tapes," Lisa said. "Now she's all pissed off."

"Oh, hey, babe, that's cool," Marty said. "Those tapes aren't shit. We make those things."

"What?"

"Yeah, we make a lot of money off them. You wouldn't believe how much money we make. The queers buy 'em as fast as we can crank them out."

Ali, partially mollified, said, "What do you mean you make them? You mean you're in them? You do that sick shit?"

"No, no, I mean we produce and direct them. C'mere, let me show you one we just made."

Bobby had rejoined them. The four of them trooped to the back of the house and into Bobby's room again.

Bobby's mother, Farah Kent, a nurse, was pulling into the driveway just then, coming home from work.

Marty found a copy of *Rough Boys* and put it into the machine. Not far into the tape, Ali heard Marty's voice in the background, coaching Larry Shafer on what to do with the dildo.

"Is that you talking back there?" Ali asked.

"Yeah. I was the director."

"Huh," Ali said, beginning to be impressed.

There was a knock on the door, and all four of them jumped. It was Farah Kent. She pushed the door open and looked in, just as the tape was reaching one of its most graphic moments.

"What's going on, kids?" she asked with a smile.

"Nothing, Mom," Bobby said, stepping in front of the television set to block her view.

"C'mon!" she said, still smiling. "What are you rascals watching?"

"Nothing, Mom!" Bobby said, beginning to whine. "C'mon, Mom. Give us a break."

"O.K.," she said, putting her hands up in the air in mock despair. "It's your business! I probably don't want to know."

"Right!" Bobby said in his cute little-boy voice.

"If you kids want a snack," his mother said, "c'mon out in the kitchen, and I'll fix you something."

Ten minutes later they were all seated at the bar in the kitchen, sipping Cokes and hungrily watching Farah Kent pull frozen mini-pizzas from the microwave.

When they returned to Lisa's house, Ali called her mother in Palm Bay. While Lisa sat nearby fuming, Ali told her mother, "I don't think this guy is marriage material after all."

THE NEXT DAY ALI WAS GONE. LISA'S MOTHER, MAUREEN, WAS AT work at her brother's garbage-hauling business. Lisa woke late, watched a soap opera for a while in bed, then went into the small kitchen and poured herself a bowl of Frosted Flakes. She was so despondent that she could eat only a few mouthfuls.

She pulled on sandals, a pair of blue jeans, and a T-shirt, pushed her hair out of her eyes, and walked out the front door. Her neighborhood, called Cedarwoods because the small townhomes in the development all had unpainted cedar facades, was arranged around a network of short streets that resembled narrow parking lots.

The heat had risen up off the Everglades in a wall that morning and was pressing down on the western edges of Fort Lauderdale, threatening rain. By the time Lisa had walked the short distance to the corner of Sheridan and Hiatus, she was bathed in sweat.

When the roaring lanes of traffic on Sheridan halted at the light, Lisa lumbered across the street in front of the stopped cars. It made her feel awkward and fat to have to walk in front of so many darkened windshields.

The Embassy Lakes Mall was on the other side of Sheridan. On a particular hump of grass in the shade of palm trees across from the Pizza Hut, there were usually kids gathered by this time in the morning, sitting and sprawled, sleeping and awake, waiting for an idea to occur. Lisa found a gaggle of middle-school students who had just finished their semester that week. But a few yards away she saw one of the girls who had been in the car the night Bobby had gone berserk and the black man had saved them.

They sat together for a while, exchanging no more than half a dozen words. All around them swirled a busy universe of young mothers in fashionable four-wheel-drive vehicles, rushing here and there on errands, some with young children in tow. The mothers got out of their cars and hurried past the adolescent vagrants in front of the Pizza Hut as if they did not see them, as if they were creatures of non-intersecting dimensions. But the natty little boys and girls whom the mothers dragged by the finger across the shopping mall parking lot almost always looked back at the young people lying on the grass. They looked at them with the ferocious, wide-eyed, unfiltered, information-sucking curiosity that only very young children possess.

Lisa smiled at a little boy whose mother was hauling him toward a video store, and the little boy smiled back. A moment later a tear rolled down Lisa's cheek.

"Hey, man," the other girl said. "What are you crying for?"

She told the girl she had tested herself in the bathroom with a kit from the grocery store. She was pregnant.

"Whose is it?"

"Marty's," she said adamantly.

"Couldn't it be Bobby's? From what you told me about them? Haven't you fucked both of them?"

"It's Marty's!"

"Well, you have to go tell him, then. He has to do something."

Lisa shrugged and allowed herself to sink deeper into a disconsolate, sweaty hump on the ground. Then, very slowly and clumsily, she lifted herself to her feet, brushed dirt off her blue jeans, and began walking toward the back of the mall to look for her cousin, Derek Dzvirko.

THE CHAMPION SHOOK HIMSELF AND SHOT AN EVIL GRIN AT THE ON-lookers who had gathered at his shoulders. Then, as the moment approached, he became steely and silent, eyes fixed straight ahead, unblinking and wrathful.

The voice said, "FIGHT!"

The combatants moved in closer, leaping and whirling, chopping at the air with their forearms.

One of the onlookers, an eleven-year-old boy whose voice had not yet changed, screamed, "Watch this shit! It's so unbelievable, man! Watch what he does."

Just as his opponent was about to close on him, Derek Dzvirko pulled back on the joystick, punched a combination of buttons on the control panel of the video-game machine, slammed the joystick forward with both of its movement buttons held down, then released all of the buttons and yanked the handle straight back as hard as he could.

On the screen of the video-game monitor, the character Derek was controlling leaped into the air and began whirling. While the character remained suspended in midair, lightning bolts exploded from his hands and struck the opponent in the face. There was an explosion of blood and flesh, after which only a blackened bloody stump remained where the head had been.

"Watch, watch!" the little boy screamed. "He's not done!"

Derek slammed the joystick forward with one hand. The fingers of the other hand ran nimbly over the controls of the machine. On the monitor, his character's right hand shot forward powerfully, piercing the chest of his victim.

Derek yanked back hard on the joystick, and his character's hand pulled back out of the victim's chest holding his pulsing blood-squirting heart.

"Eat it!" the little boy screamed. "Eat his heart, man!"

Derek slumped forward against the machine. At age twenty, he was six feet one inch tall and weighed 210 pounds, but his face was still fleshy and soft, like that of a child. He turned to the eleven-year-old behind him.

"Hey, asshole," Derek said, "I don't know how to eat the guy's heart. Nobody does."

"My brother does," the boy said accusingly. "I've seen him eat guy's hearts."

"Bullshit!" Derek shouted, waving his hands and bugging out his eyes in mock anger. "Hey, give me a break, man. I just played about two hours on one quarter. I beat every guy there is in this game. I shocked this asshole's head off and ripped his heart out. I mean, what do you want from me?"

The boys in the claque watching him play exploded in a chorus of Beavis-and-Butt-head snorts and guffaws: "Yeah, no shit, man. Yeah, no shit. Give him a break, man, no shit. Yeah. The dude's cool. Two hours on one quarter, man."

Derek Dzvirko's video-game skill would have been a disaster for the owner of the DNA Comic Store at the back of Embassy Lakes Mall—he could play for hours on a single quarter—except that Derek's presence attracted dozens of preteen boys who drifted in to watch him play. Between the money the others spent trying to keep up with Derek on the video games and the substantial sums they all spent on related comic books, the store did very well on Derek Dzvirko and his pubescent male admirers.

Derek was also a master of role-playing board games like Dungeons and Dragons, in which players took on the personae of mythological characters and then engaged in elaborate battles with each other. The younger boys' mothers did not object to dropping them off at Derek's house in a middle-class neighborhood on the other side of Sheridan Street for several hours of game playing in the kitchen. Even though Derek was twenty, he was boyish and sweet, a straight arrow who never cursed in front of adults, didn't smoke, didn't wear an ugly hairstyle, had only one small earring, always worried about getting home when his mother expected him. He was, if anything, a good influence on some of the surly kids who came to his house to play with him.

His real father had divorced his mother, Linda, when Derek was six years old. The father didn't pay child support. Linda told Derek she couldn't get any money out of his father because he had fled to Mexico. Derek sometimes wondered if he would still recognize his father. He knew his younger sister would not.

Linda had remarried, to Richard Bohnert, a flight trainer for Pan American Airlines in Miami. Bohnert was an honest, responsible, tough man who stuck by his new family. When Pan Am folded, Richard Bohnert rolled up his sleeves and went to work mowing lawns. By working long hours in the broiling Florida sun, he was able to make the mortgage payments and keep the family well fed and the cars fixed.

Derek sometimes worked with him, but it was very hard work, and Derek tended to drop out of his stepfather's work crews when he had enough money to put gas in his pickup truck and pay for a week or so of fun at the DNA Comic Store.

Derek worked hard to finish high school, even though the courses were tough for him. When he was a senior, his mother came to him one evening where he sat at the kitchen table struggling with an algebra text that should have been easy for a middle-school kid.

''You sure stick with it, don't you, sweetie?''

''Mom, I know how much you want to see me walk down that aisle.''

He looked up at her, beaming, and she saw in his face the adoring eyes of her six-year-old boy. She bent forward and kissed him, and her tears fell on his cheek.

He tried to do some things after he graduated from Cooper City High School. He applied for a job as a police officer, but he was told he needed some college credits. He tried to enlist in the army, but the army told him he was unacceptable for duty because of a tiny steel pin left in his elbow from a boyhood bicycle accident.

He took a job selling pizzas in the stands at Joe Robbie Stadium, but that was only part-time. On some days he worked with Richard, readily agreeing to go along when he needed him, ducking out if he could when the weather was too unbearably hot.

His mother was Lisa Connelly's mother's sister.

LISA PUSHED HEAVILY THROUGH THE DOOR OF DNA COMICS, THEN stopped and leaned against the doorjamb at the end of the long narrow shop rather than try to wade through the throng of Derek's sawed-off admirers.

"Derek, I need a ride."

"Shit, man," Derek said, giving himself a little space in front of his fans. "I'm busy here."

"Yeah," the boys said in a chorus of sniggering Beavis-and-Butt-head voices. "He's busy rippin' guys' hearts out. Yeah, he's busy, man."

But Derek was already headed for the door. The truth was he liked helping his cousin. His mother had spoken to him several times about her.

"She has such an attitude," Linda would say. "She quit her job at the dry cleaner's at the mall just so she could be with this boy, Marty. Now Maureen can't do a thing with her. You're a good boy, Derek. Maybe if you sort of took her in hand, she might get the idea and straighten up a little."

"I NEED A RIDE OVER TO MARTY'S," LISA SAID WHEN THEY WERE outside on the mall parking lot.

"Sure thing, babe. My ride's right behind you."

It was midafternoon, and Sheridan was relatively quiet. It took him only fifteen minutes to make the seven-and-a-half-mile drive east on Sheridan from the Embassy Lakes Mall to Marty Puccio's parents' home, on North 42nd Avenue in Hollywood.

When they arrived, Derek and Lisa found that Marty and Bobby were alone in Marty's parents' house. Marty answered the door and seemed visibly irritated to see Lisa on the walk in front. Normally when he wanted to see her, he paged her on her beeper.

"I have to talk to you," Lisa said.

"Later. I'm busy."

"Now!" Lisa shouted at him. Her voice was suddenly angry and surprisingly loud. It seemed to catch Marty's attention.

"O.K. What is it? C'mon in."

He led her into the house and closed the door in Derek's face.

Derek stood around awkwardly on the walk for a while, and then, after several minutes, the front door opened and Bobby Kent appeared. Derek had met him a few times before and didn't like him. In fact, Bobby frightened him.

Derek had seen just enough of him to guess that he had a quick temper. He was the kind of guy who would consider a fight with Derek a fair match. Derek didn't want a match.

"Hey, dude," Bobby said in a fairly mild kind of way, almost on the verge of being friendly, "what's happening?"

"Nothin' " Derek said warily.

"Hey, c'mon in, man. Let me show you what me and the Marty-Man are workin' on. It's definitely cool." He motioned with his head, and Derek followed him into the house.

Once inside, Derek could hear Lisa and Marty talking in the kitchen. It sounded like an argument. He followed Bobby to the back of the house.

In Bobby's room, Bobby flipped on his VCR. The scene of Larry Shafer playing with a dildo began to scroll laboriously across the television screen.

"This is a guy we met at the Y," Bobby said. "We got him to do all this shit. We're going to sell this tape for a lot of money to porno shops. I mean a lot of money."

Derek was trying hard not to show that he was truly taken aback. He had never seen a dildo before and really wasn't sure what it was at first. But mainly it was the prospect of seeing a middle-aged man naked on television, playing sex games with himself: Derek suddenly felt a little queasy in the stomach.

"I'll wait outside," he said, turning toward the door.

"Hey, what's the matter?" Bobby challenged him, beginning to get angry. "You don't like our fucking tape, man?"

Derek drew himself up as large as he could. "It's gross shit, man. I don't like it. At all. I am going to wait outside."

Bobby backed off. Derek let himself out of the little room and walked back through the house to the front door. On his way out, he heard Marty yelling at Lisa, telling her to "get the goddamned money and get it fucking taken care of."

Then he heard Lisa call out, "Let go of me! You're hurting me! Please let go, Marty, it hurts!"

Derek turned and went to the kitchen, where he saw Marty holding both of Lisa's wrists in the air, squeezing as hard as he could with his beefed-up paws.

"Let go of her, asshole!" Derek shouted. He was angry, ready to let Marty have it.

When Marty saw Derek suddenly looming over him with blood in his eye, he quickly dropped Lisa's arms and backed away from her.

"Jeez, man," he said, smirking up at Derek, "we're just messing around."

Derek seized Lisa's arm and held it up. "Messing around, asshole? This doesn't look like messing around to me."

Where Marty's twisting hands had left blotchy red and white hand-prints on Lisa's wrists, the bruises already were beginning to turn a striated angry purple-black.

"Does this look like messing around, asshole?" Derek bellowed at him.

Lisa groaned and collapsed against the refrigerator, holding one forearm in the other hand.

"O.K., O.K.," Marty said, beginning to whine. "Jeez, I said I was sorry."

Bobby appeared in the doorway. He shouted at Derek: "Hey, what the fuck is it with you, man?"

Derek nodded for Lisa to follow him. He pushed through the door, brushing roughly against Bobby with his shoulder. Bobby stepped back out of the way. Lisa followed.

As Derek and Lisa walked down the front walk to Derek's truck at the curb, they heard Bobby and Marty giggling and crooning through the open door, "Bye-bye, Shamuuuuu!"

"Jesus Christ, Lisa," Derek said, when they were back out on Sheridan, driving west. He looked down at her wrists, which were now swollen and awful-looking. "Damn, Lisa! Those guys are sick! They're sick!"

Lisa was silent for a while. Then she began to sniffle and then to cry. Finally she collapsed into loud racking sobs.

"Damn, Lisa," Derek said. "Why don't you tell that guy to just go fuck himself? You don't need that shit. Nobody needs that shit."

Lisa was bringing herself slowly back under control, still crying, wiping her nose on the shoulder of her T-shirt. Black rivers of mascara poured down her cheeks and smudged the shoulder of her shirt.

"Take me back to the mall," she mumbled.

"What?"

"Take me back to the mall."

"Why don't you just go home, Lisa, or come over to our place for a while? We can play Monopoly if you want."

"I don't want to play fucking Monopoly!"

"You love Monopoly."

She turned toward him and shrieked: "Take me back to the god-damned mall, asshole! I have to get some money! I have to see if anybody will lend me some money! I'm pregnant, Derek! Do you know what that means?"

Derek shrugged. "Yeah. But maybe not really. What do you mean?"

"I have to get a fucking abortion. Marty wants me to get the money myself."

Derek and Lisa stopped at McDonald's. It was midafternoon when Derek left Lisa back at the Embassy Lakes Mall. In her loose-fitting jeans and filthy T-shirt, with her thick red hair hanging down in ropes,

Lisa lumbered through the mob of smartly dressed suburban shoppers, running her traps, wandering from one spot to the next where her friends usually gathered in shoals at about this time of day.

Her dirty clothes, the horrible, obviously new bruises on her wrists, her shuffling gait, and the expression of numb despair on her face—in this sea of success and confidence, she could not have stood out more starkly if she had set herself on fire. As she passed through the shoppers, men and women quickly averted their eyes, but the children stared.

When Lisa found girls she knew, she approached them and said, ''I'm pregnant, man. I have to get an abortion. Is there any way you could spare me some cash?''

A girl in front of the Pizza Hut gave her four dollars. Almost all of the dozen or so other girls she approached said they could not afford to give her any money. A girl in front of the DNA Comic Store, someone she knew from Cooper City High School, gave her five dollars.

At ten P.M. that night, with her nine dollars wadded in one pocket of her blue jeans, she walked to the edge of the mall, waited for the light at Sheridan and Hiatus, then made her awkward crossing toward home.

The moment Lisa came through the front door, Maureen saw the bruises, saw the condition of her clothes, that she had been crying all day and wiping her face on her shirt. Most painful of all for Maureen was the terrible expression of pain and hopelessness in her daughter's eyes.

Maureen swore, cursed, raged around the house trying to bring herself under control.

''I am sending my goddamn brother over there, and he is going to beat the shit out of that little bastard. I mean beat the living shit out of him!''

If her mother made good on this particular threat, Lisa knew Marty was in very serious trouble.

''No, please, Ma, please. I love Marty! I love him more than anything!''

For a long while Maureen stood in the tiny kitchen with the fingers of both hands pressed against her forehead.

"All right," she said finally. "I don't understand this. I just don't understand what's going on with you, Lisa. Maybe I don't want to know."

"Please, Ma, don't get Marty hurt."

Maureen waved her hands in front of her face in a gesture of clearance. "O.K. Fine."

She lifted her face and shook her head at her daughter. "You need a bath, young lady."

But Lisa ran to her room, collapsed on her bed, and cried herself to sleep.

She slept fitfully and awoke several time during the night. In the dim light of the streetlamps shining through her unshaded bedroom window, she lifted her wrists and looked at them in horror.

She heard their voices so clearly, as if they were in the room with her: "Bye-bye, Shamuuuu."

And the giggling. The two of them inside the shadowed doorway of Bobby's parents' home, cackling.

The swelling of her wrists made Lisa feel even fatter. She rolled on her stomach and stared into the blackness of her pillow.

One time, one time only, when they were alone in Marty's parents' house smoking dope and drinking, when they were in the middle of intercourse, Marty leaned to her ear and whispered softly, "I love you."

She squinted her eyes into the pillow, balled her fists, and played those words over again and again in her mind. He was the Impossible Dream, the God of the Beach. His body was the body of a guy in a magazine. His face was the sweet, boyishly cute face of a child. He took her in his arms, naked, and had intercourse with her.

He loved her. And she loved him with a fury she could not contain.

She rolled over onto her back and stared at the ceiling. She squeezed her fists, even though it hurt her. She held her breath and squeezed harder, until the pain shot up into her armpits. She exhaled explosively, then breathed heavily until she had caught her breath.

It was Bobby.

CHAPTER FOUR

BOBBY MADE MARTY MEAN. BOBBY BEAT MARTY UP. BOBBY PUT MARTY down in front of other kids.

Marty was ten times the surfer Bobby would ever be, but Bobby always had to show everybody on the beach that he was the master and Marty was the dog.

Marty was mean because Bobby wanted him to be. Marty was afraid of Bobby.

Lisa sat up in her bed.

Marty wouldn't be mean any longer. The other side of Marty would come to the surface—the sweet boyish Marty who had whispered in her ear that he loved her. Everything would be fine.

When Maureen came into the kitchen at 6:30 A.M., Lisa was there with the light on, sitting at the little table with a cup of coffee, dressed with her makeup on.

"What are you doing up this early?" Maureen asked, pouring herself a cup of coffee.

"Nothing," Lisa said.

Maureen came over and examined her wrists, which were black-and-blue.

"Ma," Lisa said, "I think I might be going to North Beach today."

"Good," Maureen said. "Do you good. Who you going with?"

"Maybe Derek."

"Good. He's a good boy. Linda and I both wish you would spend more time together. Your cousin is a good kid."

"Yes, Ma."

After her mother left, Lisa watched the small television set on the kitchen counter. She sat at the table for three hours. At 9:00 A.M. she picked up the phone and paged Marty. She waited tensely to see whether he would acknowledge the page. Ten minutes later the phone rang, and she snapped up the receiver.

"Yeah, what do you want?" Marty said. His words were tough, but there was something soft in his voice that gave her hope.

"I want to see you."

There was a long silence on the other end. Finally he said, "I'm sorry about your arms."

Her heart flew up.

"I need to see you," she said quickly.

"Did you get any money?"

"Nine bucks."

"Shit, Lisa. An abortion costs three hundred and fifty."

"It's O.K. I have an idea. That's what I wanted to see you about."

"An idea about the abortion?"

"Yeah. Could we meet at the beach? At North Beach, maybe?"

Any proposal stood a better chance with Marty if it included a trip to the beach.

"I guess," he said. "How will you get there?"

"Can you pick me up?"

"I guess."

LISA PUT ON HER NEW SWIMSUIT AND A PAIR OF SLAPS, THEN COVered herself with an oversized T-shirt. She waited in the kitchen until she heard him blow the car horn, then flew out the door.

Outside the air was swampy and hot, blowing in off the sawgrass and sticking to the malls and subdivisions like a prickly wool blanket.

They rode east on Sheridan in silence. Marty kicked his mother's red 1987 Mercury Topaz in and out of traffic through Hollywood, across Dixie Highway into Dania, then out over the causeway across the fetid mangrove flats, flying above the gray choppy water of the Intracoastal Waterway, and then finally they were at North Beach Park.

The morning wind was blowing in from the Atlantic. Out on the sand the world was much cooler than it had been inland. The air was clean and bright. The glittering sea rolled in from the deep in great blue-green humps and then broke on the bars in a pearly white surf.

Lisa and Marty didn't have to talk; they knew the routine. She sat dutifully where they had dumped their stuff in a heap of towels, T-shirts, and gear, while he strode straight into the surf with his board under one arm.

Up and down the beach the day's contingent of tourists, school-skippers, and beach vagrants was just beginning to settle in.

She watched him paddle out. The sea, crashing over him, covered his brown body with a bright ceramic glaze; the muscles in his back stood out and worked like ropes; his long white-blond hair fell forward in a jagged cowl around his face.

As always when she watched him going out, Lisa felt a little light-headed and short of breath, unable to believe that she was here and he was hers.

Then he rose on the board and came dancing back toward her at the lip of a roaring white wave. The edges of Marty's surfing style had dulled—an expert observer on a serious surfing beach might be underwhelmed—but he was still almost always the most impressive thing going on this beach. Lisa looked around and saw people on the beach watching Marty come in. She heard a preteen boy sitting nearby with his parents say, ''Wow,'' and her heart swelled.

Marty paddled out and rode in on half a dozen more waves. The boy sitting nearby with his parents got up and wandered down to the water's edge, where he stood and watched shyly while Marty came in out of the sea.

Lisa came down to meet him.

"Where you from, kid?" Marty asked the boy.

"Michigan."

Marty showed the boy the board. The boy squatted and stared at its construction with intense concentration. As Marty talked to him about surfing, the boy lifted his eyes and studied Marty with hungry fascination, drinking in every detail of his body, his clothing, the hair, the way Marty spoke. When Marty's facial expression changed, the boy's face changed, too, unconsciously mimicking Marty's frowns and smiles, working his mouth the way Marty's mouth worked, learning him. Nothing in the sea itself could be as exciting as this man from its waves. He was a window.

When Marty and Lisa went back to sit by their stuff, the boy walked out into the surf up to his mid-thighs, then turned, dragging his fingers in the water, and watched from afar while Marty talked to his girlfriend.

"So what's your deal?" he asked her.

She sat as usual with her face averted, looking down between her knees or off in the distance. But then she lifted her eyes and looked him in the face.

"I want to ask you something, Marty."

Something in her tone gave him pause. He looked at her curiously, then shrugged.

"Do you think Bobby's weird?"

"Why? Weird how?"

"Weird, like weird. Like that guy in *Sleeping with the Enemy,* the psycho guy who was married to Julia Roberts. He was always washing his hands all the time like Bobby does."

"Yeah, he's kind of weird. Like that. So what?"

"Why do you let Bobby treat you the way he does?"

"What?"

"Why do you let Bobby treat you like he does? Hit you and stuff and make fun of you? He disses you right to your face, in front of everybody.''

Marty shrugged, to show that he had no intention of talking to her about any of it.

"Derek thinks you guys are queer for each other."

Marty recoiled as if physically struck. "What?" he snapped. He was beside himself. She started to talk, but he spoke over her, telling her that Derek was an asshole, a dink who didn't know anything.

They were both quiet for a while. Then Lisa turned, so that she was sitting on the sand Indian-style, facing the side of Marty's face. Marty stared out to the sea, past the boy who was still watching him.

"You know what?" she whispered.

He said nothing.

She reached tentatively with one finger and pressed it against his shoulder.

"I love you."

Marty dropped his face and muttered, "Lisa."

"I do. I love you. And I care about you. And I don't want to see you suffer. I don't want to see Bobby picking on you ever again."

Marty lifted his face and returned her gaze. "Lisa," he said, "Bobby and me . . . this shit with Bobby . . ." He shook his head.

"What?"

"It goes back to when we were kids, Lisa. Little kids. Bobby has always been like this. He's always just beat the shit out of me when he felt like it and punched me out and shit." His voice was beginning to quaver. "There isn't a goddamned thing I can do about it. I used to beg my fucking parents to let us move someplace else. . . ."

"You could move away. Yourself."

He shrugged. "How? I'm not even a high school graduate."

"Yeah," she said. "I know. Tell me about it. So there's no way to stop him? Ever?"

Marty sat shaking his head, biting a lip and looking away. "Yeah. There's a way to stop him. Kill him. But that's about it."

"That's what I was thinking."

Marty snapped around to look her in the face. "What?"

Neither one spoke for a long while. Finally, looking out to sea again, Marty said in a soft voice, "What are you talking about, Lisa?"

"Bobby."

"What about Bobby?"

"What if he was gone?"

Marty snickered. Then he turned, so that he was sitting Indian-style, too, facing Lisa, their faces inches apart. "What kind of weird shit are you talking about, Lisa?"

She didn't answer at first. But very slowly she smiled. "What if we killed him?" she said.

Marty laughed, then rocked back on his haunches, holding on to his knees. He came back forward, then peered intently into her eyes.

"What if we killed him?" he said, repeating her.

She nodded yes. Bubbling up from deep within her, a laugh erupted, a guffaw, a chortle.

He shook his head and said over and over again, "You are nuts, Lisa. You are totally insane."

She took Marty's shoulders in both of her hands and put her forehead against his. With her eyes drilling into his, she pressed the case: Bobby was always dissing everybody; he was always mean, always cruel; he beat Marty up.

Lisa said Bobby was too off-the-wall and weird even for Ali, and Ali was into just about everything weird there was. Bobby was the source of everybody's trouble. And look: He was the one who was going to finish high school and go to college and probably get rich.

"Yeah," Marty said, "and I'll be delivering pizza to him in Weston."

Lisa had never spoken this many words to Marty before, had never sat holding his face close to her face, looking into his eyes and talking. She was suddenly overwhelmed by sexual hunger for him. She pulled his mouth to hers and kissed him deeply. His hands wandered down her shoulders to her back and then forward to her breasts. Fifty yards away, the boy standing in the sea blushed, giggled, and dove into the water.

They walked down the beach together, excited, bouncing and gesticulating as they talked. They talked about how it could be done—with a gun, or poison, or maybe by hiring a hit man. They talked about pushing him out of the car in a tough black neighborhood in Miami and yelling racial epithets as they drove off.

The more they talked and the longer they walked, the more excited Marty became. He continued to shake his head and say, "You're crazy," but now his tone was admiring.

"How could we get a gun?" he asked.

"My ma has one," she said.

"Shit!" Marty shouted, bouncing on the balls of his feet. "That motherfucker has picked on me and dissed me and treated me like shit my whole life."

Lisa stopped him, grabbed him by the shoulders, and said, "Let's kill him."

He pulled her to him, tight against his chest, and kissed her deeply. "No shit," he whispered.

Lisa was the happiest she had ever been in her life.

THEY DROVE BACK TO MARTY'S HOUSE AND MADE LOVE IN HIS ROOM for several hours. They were in the kitchen snacking when his mother came home.

"How are you, Lisa?" Veronica Puccio asked.

"I'm fine, Mrs. Puccio," Lisa said brightly. "How are you doing?"

Veronica turned to watch Marty lead Lisa out to the car. "I'm doing just fine, Lisa," she said with a smile. "Thank you for asking."

As soon as Lisa was home, she called Ali's pager in Palm Bay. When the phone rang Lisa blurted the news of the plan, stumbling over herself to get it all out. Ali laughed and burbled on the other end.

"You are crazy, bitch," Ali said.

"No, I'm not. No, I'm not. Marty agrees with me. This is the way for everybody to take care of their fucking problems, because Bobby is everybody's problem.''

''So what do you want me to do?''

''Come down and help us.''

''Oh, man. What are you gonna do it with?''

''I don't know. A gun or a knife or something, I guess.''

Ali was excited. Bobby was an asshole. It was like witchcraft. It wouldn't really happen. But it would be fun.

DONNY SEMENEC WAS SITTING ON THE FRONT STEP OF HIS MOTHER'S house in Palm Bay, scratching his dog, Baron, when Ali pulled up in her Mustang. Ali got out of the car, walked to the porch, and sat by him.

''What you doin'?'' she asked.

''Just talking to my dog,'' he said sweetly.

''You high?'' she asked.

''Not enough,'' he said, chortling wetly at his own wit.

He explained that his mother was making big plans for his eighteenth birthday, a week away. ''She's gonna have a party and cake and all like that, like when you're little.''

He nodded at the pleasant tree-lined street of new middle-class homes on both sides of him. ''I think she's happy here,'' he said. ''She likes it a lot better than Taunton.''

''Whatever,'' Ali said. ''Hey, I need to talk to you about something.''

He sat passively nodding his head while Ali explained to him that she was going to drive down to Lauderdale to help Lisa, her friend, kill a guy. A couple of times, Donny rolled his eyes and said, ''Cool.''

When she was done talking, they both sat in silence for a while, and then Donny said, ''So, like, you're not really gonna do this?''

''Yeah.''

''No.''

"Yeah."

"No."

"Yeah."

Donny squinted his eyes in close concentration. "You're gonna, like, kill this guy?"

"Yeah."

He shook his head in amazement and rolled his eyes. Then he said, "But you're not gonna, like, actually kill him. Like in real life."

"Yeah."

"No."

"Yeah."

He shook his head vigorously, as if trying to get rid of a bug. "Wow," he exclaimed. "That's some heavy shit, Ali."

"Yeah."

Ali watched him carefully for a while. Then she said, "You wanta go with me?"

He was motionless.

She said, "I just got some great dope in."

Donny shrugged and smiled. "Well, yeah. Let's go."

He laughed. She smiled.

"I need something, though," she said.

Once before, for one of their witchcraft parties at the cemetery, Donny had brought along a serrated survival knife in a brown-leather sheath. His brother, Shawn, a year younger than Donny, had received the knife as a gift the previous Christmas.

Ali said Lisa needed it.

"To do it with, you mean?" Donny asked.

"I guess."

Donny got the knife from his brother. He told Shawn that he was leaving to go somewhere with Ali for a few days but to tell his mother that he would be back in time for the birthday party.

Then Donny and Ali cruised the mall in Palm Bay, looking for Heather. They found her where she always was, out in front of Blockbuster Video, hanging out. All Ali had to do was throw open the door: Before she even came to a full stop, Heather was in the backseat.

"What's happenin', bitch?" Heather asked, reaching for the fat marijuana cigarette Donny was passing to her.

"We're gonna go down to Lauderdale and help Lisa kill a guy."

Heather's facial expression was clear and smooth, the amber surface of her eyes perfectly still. Struggling to hold down the smoke, she said, "Cool."

THE MORE LISA AND MARTY TALKED ABOUT KILLING BOBBY, THE more enthusiastic Marty grew. The notion of a life without Bobby Kent was so wonderful, Marty couldn't understand why he had never thought of it before. The idea of simply banishing Bobby Kent, erasing him, taking him out of the picture entirely, was brilliant.

Marty's attitude toward Lisa changed. He began speaking to her with a respect that had never been in his voice before. In fact, Marty was listening closely to what Lisa had to say, even counting on her for ideas.

On the afternoon of Tuesday, July 13, 1993, Marty was with her in bed at her mother's house.

"We could do it like a drive-by," Lisa said. "The cops would think it was a gang thing."

"Shit, that's a great idea," Marty said.

Lisa smiled and hugged him.

ALI AND THE OTHERS ROLLED INTO THE CEDARWOODS DEVELOPMENT at about 5:00 P.M. Lisa suggested they all go across the street to the mall and have dinner at Pizza Hut. One of the waitresses on duty when they arrived was Claudia.

When Claudia saw the gang all together, she sensed something. She led the party to a big round table at the back of the restaurant. On the way over, Lisa whispered hoarsely, "We are into some heavy shit here."

They ordered several pizzas, and then, while they waited, Lisa assumed the role of mistress of ceremonies. First, she ran through the bill of particulars:

"He just about raped Ali last time she saw him," Lisa said.

Donny, who was now nominally Ali's boyfriend, had never heard this news before. He managed to lift his eyebrows and straighten his back in an expression of concern. Ali shrugged at him to show that she appreciated his support but that it was all right.

"He's beat the shit out of me and raped me before," Lisa said. "He beats up retarded people and thinks it's funny to throw a football at retarded guys' heads and stuff like that."

It wasn't clear whether Heather was listening, but the others shook their heads to show disapproval.

"The worst thing he does, though," she said, "is he picks on Marty and treats him like a dog or a slave or something. That is what just pisses me off so bad I can't stand it."

The others stared at her in silence for a moment. Then Donny said, "So what are you gonna do, Lisa?"

"We're going to kill him."

Donny shook his head. "Man, that's heavy."

"Yeah," Lisa said, nodding her head earnestly. "It is."

"So how are we gonna do it?" Donny asked.

This time there was an even longer silence.

Heather said, "We could just drive by his house, you know, when he was out in front, like on the lawn or some shit, and shoot him down."

"Nah," Ali said. "Somebody would see us."

Lisa suggested sneaking into his house when he was asleep and stabbing him.

"Hey," Donny said suddenly, "I brought a survival knife." As if struck by the happy coincidence, he smiled and said, "We could use that."

Ali said, "Shut up, Donny."

Marty objected that no one would ever be able to sneak into the Kent house, certainly not anywhere in the vicinity of the back of the house, where Bobby slept: That area was well guarded by the dog.

"The best way is to just shoot him," Marty said.

"So how do we get a gun?"

"My mom has one," Lisa said.

"No shit," Donny said.

"Yeah."

Maureen Connelly kept a .25-caliber Beretta 950 BS autoloading pistol next to her bed. The gun was not registered. Neither Florida law nor Broward County ordinance required that a handgun kept at home be registered.

"Why don't you get it?" someone suggested.

There was general agreement that getting Lisa's mother's gun would be a good first step. Then the pizza arrived, and they spent the rest of the meal talking about music.

As soon as they had finished eating the last piece of pizza, they paid the bill and rushed to their cars.

On the way out, Lisa went to Claudia, who was taking an order. She waved her over for a conference.

"Excuse me for just a sec," Claudia told her customers.

Lisa leaned to her ear. "We're gonna fix Bobby Kent's ass," Lisa said.

"Cool," she said.

On the way back to Lisa's mother's house, they all smoked dope. Once there, they gathered in Lisa's bedroom with the door closed. Lisa disappeared for a while.

When she returned, she had her hands behind her back. Slowly, dramatically, she produced her mother's pistol. She held it up before them for a while and then laid it carefully on the bed in its brown-leather clip holster.

"Holy shit," Donny Semenec said. "What's that for?"

"To kill Bobby Kent," Lisa said impatiently. "Don't you remember?"

She tilted her head away, looked at Ali, and made a circling motion with one finger pointed to her temple, indicating she thought Donny was not all there. Ali shrugged.

"It'll get blood all over," Heather said.

"Yeah," Lisa said. "We'll have to plan where we're going to do it."

They talked about a number of possible locations, but each site— the beach, the mall, the neighborhood where Bobby and Marty had lived all their lives—was marred by the possible presence of witnesses. Finally they hit on the idea of going to a remote place at night so that there would be no witnesses.

One of the group knew of an area of excavations on the far western fringe of suburban Lauderdale, in Weston, where developers were dredging new channels and piling up muck to dry for new golf-course communities. There would be roads out there with no houses at all on them yet, surrounded by barren humps of landfill. They could take Bobby Kent out there.

Maureen Connelly came home from work, poked her head in the door, and said, "Hi, kids."

"Hi, Mrs. Connelly."

Ali said, "Mrs. Connelly, these are my friends from Palm Bay, Donny and Heather."

"Hi, Donny. Hi, Heather. You kids have supper?"

"Yes, ma'am."

"O.K."

As soon as the door was closed again, Donny said, "Are we really going to do this?"

"Jesus Christ, Ali," Lisa snapped, "can you get this guy to shut up?"

"Shut up, Donny," Ali said.

He shook his head amiably to show that he would shut up.

"How are we going to get him out there?" Marty asked. "We can't just hit him on the head and drag him."

"How come?" Heather asked.

Marty and Lisa looked at her in surprise.

"He's too strong," Lisa said.

"Haven't you ever met him before?" Marty asked.

"Nah," Heather said.

"Me neither," Donny said brightly. "What's he like?"

Lisa leveled a long hard look at Donny. "He's an asshole," she said.

"Cool."

They debated several methods of luring Bobby to his death on the barrens in Weston. Lisa suggested that Ali offer to have sex with him, but Marty was not sure intercourse alone would be enough of a draw.

It was Ali who hit on the idea of allowing Bobby to "dog out" her Mustang, which meant driving it fast and making it spin and spit gravel on the flats along the new canals. She was fairly certain that the combination of sex and driving the car roughly on the gravel would be irresistible.

For a moment it looked as if Donny was going to ask something, but the rest of them stared him down, and he shrank back into obsequious silence.

Lisa said, "If Ali's down here because she wants to get laid by Bobby, then what's Donny here for? I mean, she brought her new boyfriend along so he could watch while she screwed another guy?"

"You could say they're fighting," Heather suggested.

Marty spoke up: "Nah, he won't believe that. Then what's the guy still here for, hanging around? I mean, nobody's that big a dweeb."

They all looked at Donny for a while in silence.

"Just say I'm Heather's boyfriend," Donny said.

"Hey, all right!" Marty said. "That's cool. That'll do." He put out his hand for Donny to high-five him, and Donny returned the gesture.

"Good thinkin', man," Marty said, smiling at him reassuringly.

"Yeah," Donny said, blushing. "Thanks."

*　　*　　*

MARTY USED LISA'S PHONE TO CALL BOBBY, WHO WAS JUST GETTING home after a shift at the Publix.

"Hey, man," Marty said.

"Hey, man," Bobby said.

They talked for a while about some modifications Bobby had in mind for his sound system. They agreed on a time to meet the following afternoon to lift weights together at the Y. Bobby relayed the news that he had been rejected again in an attempt to market *Rough Boys* to another porno store.

"No shit?" Marty said.

"Yeah. Well, I got some other places in mind to try."

"Hey, guess what, man? Guess who's here? I'm over at Lisa's. Ali's down. I think she wants to talk to you."

Ali got on the phone with Bobby and launched quickly into a purring, flirtatious routine. She talked about not having seen him in a long time, about missing him, about things not having worked out with some other guys.

"They didn't work out too good with us, either," Bobby said.

"Oh, I don't know," Ali whispered. "I kind of liked what I saw. I keep thinkin' about it."

"Yeah? About what?"

"It." She laughed. Then she suggested they go out somewhere and dog out her Mustang.

Bobby asked to talk to Marty again.

"What is this shit, man?" Bobby asked him.

"I don't know. She digs you, I guess. Wants some more. She's sure fine. I'm jealous."

"You over there with Shamu?"

"Yeah."

Bobby laughed. "Sick."

THEY AGREED THAT THE GROUP WOULD COME OVER TO MEET BOBBY at his house. Lisa and Ali would go with Bobby to Weston to dog out the car. That way they could get the murder done quickly and simply, and there wouldn't be a lot of kids running all over attracting attention. Lisa suggested they could just roll the body into the canal.

"That's out by the Glades, man. The 'gators will eat his ass for lunch."

The others laughed.

Lisa stuffed the gun into a small purse. Ali put the survival knife under the seat of her car.

Ali went to her car, got a suitcase from the trunk, and brought it into the house. She went into the bathroom and changed into a white tube top and a tiny skirt. She pulled her hair back and put on lipstick.

Lisa was wearing an oversized man's T-shirt over baggy shorts and a huge pair of running shoes, unlaced.

Lisa handed Ali the gun.

"What?" Ali said. "What're you giving me this for?"

"Because you're in the best position to do it. You fuck him, and then, right when he's about to come, you blow his brains out."

"Oh, man!" Heather said. "That's cool."

"Nah," Ali said, "you're the one who wants him dead."

"Ali! You said you wanted him dead, too! It's too risky if I do it. I would have to follow you, and he might hear me coming."

"No, Lisa, you do it!"

Lisa came forward, angry. "You just stuff it in your shorts like this."

She spun Ali around by one shoulder, pulled out the elastic of her waistband with a finger, and shoved the cold steel barrel of the gun down against Ali's buttocks, so that Ali jumped a little.

Lisa tugged on the tube top to make it cover the gun, pulling on it so hard that Ali had to hoist it back up in front to cover her nipples.

"I'll be right there, close by," Lisa said. "You shoot him. We'll ditch the body."

When they arrived at Bobby's house, darkness had fallen, and the first layer of the day's heat had lifted up off the city. It was still sweaty hot and humid outside, but at least the merciless flare of the sun had abated.

Bobby was waiting on the front lawn as usual. He wore khaki shorts, a white T-shirt, and expensive tennis shoes. His hair was newly slicked back.

They all kidded around for a while on the lawn. Heather and Donny were introduced as boyfriend and girlfriend.

Then Ali said, "Let's go out to Weston and mess around out on those new developments, dog out my car or some shit like that."

"Cool," Bobby said. He turned around and surveyed the rest of the group. "Everybody coming?"

"Nah," Marty said. "I'm kind of tired. I think I'll go home." He turned to Heather and Donny. "I'll give you guys a lift back to Lisa's."

"What?" Bobby said. "Where's Lisa going?"

"I'm going out there with you guys," Lisa said.

"Oh, come on, man," Bobby whined. He turned to Marty and muttered softly, "I don't want your fat bitch out there with us."

"She knows where we want to do it," Ali said.

"I can find places," Bobby said.

Ali stepped in front of Bobby. She hung her arms over his shoulders and grazed up against his chest, just touching him with her nipples, bringing her hips forward against him.

"C'mon, Bobby. She's my homie. I haven't seen her in a long time. I need to talk to her on the way out."

Bobby made a dismissive waving gesture with both hands. "Whatever. I'm drivin'." He went back into the house to wash his hands, then came out and jumped into the driver's seat of Ali's Mustang.

He turned on the ignition and barely waited for Lisa to tumble into the backseat before he slammed the car into gear and took off down the street in a screaming stink of rubber and exhaust.

"Good-bye, asshole," Marty muttered.

They wandered lost for a while on the darkened roads out beyond the last frontier of completed subdivisions, but finally Lisa was able to direct Bobby to the place she had in mind, on South Post Road. As they drove west toward the yawning mouth of the Everglades, the land to the left of them was absolutely black and formless. On the right side of the road, they saw the glittering cathedral windows of huge new homes in the Windmill Ranch Estates subdivision, home to Miami Dolphins quarterback Dan Marino and other luminaries.

Marty turned left off the pavement onto a hard-packed construction road through mounds of dredged fill dirt. Some of the mounds loomed up two and three stories above the flats—little man-made mountains.

When they were far enough away from the road, Bobby stopped. Everyone climbed out. They talked, mumbled, made small talk. No one was exactly sure what was supposed to happen next.

It was very dark. There was no traffic on South Post Road. The only sound was the whining of insects along the long black canal ten yards from their feet.

"You wanta dog it out?" Ali asked Bobby, gesturing toward the Mustang.

"Fuck the car," Bobby said. "Why don't I dog you out?" He put his hands on Ali's shoulders and yanked her up against his chest. "C'mon, baby. Give me a ride."

He slipped his hands around to her back to get a better grip. His fingers dug into her flesh, a few inches from where the butt of the gun made a bulge beneath her tube top.

Ali wriggled free frantically. "C'mon, man, give me a break!"

"Give you a break?" Bobby demanded, stalking after her. "What the fuck we come all the way out here for? Instead of I give you a break, how about you give me a fuckin' blow job, bitch?"

Ali hurried off a few yards to Lisa.

"Shit," Ali whispered in panic, "get the fucking gun off me, Lisa! If he finds it, he'll kill us!"

Bobby had paused a few yards away.

"What's the matter with you bitches?"

Lisa reached down Ali's back, snatched the gun out of her pants, and shoved it into the front of her own shorts.

"Take him down the road," Lisa whispered. "I'll follow you."

Ali turned to Bobby. "O.K., O.K., if that's what you want."

Bobby nodded, glaring darkly at her. "That's what I want."

Ali walked past Bobby and led him away from the car, down the dirt road into the blackness. Lisa could hear the crunch of their feet fading in the distance. She plodded after them, trying to walk softly on the gravel.

In a moment, Lisa could see them again, their backs ahead of her in the darkness. She could see Bobby's arm moving up Ali's back, pulling her roughly against him.

With each step, Lisa could feel the long hard cylinder of the barrel rubbing against her belly. She reached into her shorts and drew out the gun.

Now she could see Ali's head dropping down in front of Bobby, her hands pulling Bobby's shorts down around his knees. In a moment she could see Ali's head moving up and down slowly in front of him.

Bobby didn't hear Lisa close behind him. Lisa held the gun down at her side.

She lifted the gun, expecting at any instant that Bobby would hear her, turn, see the gun in her hand. She felt sweat pouring from her face, her neck, beneath her arms, on the inside of her legs.

He was only four yards ahead.

For a split second, Ali stopped and looked around Bobby's hip, straight at Lisa, letting Lisa know that she knew exactly where she was.

"What's the matter?" Bobby said to Ali.

"Nothin' " she said dully. "Just take it easy."

"Well, c'mon, bitch," he whined.

Here was the perfect shot. Ali was down below his waist, clear. He had his back to Lisa. Lisa lifted the gun and pointed it straight at the back of Bobby's head.

Her hand was shaking violently. She knew that she had to shoot now. The gun was suddenly heavy. She held it in both hands to steady it. She thought about how badly she wanted to see him dead, about the time they had beaten her with the weight-lifting belts, about Shamu and Fatso, about Marty, how much she loved him, about

Bobby ruining Marty's life and her life, too. She saw his back in front of her in the gloom, beginning to shiver and quake with cruel pleasure, and she thought how good it would feel, right when he came, to pull the trigger and splatter his guts all over the swamp.

She dropped her hands. She felt suddenly dizzy. Breathless. She turned and began walking away as quietly as she could, back toward the cars. She stuffed the gun back into her waistband.

She saw: She could not do it. She just could not do it herself. It wasn't there.

Whatever it was, good or evil, strong or weak, clean or filthy, it didn't matter, because it was not there. The stuff it took to seize another human life in one's own hand and crush it, extinguish it, put it out forever—it was not in her.

She was furious. If it was ever a game, it was no longer.

Ali and Bobby appeared from the darkness about ten minutes later. Ali was straightening her clothes and looked sullen.

There were a few words of mumbled conversation between them, and then they got in the car and drove back east on Sheridan Street in speechless silence. When Ali dropped Bobby off at his parents' home, he got out of the car without saying good night.

At Lisa's house, her mother was already in bed. Donny and Heather were awake and very stoned on marijuana. They squatted on the floor in Lisa's room, watching the Miss America contest on television.

Lisa and Ali sat on the bed for a while and watched the show. Suddenly Heather looked up at them and said, "Did you kill him?"

Donny turned, mildly interested.

"Nah," Ali said. "Lisa chickened out."

"Look at this Miss Texas," Donny said. "She is so fuckin' hot!"

"The fuck I did," Lisa said morosely.

Donny turned back to the television show.

Ali glared at her. "Then why didn't you shoot the son of a bitch while I was going down on him?"

Both Lisa and Ali turned hesitantly to watch Donny's reaction, but he seemed not to have heard and remained glued to the Miss America contest.

"Because I just thought of something," Lisa said. "On *Homicide,* they can take the bullet out of a body and trace it to the murder weapon. If I use my ma's gun, they could find out I did it."

Heather looked at Lisa blankly. "So toss it."

"Toss what?" Lisa asked.

"The gun. Toss it in the ocean. Then they can't trace the bullet."

"I can't do that," Lisa said. "It's my ma's. She'd kill me."

Heather snickered. "You're bullshit, too, bitch."

"I am not," Lisa said.

"Are so," Ali said.

After a while, Donny turned and said, "You guys need professional help."

ALI CALLED EILEEN TRAYNOR, THE ASIAN-AMERICAN GIRL WHO HAD been arrested at the Oakland Park Holiday Inn with Tom Hildebrand. Eileen suggested Derek Kaufman.

Derek Kaufman was twenty years old, six feet three inches tall, 235 pounds, and had the letters C.M.F. tattooed on one arm. The tattoo was the insignia of the gang he said he headed, the Crazy Mother-fuckers. The Crazy Motherfuckers, he said, were a division of the Davie Boys, a white gang well known to the police and greatly feared by citizens in the white middle-class suburban community of Davie.

Derek Kaufman's childhood had been normal and healthy, and he had seemed to be a fairly bright and promising boy until his parents divorced when he was eight years old. From that point forward, the clouds gathered over him in ever darker formations. He often needed counseling as a child and a teenager. His mother, Joan, said later she had been "a lousy mother" during those years.

He dropped out of high school in North Miami Beach after failing all of his courses except television production and ecology. He had no job. He had no plans. He lived in the large home of his stepfather, Ronald Esposito, just south of Weston in an unincorporated part of western Broward County, on the very edge of the sawgrass. The house was only a mile or so from the spot where Lisa and Ali had failed to murder Bobby Kent.

Ronald Esposito had been in the garbage business in New Jersey. He owned a land-development and landscape business in Florida, which involved planting palm trees for people. His house, which was a large rambling brick ranch house, was surrounded on two sides by a densely packed forest of the palms he grew for his business.

A taste for brickwork had inspired a long snaking brick wall around the front edge of the property, and the combined effect—the densely packed palms, the brick wall along the perimeter, the proximity of the sawgrass swamps—gave the place a forbidding quality.

That, and his stepfather's Italian surname, were enough to convince Derek's followers that he was, at age twenty, involved in organized crime. Of course, it helped that almost all of his followers were themselves at or near the age of fourteen.

Derek had no friends his own age. His oldest companion was seventeen but acted younger. The youngest members of his so-called gang were ten and eleven.

Derek led his lost-boy followers on criminal adventures that usually involved burglarizing parked cars and getting caught. Because he himself was no longer a juvenile, his arrests were recorded on his permanent criminal record. They included grand theft auto, fencing stolen property, and illegal possession of a concealed weapon.

When he talked about his record to his boy admirers, he invented other convictions for far more serious crimes, including murder. His size and his circumstances helped him put on a fairly convincing act, and it was natural that even a seasoned street tough like Eileen Traynor might mistakenly take him for what he claimed to be, a full-fledged, bullet-headed, cool-as-ice, down and dangerous Mafia hit man, instead of what he really was, the unemployed ne'er-do-well stepson of a palm-tree salesman.

Eileen called Derek Kaufman and told him about Lisa and her friends. She mentioned that two of the group, Ali and Heather, were hot. He said he would like to meet them. Then Eileen hung up and gave Lisa Derek Kaufman's phone number.

It made perfect sense to Lisa that she should bring in the Mafia. She called Derek Kaufman first thing the next morning, as if calling a service.

"I need to get this guy named Bobby Kent killed," she said.

Derek had understood Eileen the day before to say they wanted to have their friend beaten or terrorized. Lisa's suggestion of murder made him feel suddenly very much on the spot. "Maybe you oughta wait and think it over," he said.

"No," Lisa shouted into the phone. "I need some help right now! I need a weapon that can't be traced to shoot him with. I want him dead right away. Like tonight."

Derek gave her his beeper number and also gave her the home phone number for one of his main lads, a seventeen-year-old named Tom Lemke, with whom he had gone on many car-stereo stealing missions. He wanted the boys in his group to find out about his involvement with this new crowd.

Derek Kaufman was eager to meet the group, especially the girls. He bragged often to his boy soldiers about his sexual conquests, but in truth he was generally shy with girls and was less experienced with them than some of his youngest followers. The idea of meeting some hot girls in his role as a Mafia hit man appealed to him.

A couple of Derek's minions had pulled off a house burglary recently and, either luckily or unluckily depending on one's view, had chosen the home of a Broward County sheriff's officer. They had managed to escape with two service revolvers, but later they remembered making a number of mistakes—one of them had left at the scene his own billfold with his identification in it—which led them to believe this might turn out to be one of the many instances for which they eventually would be caught. Therefore, Derek thought, they might be eager to sell the guns while the selling was good.

Derek told Lisa he would check it out and get back to her.

Lisa called her cousin Derek Dzvirko to see if he could come over, but he said his pickup truck was out of order. She told him she might need his help with "something big" later in the day. She said she would send Ali's friends, Heather and Donny, in Ali's car to pick him up.

Heather drove. Ali didn't trust Donny with the Mustang. At Derek Dzvirko's house, they honked the horn at the curb. Derek came out and climbed in the back. He nodded hello to these two total strangers. Heather put the car in gear and without speaking started back toward Lisa's mother's house.

Donny Semenec and Derek Dzvirko were both capable of meeting someone for the first time and then spending the day with that person without ever exchanging a word. In fact, they were both capable of spending the day with someone they had known all their lives and never exchanging a syllable of conversation.

But on this occasion, in the split second when their eyes met, as Derek climbed into the cramped backseat of the Mustang, something immediately clicked.

"How's it goin'?" Donny asked.

"Cool," Derek said in his best novocaine monotone.

Donny craned around to look at Derek more closely. He smiled. Derek turned his face and stared out the window, expressionless.

"You wanta smoke some dope?" Donny asked.

They smoked a fat joint, sharing with Heather. When they were buzzed, Donny said, "What do you like to do?"

Derek shrugged. "Mortal Kombat."

"Cool," Donny said. "I love Mortal Kombat. I like to drop acid and play."

"Yeah," Derek said. "That's cool."

"You got a place to play?"

"Yeah. DNA Comics, in the mall across from where Lisa lives. You got any acid?"

Donny looked at Heather. They both exploded, laughing.

"What?" Derek asked.

Donny flipped open the glove box of Ali's car. There, stuffed in bags, boxes, and envelopes, was a stash of street narcotics big enough to blow away the entire teenage population of Embassy Lakes Mall. Donny unrolled a strip of LSD tabs, like postage stamps with the compound impregnated in glue on the surface. He handed one each to Heather and Derek. Derek put his to his tongue and sucked off the acid. Donny and Heather ate theirs.

By the time Heather dropped Derek and Donny at DNA Comics, they were both high and hallucinating mildly. They walked stick-legged, eyes popped open. Five boys hovering over the comic-book rack at the back, all around ten and eleven years old, watched the older ''men'' come in.

Immediately a Beavis-and-Butt-head chorus of exclamations went up: ''Blaaaasted! Oh-oh, I think they're wasted! Buuusted! Blaaasted! I think these guys have been experimenting with controlled substances!''

Since it was his home turf, Derek Dzvirko led Donny to the Mortal Kombat machine and dropped in the first quarter. He easily ripped several opponents apart, heaved their headless bodies onto pointed stakes in a pit, reached in, and ripped out their hearts.

On acid, they both raced in and out of the reality of the game. Sometimes they were really in it, ripping bodies apart. Derek sprouted two extra arms, and both of them grunted with pleasure and power. Donny struck such a terrible blow against his opponent that he severed his torso at the waist. The bloody legs stood quivering, rooted to the ground.

They were both experienced enough with acid to know not to fight it, not to resist if they felt themselves falling over totally into the reality of the game. That was when you started having bad experiences, when you tried not to accept the power of the drug.

Donny fought harder now, faster. His fingers flew over the controls. He turned himself into a dragon and ate his opponent. He fought the next opponent to a quick defeat.

But when the voice on the machine said, ''FINISH HIM,'' Derek shot a hand out and stopped Donny. Donny was startled. He fell away from the machine, light trailing from the corners of his eyes in fibers, the sounds of the shop and the game welling around him in a great roaring toilet flush of intelligence.

Derek Dzvirko loomed over him, Zeus-like. In a thundering voice that rose in the distance and swept over Donny like a physical wave, Derek said, "BABALITY!"

Donny was stupefied. The hair stood up on the back of his neck; his eyes were as big as saucers; he almost screamed.

He had heard of babality. He had read about it in the magazines. But he had never actually seen anyone pull it off, and, in fact, in the back of his mind, he had always wondered if it was a real thing.

Donny had played a lot of Mortal Kombat, on and off acid. He had ripped guys' heads off, split their torsos down the middle, burned their faces off, eaten them alive. He had had all of those things done to him. It didn't bother him.

But today, blasted on weed, ripped on acid, wasted from not getting enough sleep on Lisa's bedroom floor the night before, without a crumb of food in his stomach, the idea of really seeing a guy get babalized was so exciting that he thought he might actually throw up or wet his pants.

In the far distance, like a chorus of munchkins in Oz, he heard tinny little voices singing, "He's gonna hurl! Look out! He's gonna hurl!"

But he bit it back, put his hand to his mouth, and swallowed it down, let the LSD blow him right out of the universe and into the game, stood back, took his hands off the unit, and smiled sweetly at Derek.

"Do it," he said.

Derek stepped forward and took the controls.

A whisper whipped through the air around them as the preteens gathered to watch: "Babality! Babality!"

Suddenly Derek's left hand was flying over the control buttons; his right hand jerked back sharply on the stick, twisting it, fingers jabbing at the stick's fire buttons. He leaped a foot in the air and slammed the stick forward with all his might.

His opponent shrank back, seemed to physically wilt. Now Donny and Derek were deep in the game, really in it, living in the universe of Mortal Kombat, watching the defeated opponent writhe in an agony of melting flesh before their horrified eyes.

There was a ghastly shriek of agony. The dying man's flesh curled, writhed, morphed, bubbled up and splattered, turned dark and then green and then . . . pink! And it was over. The dead man had been transformed into . . .

A newborn baby!

The shop was silent for a long while. Finally Donny muttered, "Babality! Fuckin'-A, man. You babalized the dude."

First one of the onlookers said it, and then, in a chorus, they all took it up. "That is so gross, man. That is sooo gross. That is so totally gross, man, I mean it is just so totally gross. He babalized the dude."

Donny walked up close to Derek, put his hands up, and pulled Derek to him by the shirt. With his face inches from Derek's, Donny asked, "Is babality death?"

Derek shook his head no. He was so serious that he looked for a moment as if he might start sobbing. "No, man," he said, shaking his head violently. "No, man. It's worse. Way worse. Because you have to live, man. You have to live. And you're a fuckin' baby!"

Donny dropped his hands and turned away. "Oh, my God!"

"He's gonna hurl!" someone shrieked.

Then they all shrieked, "He's gonna hurl, gonna hurl!"

Donny rushed out onto the sidewalk in front of the shop, into the blasting heat of the Florida morning, and vomited into the street, right in the path of a slowly cruising Mercedes.

Derek stumbled out behind him, still mesmerized by what had happened.

Inside the shop the chorus sang, "Those guys were wasted! They were totally wasted, man, were wasted!"

CHAPTER FIVE

MARTY AND BOBBY MET AT PIZZA HUT FOR LUNCH, AS THEY HAD PLANNED the day before. Neither had much to say. They shared a large pepperoni pizza and a giant-sized soft drink with free refills.

Toward the end of their brief meal, Bobby said, "Ali gave me a blow job out there last night, and then I fucked her."

Marty nodded appreciatively. "She gave you a blow job, and then you fucked her? That's pretty good."

"Yup," Bobby said. Then he expelled a loud belch. "The power of steroids!"

Marty grinned and lifted his glass. "Steroids," he toasted.

Bobby returned the gesture. "Where'd we be without 'em?"

THEY DROVE IN BOBBY'S CAR TO THE HOLLYWOOD YMCA, WHERE THEY spotted each other in the weight room for two grueling hours. When they left, their bodies were hard as rock, and they were both exhausted and dehydrated. They stopped at a convenience store and bought giant soft drinks again. Then they reported to the Dania Publix for a short shift together at the deli.

Lisa had waited all morning and well into the afternoon for Derek

Kaufman to call. Finally she couldn't stand it any longer. She paged Eileen Traynor to find out where he lived. When Eileen didn't return the page, Lisa stormed out of the house and stalked off in the direction of the mall to find her.

Just as Lisa was walking out of the Cedarwoods development, Susan, the girl who had vomited in Bobby's car, was walking into the subdivision to see another friend there. Lisa rushed up and buttonholed her.

"Hey, you know Bobby Kent, that asshole whose car you threw up in?"

"Yeah."

"Guess what. You won't believe this shit. Guess what we're gonna do. It's so heavy! It is so totally fucking radical! You won't believe this shit."

"What?"

"We're gonna kill him."

"Oh, c'mon," Susan said.

"No shit, we are. We got this guy who does hits for the Mafia. And he's going to help us with it. We might just let him do it, or we might kill him ourselves. We're just sick of his shit."

Susan was taken aback, not so much by what Lisa was saying as by how she was speaking. Susan had never seen Lisa so revved, so wired, so alive. Lisa was gesturing wildly with her hands, talking a mile a minute. She asked Susan where she could find Eileen, and Susan told her. Lisa rushed off through traffic on Sheridan.

Eileen was hanging with some kids on the hump of grass across the parking area from the Pizza Hut. Lisa pulled her aside, to another part of the parking lot where there was a merciful blotch of shade from a feeble, exhaust-yellowed palm tree. She brought Eileen up to date on the plot and told her that she needed to know how to find Derek Kaufman's house, so that she could go there and maybe light a fire under him.

"Are you guys serious, you're going to kill him?" Eileen asked.

Lisa was nonplused. "Yeah," she said. She shrugged. "Why?"

"Well, I don't think I want to be involved in killing anybody."

"O.K. I didn't say you had to be. But would you help me find Derek Kaufman's house, so I can see if he can do it?"

"Sure."

They walked back across Sheridan to Cedarwoods, and all the way there Lisa was talking, jabbering, more excited and intense than Eileen had ever seen her.

When she was sullen and quiet, Lisa looked bovine and unattractive, but today her big brown eyes were flashing and her thick red hair danced about her face in flames. She was beautiful.

The girls—Lisa, Eileen, Ali, and Heather—gathered in the kitchen of Lisa's house and hurriedly made sandwiches of Genoa salami on Cuban bread. All the while, Lisa kept talking nonstop about the murder, how it would be done, how good it would be to get rid of Bobby. The other girls traded looks and smiles behind Lisa's back, as if to say, "The girl's snapped." Just when they had filled a plate with sandwiches, Marty arrived in his mother's car.

Lisa went to the phone and was about to call Derek Dzvirko's pager when Derek and Donny appeared out the front window, high-stepping across the street on the way home from their adventures at DNA Comics. They burst through the door, jabbering excitedly about their game. When their eyes fell on the plate of food, they elbowed through the crowd of girls at the kitchen counter and began devouring sandwiches by the fistful.

"Jesus Christ, man," Donny said to Marty, spitting food with every wet syllable, "you should have seen this guy. He babalized a guy."

Derek shrugged modestly.

"Hey, close your mouth when you eat, man," Marty muttered.

For the first time, the group noticed that Marty was in a sour mood.

Lisa came up behind him where he sat in the sofa and ran a hand through his hair.

"What's the matter, baby?"

"I don't know," he said, slumping deeper in his seat. "I'm just starting to think this whole thing is bullshit."

Lisa came around in front of him and exploded in a long, excited, rapid-fire description of the progress she had made that very morning.

She finished by telling him Eileen was there in order to take them to the home of the Mafia hit man.

"No shit?" Marty said.

"No shit, man."

His mouth swollen with salami, Donny said, "We're gonna go see a Mafia hit man?"

"Yeah," Lisa snapped impatiently. "Isn't that what I just said?"

"Man," Donny said, shaking his head somberly. "That is just so totally serious."

Marty seemed partially mollified and accepted the sandwich Lisa offered him.

After lunch Eileen called Derek Kaufman and told him they were coming out to see him. Derek asked that they park down the road, toward the back of his stepfather's property, at the point where the long brick wall surrounding the front and side of the property ended, where the forest of densely packed palm trees began.

It was a twenty-minute ride, west on Sheridan, north on Flamingo, west again on Griffin. They drove in two cars. On the way they stared out the windows at the endless new security walls along the roads and just behind them the tiled rooftops of big new homes, not yet occupied.

Eileen directed Marty to the spot at the end of the brick wall in front of Derek Kaufman's stepfather's house where they were to meet. Ali pulled up behind Marty, and they all waited in the cars for a few minutes. It was too hot to leave the cars running with the air-conditioning on; the engines would quickly overheat.

They all climbed out and stood around in a knot for a while at the end of the wall. Then Marty went back to his mother's car, reached in, and pushed on the horn a few times.

Seconds later, Derek Kaufman emerged from the darkened four-car garage at the back of the house. Lumbering down the driveway, he looked even bigger than he was. His burr haircut and punk clothes lent him a chilling aspect that was enhanced by the irritated expression on his face. He was waving his hands at them, and when he got closer, they could hear him saying, "Lay off the horn, O.K., man? Jesus shit, you're wakin' up the whole neighborhood."

Derek was approaching the back side of the brick wall, which came up to about the level of his stomach. It was clear he did not intend to come out from behind the wall in order to transact his business with them.

Eileen Traynor pushed ahead of the others and rushed to get to the wall before anyone else.

She leaned over and whispered to him, "Whatever they ask you, just say no."

But Derek Kaufman either didn't hear her or didn't understand. Or it may have been that he simply didn't agree. It was Lisa who approached next to talk to him, but Derek Kaufman's eyes were on Heather and especially on Ali, who was even more scantily dressed than usual.

"We need to know if you can get those guns for us, man," Lisa said.

Derek shrugged and danced, held up his hands and did his best cool.

"Well, hey, man, I mean, like, you got to give me some better notice than this, you know? Guns like that are kind of hard to come by just when you snap your fingers. Plus, they're not exactly free, you know."

Lisa told him they could get him some money later.

Ali, who had been standing with Donny, wandered closer to the wall. "Trust us," she said, cooing.

Derek looked Ali up and down. "Why do you want to do it with a gun?"

"I don't know," Lisa said. "It just seemed like the easy way to do it."

Still speaking to Ali, Derek said, "I think maybe you need to chill out and plan this a little better."

Some of the others started to nod their heads in agreement. But Lisa shot a quick look at Marty, who was silent, sullen.

"No," Lisa shouted suddenly. "I want it done now! Goddamn it, I want it done now! I want this son of a bitch dead! I want him dead tonight."

She turned on the group. "Listen, you motherfuckers, I want Bobby Kent's sorry ass dead tonight. Do you understand me?"

The others nodded.

"Look," Derek Kaufman said, "maybe I can help. I don't know."

He suggested they leave, search for other weapons, come up with a better plan, then call him later that evening when they were ready to do it. Lisa, Marty, and the rest of the group agreed.

Derek Kaufman pointed to a window near the rear of the house, just barely visible from where they were. He told them they were to go to that window when they came for him and rap lightly. Lisa and Marty listened soberly, making mental notes. No one in the group thought it odd that a Mafia hit man would have to arrange a Tom Sawyer signal in order to sneak out of his own house at night.

They said good-bye to Kaufman, piled back into the cars, and sped east again toward Pembroke Pines and the Embassy Lakes Mall.

Donny Semenec, who was sitting in the back of Ali's car, leaned forward and put his forehead against the back of Ali's head. He lifted his hand to pet her shoulder.

She put her hand on his hand. "What, baby?" she asked. "What's the matter?"

"Nothin'. I just love you, Ali. I truly love you."

Heather was sitting in front, across from Ali. She smiled at Ali and put her own hand on Ali's arm. "I do, too, Ali," she said.

"We're gonna be O.K., guys," Ali said. "We'll get this shit behind us, and Monday we'll be back in Palm Bay in time for Donny's birthday party at his mom's house."

The other passenger in Ali's Mustang was Derek Dzvirko. He and Donny fell back into conversation about their game earlier in the day and the phenomenon of babality.

Heather told Ali she felt like going to the beach to drop acid. Ali said it would have to wait.

In the other car, Lisa and Marty rode halfway back to Lisa's house without saying a word. Then, out of the blue, Marty began to speak. Lisa sat on the passenger seat, drinking in every word he said.

He told her a long story about being in the eighth grade and smoking marijuana for the first time. He had never smoked it, even though lots of other kids had by then. His family was strict Catholic, and he had been raised to believe the worst thing he could do in life was make his mother cry.

"She had always told me if she ever caught me messing with dope it would kill her."

Bobby, he said, had been smoking it for some time and had been wheedling and bullying him about it.

"It was so fucking important to him. If he did it, I had to do it. He just couldn't let it go."

Finally, one day when they were together waiting for the school bus to arrive, Marty gave in. Bobby promised him that the grass he had that day was very mild and would produce only a barely noticeable buzz.

In fact, it was about the strongest marijuana available at the time. Looking back, Marty now suspected it was also lightly dusted with some chemical adulterant, possibly even PCP. He took only two or three hits and was suddenly flattened. The world warped around him; sounds faded and then exploded through his head; he was terrified.

"I had no fucking idea how to handle it," he told Lisa. "All I could think of was to run."

He dropped his books at the curb and raced for home. Bobby followed a few paces behind, laughing uproariously.

When Marty got home, his parents and siblings were already gone for the day. The side door was unlocked as usual. Marty exploded through it, raced to his room, and leaped on his bed. He clutched the covers up around him, buried his head beneath the pillow, and tried to make the world stop collapsing.

"Fucking Bobby yanked the covers off me," he told Lisa with a catch in his voice, "and he just stood over me laughing this laugh that—I can still hear it, but I can't describe it."

"You know what I did, Lisa?"

"No."

"You know what I did?"

"What, baby?"

"I pissed all over myself."

Lisa put her hand on his elbow. Snuffling back tears, she said, "I love you, Marty. I love you so much. I can't even believe how much I love you. I would do anything for you."

Neither spoke again until they got back to the Connelly house.

At Lisa's there was trouble—a note from Maureen. She had returned from work briefly during the day and was not pleased by the condition in which she had found the house. She left Lisa a note telling her that none of her friends was welcome to spend another night there. Lisa called her mother at work and was sullen, but her mother was firm. There would be no overnight guests that night or anytime soon.

In the parking area in front of the house, Lisa broke the news to the rest of them that they might have to find other roosting places, at least for the next few hours until her mother went to bed. Then it would be easy for them to sneak back into the house and spend the night again in her room.

"We're calling Bobby tonight," she said. "We're going to use the same trick to get him back out there. But tonight we're going to kill him."

The others nodded agreement. Marty drove off with Derek Dzvirko. He dropped Derek at home and then went home himself.

Ali said that she had a friend nearby who could probably take her in for a few hours. She, Heather, and Donny left in the Mustang. Lisa went back into the house, went to her room, slammed the door shut, and flopped on her bed to watch television.

Ali drove to an affluent residential area fifteen minutes north of Lisa's house, to the home of a girl she had met while working for Tom Hildebrand. The girl's parents, who were upper-middle-class professionals, had no inkling that their daughter, a high school senior, had ever earned mad money by working as a prostitute. The parents happened to be out for the evening when Ali arrived.

Ali's friend took one look at Heather and Donny and smelled trouble. She warned Ali they could not stay long, and she told her they were not to smoke dope in the house. She herself had a date that evening with a boy from school, and she excused herself to go to the back of the house to bathe.

When she came back out from her bath, she was distressed to find Heather and Donny on their backs in her parents' living room, watching television with glazed eyes, beneath a thick cloud of marijuana smoke.

"Shit!" she shouted at them. "I told you not to fucking smoke dope in my house. My parents know what dope smells like, you know." She opened the front door and French doors in the back of the house.

Ali shrugged. She sat down in a chair, swinging a leg over one knee, and stared at the girl with a mischievous glint in her blue-green eyes.

"What?" the girl asked.

"Nothing."

"What? What are you guys up to? What are you all doing here, anyway?"

"Man," Ali said, shaking her head and chuckling, "you wouldn't believe it. We are into some shit that is so weird."

Donny rolled over and said, "Totally weird."

Ali spilled out the entire plot: She told the girl how they had hired a Mafia hit man who was going to come with them that very night and help them murder a boy named Bobby Kent, who was an asshole. She said they hadn't decided yet whether to use a gun or knives or some other weapon. She asked the girl if she wanted to come along.

"Well, what do you mean?" the girl asked. "Like, you're really going to kill this guy?"

"Yeah," Ali said. "It is so bizarre."

The girl sank into a chair. "Oh, man. I can't believe you all are really going to kill somebody."

"So do you?"

"What?"

"Want to come?"

The girl thought about it for a while. "Nah," she said. "If you were just going to beat him up real bad, maybe, but I don't think I want to be in on actually killing somebody."

"That's cool."

AT THE PUCCIO HOUSEHOLD, PEOPLE WERE COMING AND GOING; Marty's mother came home from work, fixed herself something to eat, and rushed off to a church meeting; his sister breezed through the kitchen, grabbed something microwaveable from the freezer, ate quickly, and left to study with a friend. Martin Puccio was working late.

Marty sat at a table in the kitchen, sipping a Coke and eating the leftover half of a hero sandwich he had brought home from work the day before. As the various members of his family drifted in and out of the room, he mumbled, "Hi" and "Bye."

When he had finished eating his sandwich, Marty went to his room and threw open the closet. As in all things, this was the beginning—choosing the costume.

DEREK DZVIRKO ATE AN EARLY DINNER IN THE KITCHEN WITH HIS parents. His father, exhausted from a tough day mowing lawns in the Florida sun, wanted to eat early and go to bed. Derek felt tired and dull, too, from his day of acid and Mortal Kombat, but no one noticed.

Toward the end of the meal, Derek told his parents that Lisa was going to come by with some friends and pick him up. His mother told him that she did not want him to stay out late and she did not want him to ride in a car with a driver who had been drinking or taking drugs. He promised her that he would be home at a reasonable hour, and he said he never rode with anyone who did drugs.

*   *   *

AT ABOUT 7:30 P.M., DONNY SEMENEC FORGOT AGAIN THAT THE GIRL whose house they were visiting didn't want him to smoke marijuana in the living room. When he lit up, she lost her temper and told them they all had to leave.

Ali beeped Lisa, who said that her mother was not home yet. Apparently she was working late or had gone out somewhere. Lisa asked Ali to go by and pick up Derek Dzvirko, then come to her house and meet her there.

But by the time Ali got to Lisa's house in Cedarwoods, Mrs. Connelly's car was parked in front. Ali kept driving and parked down the street a ways. She and Derek agreed that he would go to the front door and occupy Lisa's mother while the other three, Ali, Heather, and Donny, went to Lisa's bedroom window at the back of the house.

Derek managed to get in, say hello to Maureen, and make it back to Lisa's room in time to tell her to unlock the window. Then he came back out and sat on the sofa to watch television with Maureen and keep her occupied.

Maureen enjoyed talking with Derek. He was cheerful and seemed to have common sense. He often told her he didn't understand why other young people behaved the way they did. She told him stories of what the family was like back in the Bronx, when her grandfather was the chief and everyone else knew his and her place.

There was no trouble in the Bronx with young people misbehaving because they couldn't get away with it. They were always under the watchful eyes of their own relatives, and any aunt, uncle, or even a brother-in-law who saw a kid step out of line felt perfectly confident about taking the kid to task.

Now, since coming to Florida, it was different. Even though the family had come down more or less en masse, and even though everybody made an effort, people in the family just weren't as close as they used to be. Everybody was a long drive from everybody else; you didn't see your sister's kids running out front; people in the family lived in different neighborhoods, depending on how much money they were making, and sometimes that kept them apart.

Derek, wise beyond his years, nodded his head. He agreed that people just ran around wild too much, doing the first thing that came into their heads.

On this evening, Maureen surprised Derek by asking if he would like to go out somewhere and eat Chinese with her. She was not inviting her own daughter. It was understood that Lisa would not accept anyway. But Derek seemed like the kind of young man who could handle dinner and a little bit of conversation with an adult.

Derek looked up and saw Lisa nodding her head furiously in the background for him to go. She needed to get rid of her mother in order to do something with the others.

Derek accepted. He and Maureen walked outside to get into her car. But something at the back of the house caught Maureen's eye.

"Hey!" she bellowed. "Who in the hell is that?"

Moving slowly, sheepishly, Ali came slinking out of the shadows at the back of the house by Lisa's room. Maureen stalked back to the door, shoved it open, and shouted for Lisa to come out front.

"What the hell is this, Lisa?" Maureen demanded. "I told you I wanted these people out of here. What are you doing here, anyway, Ali? Don't your parents live in Palm Bay now? Don't they wonder where you are?"

Lisa stepped forward quickly. "She's on her way back, Ma, but she left some CDs in my room, and she was afraid to come to the door, because she thought you might get mad at her."

"I don't care if she picks up her own stuff. What, Lisa, I'm going to jump on her for picking up her stuff? What sense does that make?"

Lisa shrugged, as if to say, "Who knows?"

"Just get your stuff, Ali, and then go on. You and your friends are not welcome here, after the mess I found in my house. You all don't do anything, you don't work, you lay around and drive your cars and eat us out of house and home, and then you can't even clean up after yourselves. It makes me mad."

"Yes, Mrs. Connelly," Ali said, her voice ringing with sweet contrition.

Heather and Donny were still hiding in the shadows at the back of the house. As soon as Maureen and Derek had left, Lisa led the other three back to her room. Above her bed was a loft—a small finished section of attic, normally used for storage, that could be reached by a ladder.

They hurriedly rearranged the boxes and other items to make a screening wall at the front of the loft, then laid out a sleeping bag and blankets to make a bed for later that night. They jimmied the lock on Lisa's window to make sure it would not close all the way. It was now about 8:00 P.M.

Lisa got on the telephone. She set up a three-way conference call with Derek Kaufman and Marty. Marty said he thought it would work to tell Bobby Kent that Ali wanted to see him again and that this time they were all going to go out to Weston and race Ali's Mustang against Marty's mother's Topaz.

Derek asked how strong Bobby was, and Marty told him Bobby was very strong. Derek suggested they might all need some kind of protection, in case Bobby went berserk on them before they could get him dead. He thought baseball bats might be a good idea. Lisa said she would get Derek Dzvirko to round up some bats as soon as he got back from the Chinese restaurant.

When they hung up, Marty called Bobby and asked if he could come down the block to see him. By then Marty had decided on his costume for the evening but had not yet put it on. He walked down the street to Bobby's house, where he met him on the lawn. Both were wearing shorts and T-shirts.

Marty explained to Bobby that Ali wanted to see him again, and they were all thinking about going back out to Weston where Bobby, Ali, and Lisa had gone the night before. Bobby was noncommittal—not sure he felt like it. Marty urged him to come along, and Bobby finally agreed. Marty said they would drop back by for him in forty-five minutes or so.

As Marty was turning to leave, Bobby came up behind him and slipped his arm around Marty's neck. "You're my best friend, Marty."

"Yeah."

Marty was uncomfortable. Sometimes, at moments like this, Bobby would do something like choke him and throw him down.

But this time he dropped his arm away gently and gave Marty a pat on the butt. "See you later, bro'," Bobby said.

"Later."

When Derek came back with Maureen Connelly, Ali and the other two slipped up into the loft. Lisa came out into the living room, pried Derek away from her mother, and led him into her bedroom. She closed the door, and the others came down from the loft.

Lisa explained to Derek that she needed him to get some baseball bats.

"We gotta have some more weapons. Ali can drive you."

Derek was slow to answer. He turned his face from her.

"What's the matter?" she asked.

"I don't know," he said. He wouldn't look at her.

Lisa sensed that sending him to dinner with her mother might have been a mistake—an exposure to the wrong kind of influence.

Ali was also watching Derek's face carefully.

Lisa said, "My ma say something?"

"Nah. I just . . . I don't know. Everything's cool."

Ali slipped off the end of Lisa's bed and came to him. "My back hurts, Derek," she said. She looked up at him, kittenish, and made a mock whimper. "I think I have a tension backache. Will you massage me?"

Derek shrugged. He was interested.

"Me, too," Lisa said quickly. "I have a backache, too. I want a massage."

Both girls lay on their stomachs on the bed. Derek shrugged again, then took a sidesaddle position on the bed between them.

He slipped his hands up under Ali's tube top and worked her delicate back with his thumbs. She made sensuous ooh and ahh sounds and deliberately wriggled so that his hands slipped down to the borders of her breasts.

"Hey, watch it," she said, giggling.

He was embarrassed and turned to work on Lisa's back, but in her case he kept his hands outside her clothing.

"O.K.," he said, rising to his feet. "I'll go see what I can do."

Lisa went to the door, opened it a crack, and listened until she heard the sounds of her mother in the bathroom showering. Then Derek and Ali tiptoed out through the house to Ali's car.

Derek asked Ali to take him to the DNA Comic Store so he could use the phone there. She waited in the mall parking lot, right between DNA and Pizza Hut, while Derek called Babbages, a computer software store at the mall, and asked for Chris Hoadley, a kid who worked there. The manager said he was closing up and Chris Hoadley was probably at home.

Derek reached him at home. Derek knew that Chris Hoadley's brother was a baseball player. Chris had mentioned once that his brother probably had a couple of thousand dollars' worth of aluminum baseball bats—not hard to do in a day when one bat could easily cost $300.

Derek explained to him that a kid named Bobby Kent had raped this girl named Ali Willis, so Derek and some other kids were going to take him out in the Everglades and beat the shit out of him, or maybe wreck his car, or maybe even both. He said Hoadley could come along if he wanted to, but Hoadley said he couldn't because he had summer school the next day.

Hoadley agreed to lend Derek his brother's bats. He said he would put them just outside the front door of his house, behind the bushes. But he said Derek should ring the bell and come in because his parents would get paranoid if somebody stopped a car out front and started walking around on the lawn.

Chris Hoadley had already placed one aluminum bat by the door— a 32-inch, 25-ounce, blue and silver Easton—when his older brother discovered what he was doing and stopped him. Chris explained that some guys he knew from Embassy Lakes Mall were going to go out in the Everglades and beat the shit out of a guy who had raped a girl. They needed the bats to beat him up with and maybe to use also on his car.

Chris's brother said he didn't want his bats used for something like that. Chris said nothing to his brother about the bat that was already out front.

A short time later, Ali pulled up in front of the Hoadley home on a quiet street in a pleasant middle-class residential area. Derek eased out of the Mustang and rang the bell.

Chris met him at the door and ushered him in. Both of Chris's parents made a point of getting to the front of the house so that they could meet and examine this new young man who was dropping by to visit their son.

Even though Derek was big and was wearing all black clothes that evening, his appearance was considerably softer than that of many of the young people Chris Hoadley's parents saw every day at the Embassy Lakes Mall and at their son's high school. Derek didn't have any major perforations on his face—a small diamond stud in one ear—and there were no obscenities carved into the side of his scalp. He was a little overweight, but he looked as if he might actually get outdoors every once in a while and engage in work or other moderately strenuous activity.

Derek was genially polite. He made a remark about the night being very hot. Mrs. Hoadley offered him a cold drink, but he demurred. Both of Chris's parents hovered near the foyer for a while, until it was clear that they wanted to know why Derek was there.

"So, you can't come play baseball with us tonight?" Derek asked.

"Nah," Chris said. "School tomorrow."

"Chris's brother is the baseball player," the father said.

"Yeah, well, we're just messing around really," Derek said. He looked at Chris expectantly. Chris said he would show Derek out.

Once on the porch, Chris reached behind the bush and then handed Derek the Easton baseball bat. When Chris came back in the house, his mother said, "He seems like a nice young man."

"Yeah," Chris said, "he's pretty cool."

*   *   *

IT WAS ALMOST 10:00 P.M. DEREK AND ALI TOOK THE SINGLE BASE-
ball bat they had been able to procure back to Lisa's house. They
parked a few doors down, left the bat in the car, and went to Lisa's
bedroom window.

Lisa already had another assignment for Ali. She needed her to
drive to Weston and pick up the Mafia hit man.

When she had last spoken to him, Kaufman had delivered disap-
pointing news. He had been unable to come up with the proper kind
of weapons from his usual mob sources. Because it wasn't a sanc-
tioned mob hit, the people who normally supplied him with guns
didn't want to get involved.

The good news, however, was that Derek Kaufman was willing to
come along and supply certain kinds of advice and assistance. Lisa
needed Ali to go pick him up.

Ali was afraid to go get him alone. She asked Heather and Donny
to go along, and they agreed.

At this time of night, and knowing the way already, they made
good time. They parked where Derek Kaufman had told them to,
walked through a gate in the wall and up the driveway to the part of
the house where he had said they would find his bedroom window.
They rapped lightly on the only window that was lighted; lace curtains
parted, and Derek Kaufman's large buzz-cut head appeared, framed
by lace like the head of a monstrous bride.

"Be right out," he said softly through the closed window.

Twenty minutes later they were all crowded together in Lisa's bedroom, beginning to make some serious plans.

"I've been on the phone with Marty," Lisa said in her chairperson
voice, "and we have made some decisions. We're going to get Bobby
out to Weston where we dogged out the cars last night, and then we're
going to beat him and stab him. Our plan is for Ali to do it."

"Hey, no shit!" Ali objected. She said that she didn't want to be
the one who had to run the risk of screwing it up somehow and getting

the crap beaten out of her or even being killed by Bobby when he figured out what was going on.

Lisa made a long, jabbering, breathless speech about how Ali was the one who would be in the best position, since she was the one who would be having sex with him when he got it.

Ali countered that it made more sense for Derek Kaufman to sneak up and stab him from behind, but Kaufman said Bobby Kent was *their* friend, and it was their deal, and he was only along to lend his expertise and advice.

Derek Dzvirko said it seemed to him that Lisa was the one who was so hot to see Bobby Kent killed in the first place: Why wasn't she taking a more active role?

At that point, Donny Semenec rose from where he had been lying on his back on the floor. He hitched up his blue jeans and said, "Well, if you don't have the balls to do it, then I'm gonna do the fucker."

"Oh, Donny, shut up," Ali said.

A scratchy, humorless laugh erupted from Heather. "Donny!" she said, imitating a character on *Saturday Night Live.* "The Donny Man! Donny Big Man! All right!"

"Hey, fuck you guys, too," Donny said, but he was already smirking and sinking back to the floor. "You guys are bullshit. Nothin' but bullshit. I'll do it. I'll cut that motherfucker."

Lisa did a quick inventory of the arsenal. So far, not counting her mother's gun, which she didn't plan on even taking this time, they had Donny's brother's survival knife and one aluminum baseball bat. But Marty was planning on bringing some stuff of his own.

IT WAS TIME FOR MARTY TO ROBE. HE STOOD BEFORE THE FLOOR-length mirror on the outside of his bathroom door, naked. He squeezed a fist in a palm and did a biceps and pectoral flexing pose. He was, in his own eyes, a magnificent specimen, clean and perfectly defined in every inch of his physical being. He was greatly pleased with what he saw.

He turned, walked to his closet, and with both hands swept open the folding doors. From a set of white wire shelves sitting on the floor at the back of the large closet he took clean underwear—white socks, light blue boxer shorts, and a white T-shirt—and put them on.

He then carefully lifted a pair of baggy black creaseless cotton pants from the clothes rod. He sat down and pulled on an immaculate white pair of Adidas running shoes.

He pulled out a red bandanna. He turned to face the mirror on the bathroom door and tied the bandanna around his head, pirate-style.

He pulled his brother's black trench coat from the closet and put it on. It was a size too large for him and hung around him like a cape.

He presented himself to the mirror and smiled. He was ready.

ON THE WAY TO MARTY'S HOUSE IN ALI'S CAR, LISA TALKED A MAN-tra of blood. Over and over again she described how they were going to stab the motherfucker, slit his throat and bleed him like a pig, slice his guts open and spill his intestines out on the dirt, beat his head in with the baseball bat until his fucking eyeballs fell out.

Ali drove and shook her head back and forth slightly, almost imperceptibly, as if listening to music.

Donny was very high again on something, sitting in the backseat holding on to the rear strap with one hand, his forehead pressed against the roof. He muttered, "If you won't do it, I'll cut that fucker for you. I'll do it. If you won't do it, I will."

Heather stared out the side window, chewing gum, eyes dead as soap.

"So weird," Ali whispered. "This shit is so weird."

They pulled into Marty's driveway and tapped the horn. For a moment there was no response, and then suddenly, so that Ali and Lisa were startled, the garage door began to lift, light flooding out from beneath over the driveway, gradually blinding them.

They saw him in an outline of shadows at first, the flowing black trench coat, blood-red bandanna cocked across his forehead, face a mask of ice. Marty was standing next to his mother's car, dangling the keys from the fingers of one hand.

FRED AND FARAH KENT ATE DINNER WITH THEIR SON IN THE KIT-chen—a calm, almost wordless gathering over a combination of Middle Eastern and American dishes. Fred and Bobby sat at the table for a while after dinner, while Farah did the dishes.

Fred spoke.

"Ali is back in town?"

"Yeah. She's visiting Lisa."

"You went out with her?"

"Yeah. Kind of. Last night. We drove around in her car. We didn't really, like, 'go out.' But I saw her. Why?"

Fred shrugged. He didn't have to say anything. Bobby knew all too well that Fred objected to his seeing Ali. He had met her only a few times, always when she was in town visiting Lisa, but Fred Kent didn't need to do an in-depth analysis to come to a conclusion about Ali Willis.

She was trash. She dressed like trash. She spoke like trash. She had the manners of trash. Carried herself like trash. Fred didn't know her parents or have any idea why they allowed their adult daughter to drive around in an expensive sports car, unemployed, not in school, spending money like water. He had stopped a long time ago trying to understand why so many people in Florida, even people with money, were unperturbed when their young-adult children persisted in leading lives of complete aimlessness.

Bobby rose from the table and went to the bathroom to shower. He appeared again half an hour later, scrubbed, combed, smelling of musky cologne.

Fred was helping Farah in the kitchen.

"Where are you going tonight, Bob?" he asked.

"Out with my friend."

That would be Marty. That was what the phrase meant. Bobby

almost never referred to Marty by his name. And Marty was certainly never *a friend*. He was *my friend. The friend.*

The car horn sounded outside, and he was gone.

So hard, so very difficult and perilous, to raise a son. No matter how loving a shelter his family may provide, sooner or later the son must and will embrace the world around, hungrily. But how can the parents know who or what is right? If there was any comfort at all for Fred Kent, it was that almost everyone else in South Florida was in the same boat. Whether they came from Iran or New Jersey, they were all at sea now.

LISA LEAPED FROM THE CAR AND RAN UP THE DRIVEWAY TO GIVE Marty a hug. Derek Dzvirko followed slowly and asked Marty if he could go inside to use the bathroom.

"Number one or number two?"

"One."

"Just go in the alley, O.K., man?"

Derek shrugged and walked off obediently toward the back of the house.

Derek Kaufman and Donny Semenec joined the group at the top of the driveway. Donny was staring at the lurid homemade tattoo on Derek's forearm—the letters C, M, and F, curling through the thick dark hair on his arm like a livid worm.

"Hey, man?" Donny said, with his head down, bent at the waist like Groucho, and jabbing with one finger to point out Kaufman's tattoo. "Hey, man?" he said again, smirking and snickering.

Kaufman stared at him as if he were a red ant at his feet.

Donny said, "What's that mean? C, M, F. What's CMF?"

Lisa shook her head in disgust. She muttered to Ali, "We already told him what it means, didn't we? Jeez. What's with this guy?"

Ali came over to Donny and slipped an arm around him from the side. "Hey, babe. It means Crazy Motherfuckers. He's their godfather. It's a division of the Davie Boys."

Donny stood up straight. "No shit. Davie Boys. The godfather. It's Crazy Motherfuckers?"

"Yeah," Ali said.

"No shit."

Marty approached Derek Kaufman.

"Hey, man," he said.

Derek cocked his head slightly in response but did not speak. Now it was Marty's turn to grovel.

Marty bent over, pulled up a leg of his loose-fitting pants, and extracted a length of ¾-inch galvanized water pipe, strapped to his calf with knotted strips of white cloth. He offered it to Kaufman.

"Do you think this is heavy enough?" Marty asked meekly.

Kaufman stared at it, then finally took it in his hand. He bounced it against an open palm a couple of times. "What, to kill a guy?"

"Yeah."

"Maybe. If you hit him right."

"What do you figure, like the back of the head?"

"Yeah. Back, front. It don't make that much difference. You just got to hit him hard enough."

Marty snickered. "Yeah. I guess that's always the important thing."

"Yeah," Kaufman said woodenly. "You got to whack the guy. You can't just smack him, like you're in a fight, and you're real mad, and you want to hurt him. I mean, you know, you're not trying to hurt the guy. You're trying to kill him."

"I got something else," Marty said, grinning.

Kaufman nodded, unsmiling.

Marty reached into the waistband of his pants and extracted a scuba diving knife in a sheath. He pulled it out of the sheath and showed Kaufman its long, straight, razor-sharp blade, made for hacking and puncturing.

"That's cool," Kaufman said.

Donny went to Ali's car and retrieved the bat Dzvirko had borrowed. He brought it to show to Kaufman. "Do you think this is good enough?"

Kaufman shrugged. "For what? Play baseball with?"

"No," Donny said, shrinking away, smirking.

"For what? What're you showin' me a baseball bat for? For what? What do you want to do with it?"

"The guy," Donny whined.

"What guy?"

"Bobby Kent."

"What about Bobby Kent?"

"The guy we're gonna kill. Is this bat good enough? You know. To do it with? To kill him?"

"I don't know, man."

Donny slumped, frustrated. He took the bat back to the car, dumped it on the floor of the backseat, and withdrew the serrated survival knife from under the driver's seat. He brought it to Kaufman.

"You think this is sharp enough?" He held it up, offering it to him.

"I don't know, man," Kaufman said. He shrugged and turned away to show that he wasn't very interested.

Derek Dzvirko had reappeared after his trip to the alley and was listening from the sidelines.

"What I wanta know," Dzvirko said glumly, "is, are we just going to beat the shit out of this guy, or are we going to kill him? That's what I want to know."

No one spoke.

Then Marty came forward, still brandishing the pipe in his hand. "Look, I want this motherfucker dead tonight. And I don't want any bullshit about it."

Lisa came to his side and took him protectively by the arm. "No shit, man. I mean, look, the son of a bitch raped Ali."

"Yeah," Donny said. "That's what pisses me off about him."

"And, I mean, just think about it," Lisa went on, revving up. "Marty just about doesn't have a life because of him. Bobby beats the shit out of him if he does anything Bobby doesn't like. He makes him work on his car all the time, and he won't even let him spend time with his own family."

"That sucks, man," Derek Kaufman said. "Let's do it. A guy like that needs to die."

Donny started prancing around on the edge of the group with the survival knife in one hand. "I'll kill the fucker, if you guys don't." He repeated it over and over again, more or less to himself. "I'll kill him. I'll kill him."

Lisa and Marty nodded their heads as they watched Donny circle them; Ali and Heather shook their heads in agreement; Kaufman nodded; but Dzvirko was still holding himself aloof, not really joining in.

"O.K.," he said, "but I want to know, are we going to just beat the shit out of this guy really, and scare him, or do you guys actually think we're going to kill him?"

Marty came close to Dzvirko and looked him in the eye. "Man, I want this son of a bitch dead. Tonight. I mean, I want him dead!"

Marty began to do a little jive shuffle in a circle, pumping his forefinger up and down, neck and face bent down. "I mean I want him dead! Dead! I want this mo'fucker dead!"

"Yeah!" Donny cried. "All right!"

"I want him dead!" Marty chanted.

"Yeah!" the others sang back in response. "All right!"

"Dead!"

"All right, man! Yeah!"

Derek Kaufman stepped to the center of the little group and put one hand in the air, barely waving it at his shoulder. The others fell silent.

"Look, uh, people," he said softly, "I got to know some shit here."

For a moment no one spoke, and then Lisa said dully, "What?"

"Well, see, people, you know, this ain't exactly a game for me. I mean like a bunch of little kids playing make-believe or something."

"Hey, man," Marty said. "Who said it was a game?"

"I know, all right, I mean, like, just chill, dude, I hear you, but, like, I need for you people to understand some shit."

Derek half closed his eyes, bent forward, and put both hands out in front of his shoulders, fluttering the fingers as if his hands were little wings.

"See, like, you people brought me into this shit, you need to know, I'm like, me and my people, we're what you would call serious people. I mean, you understand, right? You know what I mean by serious?"

"Yeah," Donny said brightly. "We know what that means."

Derek moved up on Donny. "What does that mean, my man? When I say I'm like, serious, what does that mean to you? Tell me."

Donny shrugged. "It means you ain't playin'. Hey, I know what it means. What the fuck, man, I said from the beginning I'll kill the fucker. I said that first. I was the first one. I mean, you know, don't be callin' me a little kid."

Kaufman stared at Donny icily, and Donny stared back at him. Then Kaufman turned and pointed a finger at Derek Dzvirko.

"You sure you're up to this shit, boy?"

Dzvirko gazed at Kaufman, his face a numb-lipped mask of dismissal. He did not speak. The two continued to stare each other down.

Finally Donny blurted, "Hey, man, this dude is cold, I mean, he is cold, I just been hangin' with him a couple days now, and I seen this dude do shit you wouldn't believe."

Kaufman began to nod his head. "Right," he said, still staring at Dzvirko. "Well, that's good. That's good. Because, tonight, we're gonna take a trip. A trip to a different place. And I just got to know if everybody's got the balls for it."

"We got the balls," Marty said. "Don't worry about it."

"Yeah," Lisa said. "We got the balls to do whatever we want to do."

Kaufman seemed satisfied. "Good. That's cool. Well. Let's go kill the guy."

At that moment a bright bar of light appeared behind them, inside the garage at the edge of the door to the house. The door swung farther open, and Marty's mother looked out. Her golden hair was backlit by the neon bulb in the hallway behind her, so that her head was enveloped in a halo.

Marty turned. "Hi, Mom," he said.

"Hi, Loverbug," she said. "What are you kids up to tonight?"

"Nothin'," Marty said. "Just going to a movie."

"O.K., then," she said. "Drive carefully. Be careful with my car, honey."

"Yes, Mom. I will."

The door pulled closed, and she disappeared.

"LET'S MOVE," MARTY SAID.

Derek Kaufman got into the back of Marty's mother's car. Derek Dzvirko opened the other back door and got in next to him. Marty and Lisa got in front. Donny and Heather piled into Ali's car—Donny in the back.

Marty peeled out of the garage backward, engine roaring, tires shrieking on the smooth concrete driveway. Then, with Ali following close on his bumper, he floored the Topaz up the block, spitting gravel all the way to the far end, where he stamped hard on the brake and came to a sliding stop in front of Bobby Kent's house.

The front of the house was blank. Then Bobby stepped out from the shadows at the front door.

With his hair combed straight back, neck and chest muscles bulging beneath the crisp white Ocean Pacific T-shirt his mother had ironed for him, splay-legged in brand-new blue jeans and spotless Aero-Jam sneakers, a mischievous smirk flickering at his lips, he was a vision of young masculine beauty.

When the chariots at the curb were silent, he dipped his head forward in greeting, grinned maniacally, then tipped forward with his fist against his forehead in the pose of Atlas bearing the world.

Marty leaped from his car, bounded across the grass and slapped hands with him. "Hey, man! What's happenin'?"

"You tell me, dude," Bobby said. He nodded toward the cars. "Who're all those assholes?"

"Some dudes Ali brought down with her from Palm Bay."

"Some dudes? Hey, what the fuck, man? I thought she wanted to fuck me!"

"She does, man. She keeps talking about it. That's what she wants, man. But we're gonna dog out her car, too, man, see if it can beat my old lady's car."

Bobby guffawed. "No shit, man. A five-point-o? Against your old lady's Topaz? Give me a break, man. What kind of a race is that? That's a bunch of shit, man."

"Hey, c'mon, dude, chill," Marty said, spinning and shucking on the grass in front of him. "We're just going to go out to those sand dunes in Weston where you guys went the other night and dog out the cars. You did O.K. out there, from what I hear."

Bobby cupped his crotch with one hand and made a wild humping motion with his head thrown back, shrieking a high-pitched, "Wa-hooo!"

"All right!" Marty said. "Well then, let's roll."

Bobby walked to Ali's car and pulled open the passenger door. "Get in back, bitch," he said to Heather. She came out of the car smiling broadly. There were sparks between her eyes and his. He made a show of staring at her ass and legs while she climbed into the back of the car with Donny.

"MMMmmm," Bobby said appreciatively. "I'll keep you in mind, baby.

"Hey," he said to Ali. "Get the fuck over here. I'm drivin' this piece of shit."

While Ali moved to the passenger seat, Bobby strode around the front of the car and climbed into the driver's seat. "Show me how to shift this thing," he said. He reached over, grabbed her hand, and pressed it down on his crotch.

"Ooooo," Ali said, smiling. "He's hot!"

Heather laughed in the backseat, and then Donny laughed uncertainly, not quite sure what the joke was.

"Shit," Bobby said. "I'm not hot, baby, I'm just big!"

Bobby turned the key, slapped the shift handle into drive, and stamped down on the accelerator. The Mustang shuddered and squealed out onto the street, throwing a curtain of gravel and dirt behind. He swung the car a few inches wide of the Topaz, careened around the corner, and headed off toward Sheridan.

Marty climbed back into the car.

Slumped in the backseat of the Topaz where Bobby had not yet seen him, Derek Kaufman muttered, ''That guy's an asshole to drive her car like that.''

''Hey, tell me about it,'' Lisa said. ''See what the fuck I'm talkin' about?''

''Yeah.''

''We gotta kill that fucker.''

''Yeah.''

In the Mustang, Bobby told Ali to put some music on her system. She shoved in a tape by Cypress Hill, a West Coast rap group, singing ''Dead in the Brain,'' an ode to mental numbness.

Bobby put a fist in the air and shouted, ''All right, I love these dudes!,'' then rocked back and forth in his seat, roaring in and out of dense traffic moving west on Sheridan.

''Yeah,'' Donny snorted in the backseat. ''These guys are really excellent. Hey, dude, did you catch them when they were here?''

''No shit, man,'' Bobby said. ''Did you?''

''Yeah. I came down here with this friend of mine and we got totally wasted.''

''Yeah, no shit. So did the whole fucking crowd. They were the dudes who had this huge statue of a fat Chinese guy, right?''

''Yeah,'' Donny said. ''A Buddha.''

''Right. A Buddha dude!''

Donny laughed. ''Yeah, Buddha dude, dude. With this gigantic marijuana leaf on his belly.''

''Right,'' Bobby said, laughing. He plowed through a yellow light and turned right on University, drove north past tall beige walls protecting a new unoccupied community from the world, then turned left or west on Griffin. ''They played this song, and everybody brought out all these tons of marijuana, man, and lit up.''

"Yeah," Donny said, rocking and laughing in the backseat. "I lit up, too."

There was a momentary silence in the car. Bobby picked his way through traffic, driving past the gated golf-course communities of Cooper City. He turned and stared at Ali.

Ali looked over her shoulder toward Donny and then at Heather in the backseat. They gazed mutely into her eyes, like puppies waiting to be fed.

"Oh, shit," Ali said, "O.K." She brought a prerolled joint out of the glove box, lit it, and handed it around. "Might as well get high."

Bobby shouted out the lyrics of the song between drags on the joint. Donny joined in with him. When the song was over, Bobby said, "What's your deal, man?"

"Huh?"

"What are you doing here?"

Donny stared at Ali, blushed, and then turned toward Heather for help. Heather stared back at him blankly.

Ali said, "Donny is Heather's boyfriend. He's here with her."

"So you live in Palm Bay?"

"Yeah," Donny, nodding enthusiastically.

"So why'd you come down?"

Bobby craned around and looked at him. Donny stared back, stunned, as if struck between the eyes with a brick. He shrugged and whispered, "I don't really know."

"I wanted my friends to see you," Ali said. "See what a fine-looking dude I'm going out with."

Bobby snickered. "You call that goin' out?"

Ali shrugged and was silent. She turned away, a little hurt. "I don't know," she said, softly to the window.

"I call that a blow job," Bobby said. "A damn fine blow job, but a blow job just the same."

Heather leaned forward, a hint of animation flickering far back in her eyes. "What do you call 'going out,' dude? What's your definition?"

Bobby shrugged, checking the rearview mirror to make sure Marty was still behind him. "I don't know. What's your name again? Feather?"

"No, my name is not Feather. My name is Heather."

"Well, let me ask you somethin', Heather? Are you a hooker, too? Like your friend here?"

Ali muttered, "Shit."

Heather said, "I think you better watch your little mouth, dude, or my boyfriend might get pissed off."

"Who's that? Lonnie? You talkin' 'bout Lonnie here in the backseat gonna get pissed off at me? Pissed off at me and then what? Lonnie. Here, Lonnie!"

Donny bobbed his head and guffawed. "It's Donny, dude. The name is definitely Donny."

"Whatever. Donny, you know your girlfriend here is a hooker?"

Donny stared back at him, speechless.

Ali said, "Marty tells me you guys have turned a few tricks yourselves."

Bobby reached down and turned off the music. "Is that what Marty Puccio says about me?" He drove on in silence for the next couple of miles, staring straight ahead.

In the other car, the two Dereks were in the backseat, also talking about rap music. Derek Kaufman had an easy laugh that surprised Dzvirko.

After a while Kaufman fell silent, as if thinking.

"What did that other dude mean earlier when he said he had seen you do some amazing shit?"

"Who, me?" Dzvirko asked. He was aloof, cold-eyed. "I don't know what the dude thinks he saw me do. It could be anything, you know."

"Yeah, but what? What's he talking about? You do somebody, or something like that?"

"I got down on a guy earlier today."

"You kill him?"

"Nah. It wasn't like that. I mean, this was like, at the mall, you know. Nah. I just put a little disciplinary action on him."

"Disciplinary action, eh?" Kaufman smiled, then laughed. "I like that. You put some disciplinary action on the dude."

"Yeah."

"Like we're gonna do for this dude tonight."

"Yeah."

Neither one spoke for a while. Then Kaufman said, "What are we gonna do to this guy? Like just beat the shit out of him or what?"

"I don't know, man," Dzvirko said. "They say they want to kill him."

In the front seat, Marty and Lisa were listening to the music on the stereo, not talking. Marty was having a hard time keeping up with Bobby's driving. Bobby would know that. He always did this, if Marty had to follow him somewhere—drove like a total asshole so that Marty would be worried about the cops the whole way. But Marty kept his foot on the floor and wrenched the car in and around traffic to keep up with him.

"So how is it going to go down?" he asked, over his shoulder.

Kaufman and Dzvirko traded looks.

"You talkin' to me?" Kaufman asked.

"Yeah. I just wondered if you had any thoughts. I mean, we got, what?, we got you, me, the other Derek, Donny . . ."

"Who is Donny?" Kaufman asked.

Lisa turned to the backseat. "Ali's boyfriend from Palm Bay."

"Ah, jeez," Kaufman said. "That guy? That guy's retarded or some shit, isn't he?"

"No, he's not," Lisa said sharply. "He just gets high a lot. He's as normal as you or me."

"Well, shit," Kaufman said, smiling at Dzvirko. "That might not be saying too much."

"Look," Lisa said, "we brought you along because you're supposed to be the big hit man and the gangster and all like that."

"Yeah?"

"Well."

"Well?"

"So what should we do?"

Kaufman turned away and looked out the window for a while. "Well, you know, like you gotta have a plan. Like you gotta have a signal and all like that."

"A signal?" Lisa asked.

"Yeah, like, like you said the deal was, we're gonna tell him we're gonna have some car races. But, like, the real reason he's here is because of the fox."

"The fox?" Lisa asked.

"Ali," Marty said. "The real reason Bobby's here is because he thinks Ali wants to fuck him."

"O.K.," Lisa said. "So?"

"So," Kaufman said, "I suggest we do the following. We have, uh, what's her name?"

"Ali," Lisa said.

"Yeah, Ali. We have Ali kind of lead him off somewhere, and then the rest of us are behind them or sneaking up or something, and then somebody gives the signal."

"And then what?" Lisa said.

"Then we kill him."

They rode in silence for a while, following Bobby through a trackless void where there were no developments, only shadow and the distant bones of lighted freeway overpasses—gray humps held up against the blackened sky.

"So what's the signal?" Dzvirko asked.

"Well, I don't know," Kaufman said. "I have to wait till we get out there, so I can check out the scene a little. This has to be done right, you know."

Five minutes later, the two cars crunched to a halt on a sandy barren on the south side of South Post Oak Road in Weston.

* * *

THE SIDE OF THE ROAD WHERE BOBBY AND MARTY PARKED THE MUS-
tang and the Topaz was a broad barren shoulder, sloping down gradually for fifteen to twenty yards before it met the trash-strewn banks
of a canal. The company that had dug the small curling system of
canals a few years earlier had left twin peaks of dredge a hundred
yards or so from where the two cars had stopped. The lower one was
about thirty feet high and the other was between forty and fifty feet
high. The area behind the mounds was a dark waste of weedy banks
along abandoned canals. When the car lights were on them, the
mounds appeared like huge heads peering over the horizon, and when
the lights went off, the heads disappeared.

Bobby got out of the Mustang, stretched his arms high above his
head and then shouted, "Oooee! C'mon, baby. It's rockin'!"

Ali got out of her side of the Mustang and sidled up to him. She
was wearing the postage-stamp skirt and the little white tube top. Her
legs were long and lithe in the moonlight, and her lips were a glistening blue. She grinned, slinking toward him, and rubbed her silky
shoulder against his chest.

Bobby took one finger, ran it down her cheek, then down her neck.
She twisted and curled around his finger.

"Hey," he said, his voice gone soft. "Let's take a walk."

Ali turned, lifted her eyebrows knowingly, then put her arms back
and pushed herself forward, grazing him with her nipples.

"Let's do," she said.

As soon as Ali and Bobby had turned their backs and started off
down toward the canal bank, the others climbed from the cars. Donny
Semenec and Heather Swallers emerged from the backseat of the Mustang. From the Topaz came Marty Puccio, Lisa Connelly, and the two
Dereks, Dzvirko and Kaufman.

They milled aimlessly for a moment, then gathered in a circle
around Kaufman.

Marty said, "He's gonna tell us what to do."

"Yeah," Kaufman said, bobbing his head nonchalantly. "Well,
like, I did have a few ideas. Like, I think you should tell him what
we're doing now, uh . . . does that five-point-o have T-tops?"

Lisa said the car, a convertible, did have T-tops—removable roll bars that could be snapped into place like a helmet over the driver for protection in case the car flipped over.

"They're in the trunk."

"Call down there and tell him we're putting the T-tops on, so he won't get suspicious what we're all doing up here," Kaufman said.

"Man, I can't believe this shit," Donny said.

"Shut up," Lisa said. She turned toward the canal. Ali and Bobby were barely visible in the gloom.

In a braying voice, she called, "We're puttin' on the T-tops!"

"Wow," Heather said, holding her hands to her ears. "You shouldn't yell like that!"

"Well, sorry," Lisa said defensively. "I mean, it's not like somebody's gonna hear us out here."

Heather came closer, staring blankly at her and shaking her head. "No," she said, "you just shouldn't yell. Somebody might hear. They would know somebody was being killed."

"O.K., Heather," Lisa said, irritated. "I'll keep it in mind."

Lisa reached into the Mustang and released the trunk. Marty lifted the trunk lid and removed the baseball bat. He handed it deferentially to Kaufman, who held it by the neck with the fat end resting on his shoe, bouncing it on his toe.

"So who else has a weapon?" he said. "You got the diving knife?" he asked Marty.

"Yeah."

"So get it out." He turned to Donny. "You planning on doing anything?"

Donny stared at him strangely. His face twisted slowly into a beady-eyed grin. Then he whipped his right hand around from behind him and held up the survival knife he had borrowed from his brother.

"Fuckin' right," he said.

* * *

146

NOW THEY ALL GATHERED AROUND DEREK IN A SEMICIRCLE AT THE back of the Mustang. Lisa breathed heavily, her face a shiny mask of sweat. Marty was grim, gulping, holding the sheathed scuba knife in his hand. Donny Semenec grinned at Kaufman, nodding yes, bouncing on his feet. Heather stood with her back to Kaufman, staring down toward the darkness at the canal, blank and still as a pillar of salt.

Marty gripped the sheath with his left hand and eased it slowly down off the blade so that it wouldn't make a scraping sound. He looked around, then bent at the knee and slipped the sheath beneath a low-growing shrubby weed.

Derek Dzvirko was on the edge of the group, fidgeting as if about to dart but rooted to the sand, picking at his hair and sniffling, wiping his nose.

"So?" Dzvirko said. "So what? So what do you want to do?"

Kaufman shook his shoulders loose and threw his head back. Now Heather had turned toward him, and they were all watching him.

"Yeah," he said. "So, I don't know. What are you guys gonna do?"

Lisa stepped forward suddenly and hissed, "I want this fucker dead, now."

"Right," Kaufman said, nodding, "I got that. O.K. So here's what I think we should do. We need a signal. So, Heather, you go down there and talk to them. When you see it's O.K., like he doesn't suspect anything, then you yell out, 'Are there any alligators in there?' Then, when we hear that, we know it's time. You got that?"

Heather stared at him. "Alligators in where?"

"In the canal. It's a signal. Just say something about alligators. Then we'll do him."

"Say alligators, and then you'll kill him?"

"Yeah," Kaufman said. "It's a signal."

He looked at Donny Semenec, who was grinning with the knife in his hand. "You go down there with her, like holding hands, like you're going out. When she gives the signal, do it."

He turned to Marty. "You back him up."

Then, to Derek Dzvirko: "You and me back them up up here. That way he can't get away."

He turned back to Heather and Donny. "So. Go. Just do it."

Heather turned, her shoulders stiff, and began to walk down into the darkness by the canal. Donny went to her left side and put his right hand up behind her back to hide the knife.

ABOVE: Much of the plotting and meeting happened in a corner of a shiny new shopping mall, in a scene of typical middle-class affluence.

BELOW: The conspirators met Derek Kaufman here at this wall behind his parents' home.

BROWARD COUNTY SHERIFF'S DEPARTMENT
SUSPECT IMAGE

WILLIS, ALICE

BROWARD COUNTY SHERIFF'S DEPARTMENT
SUSPECT IMAGE

CONNELLY, LISA MARIE

BROWARD COUNTY SHERIFF'S DEPARTMENT
SUSPECT IMAGE

SWALLERS, HEATHER JUNE

LEFT: Maureen Connelly, a single parent, raised her daughter, Lisa, in this modest townhome across the street from the Embassy Lakes Mall.

BELOW: Fred and Farah Kent lived their version of the American dream here, a block from the Puccio Family.

BROWARD COUNTY SHERIFF'S DEPARTMENT
SUSPECT IMAGE

DZVIRKO, DEREK GEORGE

BROWARD COUNTY SHERIFF'S DEPARTMENT
SUSPECT IMAGE

KAUFMAN, DEREK LEON

BROWARD COUNTY SHERIFF'S DEPARTMENT
SUSPECT IMAGE

SEMENEC, DONALD DANNY

ABOVE: Mug shots. BROWARD COUNTY SHERIFF'S DEPART-MENT

BELOW LEFT: Marty Puccio grew up in this house just down the block from his best friend, Bobby Kent, in Hollywood, Florida, a town bordering Fort Lauderdale.

BELOW RIGHT: Derek Kaufman lived in an area of big acreages, horses, and privilege. He wanted to be a Mafia hit man. BROWARD COUNTY SHERIFF'S DEPART-MENT

BROWARD COUNTY SHERIFF'S DEPARTMENT
SUSPECT IMAGE

PUCCIO, MARTIN JOSEPH

LEFT: The desolate murder scene was just across the road from a new development of big homes on cul-de-sac streets. BROWARD COUNTY SHERIFF'S DEPARTMENT

BELOW: Bobby Kent's best friends had believed the alligators would eat his body before the police could find it. BROWARD COUNTY SHERIFF'S DEPARTMENT

ABOVE: The murder took place here, across a murky canal from a dune of dredged muck.

BELOW: After the killing, the group gathered on this beautiful Florida beach in the predawn hours and planned what they were going to say. BROWARD COUNTY SHERIFF'S DEPARTMENT

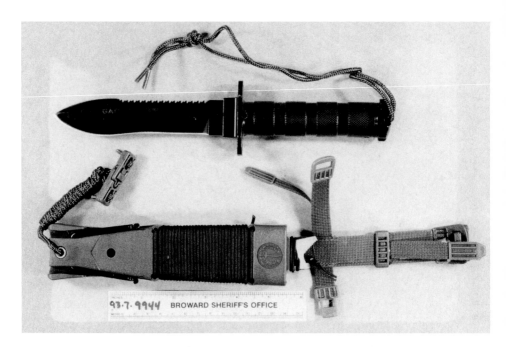

ABOVE: Lisa Connelly and Marty Puccio told Bobby they were going out to drag race and have fun, but on the way they hid survival knives in their boots and under the car seat. BROWARD COUNTY SHERIFF'S DEPARTMENT

RIGHT: Police found one of the murder weapons, a bat, returned to its owner and polished up, sitting in the closet next to the family vacuum cleaner. BROWARD COUNTY SHERIFF'S DEPARTMENT

RIGHT: Every hole and tear in Bobby's shirt was important evidence in the trial.
BROWARD COUNTY SHERIFF'S DEPARTMENT

BELOW: This is the high-powered car, a gift from her parents, driven by Ali Willis, a high school dropout and drug user involved in a teenage prostitution ring.
BROWARD COUNTY SHERIFF'S DEPARTMENT

Lisa buried the weapons at the foot of the boardwalk, then dug them up and threw them into the sea.

CHAPTER SIX

WHEN HEATHER GOT HALFWAY TO THE BANK OF THE CANAL, DONNY stopped and let her go the rest of the way by herself. She found Bobby and Ali looking at the water. They turned and saw her behind them, but they did not speak.

"Are there any alligators in there?" Heather mumbled.

It was pitch-dark with the car lights turned out, and there was no traffic on South Post Oak Road. In the far distance there was an occasional whine of truck tires high in the air on freeway overpasses. On the low, flat earth insect noises and the membranous harping of frogs thrummed and hissed.

Bobby said, "What?"

Ali turned and looked at Heather. Then she turned back toward the canal. "She asked, are there any alligators in there?" she said softly. She didn't know it was the signal.

"In there?" Bobby said, turning toward the canal. "Huh. Why don't you go for a skinny-dip and see?"

Heather turned to face back up the slope toward Donny, who was a few yards away. Raising her voice, she said, "I asked him if there are any alligators in there."

Marty was still waiting at the car with Kaufman and Dzvirko. They stood riveted to the spot, motionless, all of them staring down toward Donny's back and Heather's voice, none of them moving a muscle, none of them turning an eye toward the others, all of them suffocating in a gelatin of night and horror.

Donny broke free. He threw himself running down the slope with the survival knife in his hand, arms flailing, feet flopping on the sand in untied sneakers. Bobby didn't hear him coming or didn't care. He was still looking out at the flat black canal, snickering over his idea—the thought of Heather, naked, slipping down into the filthy water and swimming out to discover if there were alligators waiting.

Flailing and still running, Donny made a looping arc with the knife loosely held in his right hand. He stuck the tip of the knife's long blade into the back of Bobby's neck, low on the neck, just to the right of the bony prominence at the base. It went in barely an inch.

Donny yanked the knife back abruptly and stumbled backward, backpedaling, gasping for air, desperate to regain his footing.

Bobby winced, twisted around, and threw his right hand to his neck. He revolved the rest of the way to face Donny and started walking toward him, his face blackening with rage, eyes beginning to bulge. But when Bobby pulled his hand from his neck and looked at it, he was shocked to see it covered with blood. He looked up and saw Marty running toward him on his right side.

"Oh, fuck!" Bobby shouted. "I'm bleeding! Marty! Marty, I'm bleeding!"

Heather put her hands to her ears and raced back up to the Mustang. She yanked open the door, dug her way into the backseat, and then crouched on the floor with her hands over her ears, rocking and whimpering.

Bobby turned toward Marty imploringly, hands outstretched. Marty stabbed forward with the scuba knife from a lower position directly up into Bobby's belly. The knife met only soft tissue and plunged smoothly, deep into Bobby's abdomen. Marty, staring into Bobby's eyes, twisted the knife hard and pulled it back out with an upward movement, ripping Bobby's belly open and drawing out part of a loop of his lower intestine.

Bobby looked down at his intestine hanging out over the front of his crisply pressed blue jeans. Now the others were closing around him.

"No, help me, Marty!" he screamed. "Marty, I'm sorry! Please, whatever it is, I'm sorry, Marty, I'm sorry!"

Marty brought the knife back around as fast and hard as he could, but Bobby threw up his arm and caught the tip of the blade on his thumb. The knife cut the thumb open and then was deflected into Bobby's right biceps, penetrating less than two inches.

Now Donny was back at him like a dog, hacking and stabbing him two more times in the back but failing to make a solid connection either time.

Bobby turned toward Donny as if in slow motion. Donny hacked at his face but missed again. The knife made a glancing slice across his scalp.

Bobby began to walk slowly up the bank, his face and chest sheeted with blood. Marty and Donny backed away from him for a moment and watched him walk away, staring stupefied at his back.

Bobby exploded into a dead run, racing for the darkness and a chance to escape. In spite of the blood covering him and the severity of the gut wound Marty had dealt him, Bobby was still capable of moving with strength and speed. All of a sudden, Derek Kaufman was terrified. In a high shrieky voice that had lost its hit-man cool, he shouted, "He's getting away! He's getting away! We have to get him! You can't let him get away!"

Kaufman and Marty ran after him, Marty up the slope with the scuba knife, Kaufman down the slope with the bat.

Ali ran for the Mustang, yanked on the door, and lost her grip, stumbling backward, then came back and grabbed the handle again and pulled until she got it open. She hurled herself into the driver's seat, pulled the door shut, and sat with her fingers at her mouth. It was dark outside the car, as if the windows had been painted black. Ali could hear nothing.

The passenger door across from her was ripped open from outside, and Ali screamed. Derek Dzvirko's big face appeared, twisted and screaming. He jumped into the car and slammed his door. "Go! Just go! Get the fuck out of here! Go!"

Ali turned on the ignition and pulled on the headlights. Bobby was on his back on the ground directly in front of the car. He had been running away from the parked cars, but he must have looped back around. He lay splayed on the ground with his arms and legs wide, his head toward the car.

Kaufman screamed at Marty, "Finish him!"

In the headlights Ali and Derek Dzvirko could see the black outline of the two tall mounds of dredge in the distance, like watching heads.

Donny and Derek Kaufman were standing a few feet away from where Bobby lay. Marty was on him.

"FINISH HIM!" KAUFMAN SHOUTED AGAIN.

Marty was straddling Bobby's broad chest with his knees on Bobby's upper arms, pinning him down. Bobby was weakened but still struggling, imploring them to spare him.

"Please," he said thickly, sputtering blood from his lips. "Please, Marty."

Marty reached forward, grabbed Bobby's head by the hair with his left hand, and slammed his head back so hard against the sand that he fractured one of the vertebrae in Bobby's neck. With his right hand, Marty brought the sharp edge of the scuba knife down on Bobby's throat and began to saw back and forth, opening the throat from one side to the other. Marty pushed down so hard with the blade that he crushed Bobby's voice box.

Blood was spilling fast from Bobby's neck and mouth now, as well as from his abdomen. But he was still alive and conscious. His head was twisted up at an odd angle because of the damage to his neck, and he could no longer make any sounds, but he continued to move his lips and implore with his eyes.

Lisa was standing next to the Topaz, watching. She was breathing hard and quickly, snatching her breath rhythmically, making a sound midway between panic and sexual pleasure.

Marty lifted back slightly, allowing his knees to rise up off Bobby's arms. He was no longer afraid of Bobby. He lifted his right hand high in the air and then brought the scuba knife down hard, plunging it into Bobby's upper left chest, through the ribs, all the way through his heart and through the back of the upper chest cavity and the back of the rib cage just below Bobby's uplifted shoulder blades, so that the tip of the knife dimpled but barely missed breaking through the skin of Bobby's back.

Marty rose from Bobby. The headlights of Ali's car bathed him in white light against the black sky, as if he were a figure in a black-and-white photograph. He was soaked in blood, knife dangling loosely from his right hand. He was breathing heavily. He stared into the headlights for several seconds, gasping for air, before he seemed to realize that the lights were on him.

''Turn the goddamn lights off!'' he shouted suddenly.

Then Kaufman joined in: ''Shut the fucking car off! Shut it off!''

Derek Dzvirko was shouting again into Ali's ear, grappling for her hand to keep her from turning the car off.

''Go! Jesus fucking shit, bitch, get out of here!''

Then suddenly they were all silent.

At once, like a spell that fell on all of them at the same instant, a sound had come. It separated itself from the distant whining of the highway in the invisible distance and from the monotonous twanging of the frogs hidden by the canal. It was distinct, very soft, barely audible but all around them, and, when they listened, they all heard it clearly.

The gurgling of a baby.

Marty looked down. Ali and Derek Dzvirko stretched their necks forward to see out the windshield and down over the hood of the Mustang where he lay. Derek Kaufman and Donny Semenec came forward, closer to him.

Still alive but ebbing, immobilized by his wounds, Bobby was turning his head back and forth slowly, pleading with his eyes and trying to cry out, but the sound that bubbled out of his open throat and lips was the soft plaintive whimper of an infant.

Kaufman stepped forward, put a hand on Marty's shoulder, and pushed him away from Bobby.

Kaufman lifted the bat midway, perpendicular to his own belly, and strode around Bobby to his head. He took a position spraddle-legged in the sand between Bobby and the Mustang, with his back to the Mustang, so that Bobby's head lay before his feet like a ball.

Kaufman shifted his hips in a batter's stance and lifted the bat high up into the air above his head.

Marty screamed: "Turn those goddamn lights off, Ali!"

She reached forward, turned off the key, and killed the lights.

There was a moment of pitch-black darkness inside the car. They could hear the gurgling noise from Bobby's throat, a bit louder, more urgent. Then they heard a whoosh and the wet crackling thud of the bat on the side of Bobby's face.

Then there was silence.

Derek Dzvirko was just tuning up, about to begin screaming at Ali to start the car and get away, when suddenly the car door next to him flew open. Standing outside glowering at him was Derek Kaufman with the bat.

"What do you want, man?" Dzvirko asked in a high-pitched whimper.

"Get out," Kaufman said solemnly.

Suddenly Dzvirko was so frightened that he went numb, as if his heart had stopped beating. He nodded agreement, to show that he would do as he had been told, but he fumbled with his arms and legs trying to get out.

"Get out!" Kaufman roared, backing away with the bat.

A spray of urine escaped into Dzvirko's pants. He hauled himself quickly out of the car and stumbled toward Kaufman, who backpedaled away from him with the bat in both hands. When Dzvirko recaptured his balance, he threw his arms up in front of his face, anticipating a blow, but Kaufman flipped the bat casually in the direction of the Topaz.

"Help me carry him," Kaufman said.

Heather, who had been curled in a ball and rocking on the floor of the backseat, straightened, rose to her knees on the car floor, turned, and looked out the open passenger door of the Mustang to where Dzvirko stood with his back to her.

"Is he dead?" she asked in a dull murmur.

"Oh, fuck," Ali whispered in the front seat. She was doubled forward with her hand in her mouth, gnawing her fist. Her voice shook and she trembled as she spoke. "Fuck, fuck, fuck, fuck."

"Is he dead?"

"Shut up, Heather."

"Is he dead?"

"I think . . . yeah, he's dead, the fucker's definitely dead. They just beat his head in with a baseball bat."

Heather sat up on the right side of the backseat, staring forward over the seat in front of her, searching the opaque blackness of the windshield.

"Can we go?" she asked quietly.

"Shut up, Heather," Ali said. "Just shut up." She was leaning across the passenger seat, peering out the open passenger door to see what was going to happen between the two Dereks.

"Help me pick him up, man," Kaufman said.

"Why?" Dzvirko asked. He hadn't looked down at Bobby.

"Because we have to get him out of sight, asshole. Hey! Somebody get me some fucking gloves."

Lisa walked to the Topaz, reached into her purse, and withdrew a pair of rubber surgical gloves. She brought them to Kaufman. He pulled and snapped at them until he was able to jam his huge hands into them.

"Get his wallet," Kaufman said to Dzvirko.

"What?"

"I said, get his goddamned wallet, asshole. What's the matter with you?" Kaufman walked closer to Dzvirko. "I asked you a question."

At the instant when Bobby had charged up the slope toward him, Kaufman had seemed on the edge of cracking, but now, with Bobby flat on his back, his face smashed into a sloping mush, blood oozing from holes all over his body, neck gaping open like a second mouth, Derek Kaufman was suddenly alive, alert, supremely confident, and believable in his role.

"What?" Dzvirko mumbled, chin quivering.

"I said, what's the fucking matter with you? How come you're standing around looking like a stupid motherfucker instead of doing what I goddamn tell you to do?"

"I don't know," Dzvirko said. He smirked, then looked as if he might start crying. "I'm scared."

Kaufman put his arm out and held his finger under Dzvirko's nose. "I will tell you when to be scared, motherfucker. When I tell you to be scared, then you need to be so goddamned scared your fucking heart stops. Until then, you do what I tell you to do."

Dzvirko nodded obediently, gulping for air.

"Get his wallet," Kaufman said.

"His wallet?"

"His fucking wallet!" Kaufman roared.

Dzvirko began shaking his head yes, shaking it and shaking it but backing away. "O.K. But why do we want his wallet?"

Kaufman stalked him, staying close to his face. "So that if somebody finds his goddamned body, they won't be able to identify him. Now bend down and get it!"

Pushing his face into Dzvirko's face, Kaufman shooed him around, Dzvirko stumbling backward in the sand, until Dzvirko was next to where Bobby lay.

Still staring up at Kaufman, Dzvirko began to bend at the knee, lowering himself toward the ground without looking at Bobby. Then finally, when he was kneeling next to him, he turned his head slowly and looked.

The body was motionless. Bobby's eyes bugged bizarrely from his face, almost hanging loose from their sockets. His chest was black with syrupy blood.

"Get his wallet," Kaufman said.

Dzvirko reached, hand shaking, toward the hip pocket of Bobby's jeans. He snatched his hand away suddenly from the body. There was blood dripping from his fingers.

"What's the matter with you?" Kaufman asked, towering directly over him.

"Blood," Dzvirko whispered.

"Get the fucking wallet."

Dzvirko forced his hand back toward the pocket. He was shaking so badly he thought he might pass out. He felt the scratchy surface of the denim against his fingers, then the slick puddling of blood at the lip of the pocket. He forced his fingers through until he felt the edge of Bobby's wallet. He pulled on the wallet, then caught his breath when he thought he saw the body twitch on its own power.

The body, though, was motionless. When Dzvirko pulled on the wallet, Bobby's ass had merely rocked slightly in the sand. The wallet came out. Dzvirko reached up with one hand over his head to offer it to Kaufman.

"Don't give me that shit," Kaufman shouted at him.

Still holding it over his head, Dzvirko muttered, "Well, what the fuck do you want me to do with it, man?"

"Get rid of it. Toss it out there across the canal where nobody will ever find it."

Dzvirko rose slowly. He shambled down to the water's edge, shoulders low, wallet in one hand hanging loosely at his side. He reached back and hurled the wallet into the night.

"Now get up here and help me move this," Kaufman said.

Dzvirko came slowly back up the hill, stumbling like an obedient Igor. He stopped a few feet away from the body, reached up with both hands, and peeled his knit shirt up over his head, revealing a flabby white gut and saggy chest.

"What are you doing?" Kaufman asked.

"Don't wanta get blood on my shirt."

"Well, we're not gonna hug him, asshole. You grab his feet and I'll get him by the hands."

Dzvirko stooped over Bobby's feet, examined them for a moment, then reached down and clutched the cuffs of his blue jeans in-stead.

Marty, who had been standing higher on the slope behind Donny, said, "What are you going to do with the body?"

"We'll put him in the canal," Kaufman said. "The 'gators'll get him. By the time anybody ever comes out here, there won't be any-thing left to find."

Donny said softly, "Cool."

Kaufman stooped and grabbed the body by the wrists.

"Lift!" he said.

Together they hauled up on the four limbs, and the body rose into the air. They both walked sideways toward the canal a few steps, stumbling on the uneven ground, looking back and forth from the ground to the body, both of them riveted by the misshapen head and face, its sightless eyeballs already beginning to solidify in the air.

Bobby opened his lips and uttered a wheezing cry.

Dzvirko screamed and dropped the legs. Kaufman cried out and dropped the arms. Bobby fell to the ground, bounced up on his side, arms flailing, then fell on his back again, new blood pouring from his mouth. His lips twisted open and emitted a long gurgling moan.

IN THE CAR, HEATHER SAID DULLY, "HE'S NOT DEAD."

"Jesus, Heather," Ali gasped, "will you shut the fuck up?"

Higher on the slope, Donny said, "Gross."

Kaufman's hit-man cool had escaped him again. He stumped around in a circle for a while, gasping and snorting snot up his nose.

Dzvirko stood exactly where he had dropped the body, motionless, staring down at it. "Now what, asshole?" he asked bitterly.

"What?" Kaufman asked, trying to sound angry.

Marty came forward, staggering, staring at the body with a finger outstretched. With each sentence, Marty's voice seemed to slide up another octave: "We stabbed the fucker. We cut his fucking throat! We beat his head in with a bat!"

Beginning at Bobby's ankles and sliding up the length of his body, a long writhing curl shook his shoulders. His head twisted around as if searching, eyes lolling, and he cried out.

"That is so weird," Donny said.

"Why isn't he dead?" Marty shrieked. "Why isn't he dead?"

Kaufman and Dzvirko stood staring at Bobby, both of them equally stupefied, speechless.

"You could just go ahead and throw him in the water, anyway," Donny said. "It's not like he's gonna swim."

Dzvirko and Kaufman looked at each other, looked at Bobby, then simultaneously stooped and picked him up again.

Marty followed them to the water. "Will he drown?" he pleaded.

"Shit, man," Kaufman said, "what do you think? Look at him."

Marty bent over Bobby and took a long last look at his mangled face. Then as if in absolution he waved his hand and nodded for the body to be taken.

Kaufman and Dzvirko swung the body back behind them, then swung it hard out over the water and let it go. But Dzvirko's grip was slippery, and Bobby splashed down half on the sand.

Kaufman waded out a foot or so. The bottom dropped off steeply. He tugged on an arm and managed to pull Bobby off the bank. He pulled him out into the water. As Bobby went down, his mouth opened a last time and emitted a white bouquet of bubbles.

Dzvirko retrieved his shirt and pulled it on. Marty walked to his mother's car and stood waiting. Donny went to Ali's car. Lisa stood by the Camaro's open door. Donny asked her with his eyes to move, then slipped around her and got into the backseat with Heather.

"Is he dead?" Heather asked.

"Gettin' there," Donny said.

Derek Dzvirko walked to Ali's car. "Will you take me home?" he asked.

Ali nodded, and he climbed into the front passenger seat.

Lisa went to the Topaz and stood by the open passenger door.

"Where's everybody going?" Kaufman asked.

Dzvirko leaned out of Ali's car. "Hey, man, where the fuck do you think we're going, Disney World? We're going to get the fuck out of here, man, that's where we're going."

Kaufman stomped toward Ali's car, lifted his foot, and kicked the door shut on Dzvirko. Then he reached forward and yanked it back open.

"Like fuck!" he screamed. "Like fuck you are!"

The others watched him carefully, but no one spoke. Kaufman was red in the face, sucking his breath in gasps and shaking.

"Let me tell you people something," he shouted. "Nobody is going home until we have agreed on our fucking alibis, because I am definitely not going to have this shit put on me! I will tell you this, we had better get our goddamn stories right, because, if shit happens to me, if one fucking thing happens to me, then I will come after the rest of you, and you will wind up fucked up worse than this motherfucker over here in the ditch. Do you understand me? Do you fucking understand me?"

Marty nodded. "O.K. But I want to get out of here before somebody finds us. How about we go to the Publix mall near my house, on Sheridan, and meet there, and we'll chill out a little bit that way and then get our stories right, O.K.?"

Kaufman agreed. Marty motioned for him to ride with him. The headlights came on, doors slammed, the engines roared to life, and within seconds both cars had spun off the shoulder onto the pavement, kicking up rooster tails of sand.

For ten minutes or more after they had left, the place where they had killed Bobby was silent, empty, and smooth. His face lay half below the silky black sheet of the water's surface, half above, one huge eye staring up lidless at the moon. The sheath to Marty's scuba knife lay still and gray on the sand beneath the clump of weeds where he had placed it. Then the water began to wrinkle, and then to roil, as sand crabs rushed in hungrily to the feast.

*　　*　　*

ALI WAS IN THE LEAD, FLOORING THE MUSTANG EAST ON GRIFFIN through light traffic. She was shaking her head while she drove, biting her lip and bobbing her body slowly back and forth against the seat back.

Heather leaned forward and put her hand through from the back to touch Ali's shoulder. "You shouldn't feel bad, Ali," she said. "He deserved to die. He probably would have hurt you or your baby, even."

"What do you mean?"

"I don't know," Heather said. "I don't know. I just don't think you should like, you know, have a guilt trip or something."

In the Topaz, Kaufman was sitting in the back next to Dzvirko. Lisa and Marty were in front.

"We have to go get our shit together," Kaufman said. "That didn't go down right. People just weren't cool. They weren't cool at all. If some little fuck starts spilling his guts and puts any of this shit on me, I will definitely kill the motherfucker."

"We shouldn't go to the Publix," Lisa said, interrupting him.

"Why?"

"Too many people. Too many kids hang there. They'll see us there together. We should go to South Beach. We can chill there and get our shit together about the alibi."

"Well, you better tell them," Kaufman said, nodding toward Ali's taillights two car lengths ahead of them in traffic.

Marty jammed his foot down harder on the gas and surged ahead wildly through the lanes. When Ali stopped at the light at the corner of Sheridan and Hiatus, Marty pulled up next to her. He honked the horn, and Lisa screamed, "South Beach!" at them. Ali gave her a thumbs-up to show they understood, and the two cars roared off down Sheridan, through the new communities in the west, then through the older neighborhoods in western Fort Lauderdale proper, where Marty and Bobby had grown up, through Dania and across the causeway, south along the beach road and finally to the small public lot separated from the beach by a narrow boardwalk.

They got out of the cars slowly, first Ali and Derek Dzvirko from the Mustang, then Marty, Lisa, and Derek Kaufman from the Topaz. Donny Semenec pulled himself from the driver's side door of the Mustang slowly and deliberately, like a snake. Finally Heather came out of the other side of the Mustang. The others stood around uncertainly near the cars. Heather walked straight to the boardwalk and led them over it to the beach.

It was 1:30 in the morning. The skies had been cloudy early on the previous day, but now a strong ocean breeze had blown the weather back inland. In the distance, at the far ends of the beach, were soaring clusters of brightly lighted beach hotels. The beach itself was almost phosphorescent in the moonlight, a silver strand hanging between star mountains. As each of them came to it and took a position, sitting or standing, the only sound along the beach was the patient hiss of the sea and the woody clattering of the palm leaves overhead. At sea, barely visible on the dark horizon, a ship's lights winked up and down behind the swells, as if stars were drowning there.

Heather stared out toward the ship. Ali sat behind her on the stairs leading down from the boardwalk to the sand.

"I almost passed out driving here," Ali mumbled.

"Why?" Heather asked over her shoulder, still looking out to sea. "I don't feel bad. I just, like, when they were doing it, I just blanked." She turned and looked at Ali.

"Have you got any weed?"

Ali shook her head no.

Just off to the right of them was a wooden lifeguard station. Derek Kaufman was leaning against it with one arm. "Where's the knives and shit?" he asked.

"In the cars," Marty said.

"Well, go get them. We have to get rid of them."

Marty climbed back up the steps to the boardwalk, and Lisa followed him. Ali rose and went, too. Heather decided to follow.

When they opened the Topaz and began looking for the weapons, Lisa said, "It smells like blood."

"What?" Ali asked. "You're crazy. I don't smell anything."

Marty was on the other side of the car with the door open, looking for the weapons. Lisa was standing on the lot next to the open door, stooping forward with her head inside the car. "It smells like blood in here!" she said. "Come here. You can smell it."

Ali went to the other side, opened the door, and sniffed. "I don't smell anything," she said.

Lisa plunged into the car on her knees on the floor and began hurling out litter and trash behind her. "It stinks! It stinks of blood!" She was breathing heavily again, the way she had when Marty was sitting on Bobby's chest stabbing him.

Marty came up behind her and put his hand gently on her shoulder. "Lisa," he said.

She backed out of the car and stood up.

His lower lip was trembling and his eyes were moist. She gazed into his face trying to comprehend, then took him by both hands.

"What is it, baby?" she asked softly. "Is something the matter?"

"Lisa," he said. His lip was trembling.

She shook his arms, gently at first, then harder. "What is it, Marty? What's the matter with you?"

"I don't have the sheath," he whispered.

"What?"

"I don't have the sheath to my diving knife. I left it back there."

She stared at him, speechless. Then she said, "You bent down and put it under a bush, I saw you."

"Yeah."

"You didn't get it?"

"No."

"Oh, God."

Marty pulled her to him sharply. "I can't go back," he said.

"You have to."

"Somebody could be there by now."

"You have to go, Marty. You have to get it. You'll get caught if they find it. They can get fingerprints from it."

They all turned at once and looked toward the steps leading down from the boardwalk to the parking lot. Derek Kaufman was at the top of the stairs, leaning on a rail and glaring down at them.

"What's the matter?" he asked.

When they told him, Kaufman was surprisingly calm. He came toward them. "You forgot the sheath. We have to go back. I was coming to tell you we have to go back anyway. We didn't cover the tire tracks; we might have left other shit out there. We just got freaked, and we left too fast."

Lisa backed away from him, shaking her head, beginning to hyperventilate again. "I can't go back there, man. I'm not fucking going back out there."

"Lisa," Marty said, "you said yourself I might get caught if we don't go get the sheath."

"So you get it. I'm not going back."

Ali found some dope after all in the car for Donny, Dzvirko, Lisa, and Heather to smoke. Then she got in the Mustang and drove Marty and Derek Kaufman back up the beach road to Sheridan and inland toward Weston.

It was a twenty-five-minute drive. During the entire trip, not one of them spoke. Then, just as they were pulling off South Post Oak Road, Kaufman said, "First we have to find the sheath and look for anything else we might have left. Then we have to get some branches or something and smooth over our tracks."

"Why?" Ali asked.

"They can tell tire tracks," Kaufman said. "I've seen it in movies and stuff."

As they rolled toward the spot on Post Oak Road where they had left him, all three were wound tight, prepared at any instant for lights to come on and sirens to race shrieking at them from the darkness.

They stopped the car and stared out into the darkness from the side of the road. They rolled the windows down. They could hear nothing. Nothing seemed to be moving.

Within seconds after getting out of the car, Marty had retrieved the sheath. He and Kaufman made a hasty reconnaissance of the rest of the area and concluded nothing else had been left. Then they walked back over the tracks their tires had left in the sand and scuffed them with their feet to obscure them.

"O.K., let's get the fuck out of here," Marty said.

"Nah," Kaufman said. "We need to go see if he's still there."

Marty gazed glumly at him. "Shit, man," he said softly. "I really don't want to do that."

"Well, we got to, man. We're here. We need to know if somebody found him yet."

Kaufman led the way. Ali stayed up by the car.

"He's here," Kaufman whispered hoarsely.

Marty came up behind him. Both of them leaned forward at the waist to examine the body.

Something darted near the face and splashed. They both shouted and leaped backward.

"Shit!"

"What the fuck was that?"

Marty walked back down and peered. He saw small quick movements all along the bloody flesh of the face and down by the belly where the intestines were floating out loose from the body. He staggered backward, holding his stomach.

"They're eating him," he gasped. He bent more sharply forward at the waist, and a river of vomit gushed from his throat.

Kaufman stepped around the vomit and went down to look. "That's so sick, man," he said. "That is so gross. Nature sucks, you know it?"

Marty was wiping strings of vomit from his chin with the backs of both hands. "No shit," he said.

BACK AT THE BEACH, LISA HAD RESUMED THE TASK OF CLEANING out the Topaz with a ferocious energy. She even threw out a pile of newspapers and magazines that had been slopping around in the trunk for months, waiting to be dropped at a recycling center. "I can still smell the blood," she said.

Heather said, "I don't smell it."

Donny was sitting at the top of the steps enjoying a fresh high from Ali's dope. He shrugged and smiled sweetly. "If she smells it, she smells it. People are all different, you know."

Lisa finally slammed shut the doors of the car and then gathered up the bloody baseball bat and knives and started back over the boardwalk with them.

"Where are you going?" Donny asked.

"To bury this shit," Lisa said.

"Cool." He got up to follow, and Heather and Derek Dzvirko came after. They all traipsed after Lisa across the boardwalk and down the steps at the far end to the beach. Lisa slogged across the sand to the lifeguard station, where she dropped the bat and knives and then fell to her knees. With her hands she began furiously burrowing in the sand. The rest of them stood at a distance and watched her.

When she had made a small depression in the sand, she reached for the knives and bat and dragged them into it. Then she leaned forward, grunting, and dragged sand back over them. She rose to her knees, breathing heavily. Then slowly, pushing herself with one fist in the sand, she got to her feet.

She looked down at her feet. Then, kicking as if at an invisible attacker, she kicked her sandals off and sent them flying several feet.

"There's blood on my shoes," she said. "Christ! There's fucking blood on my shoes!"

She stalked over and retrieved her shoes, then went to her knees again where she had buried the weapons. Clawing at the sand with both hands, she unearthed the knives and bat, then put her shoes with them and covered them again.

She stood up and stared at the spot on the beach. "Some dog will just come dig this up," she said. "You know, people bring their fucking dogs out here. It's against the law. They do it anyway. They bring their fucking dogs, the fucking lifeguards don't do shit.

"If . . ." she started. Her voice faltered. She turned to implore the others, who were in a knot a few yards away, watching her, their faces blank.

"If they find this shit, if they find the . . . the blood, if they find the blood, the stuff with the blood . . ."

Her lower jaw was trembling.

"Maybe you should just try to chill, Lisa," Heather said.

"No, no, I can't handle being caught," Lisa said. "I can't handle that. I can't . . . I definitely cannot be caught for this shit. I mean, do you guys realize . . . you know what they would do, right, I mean, they're going to say, you know what . . . I mean you guys know what we fucking did, right? Right?"

Heather shrugged. "I didn't do shit," she said.

Derek Dzvirko shrugged. "I definitely didn't."

They all turned to look at him.

"I didn't kill anybody. I went along for the ride."

"You helped drown him," Donny said.

"Hey, listen, fucker," Dzvirko said, jabbing on Donny's chest with a finger, "I just helped carry the body because that fucker Mafia guy was gonna beat the shit out of me and maybe kill me, too, if I didn't."

Lisa interjected, "I didn't do shit."

Dzvirko was still working on Donny. "You stabbed him first, asshole."

Donny held up his forefinger and thumb to show a tiny amount. "I stuck him about that much," he said, whining.

Lisa fell back to her knees and began scooping out the sand again. In a moment she had pulled out the knives, the bat, and her sandals. She carried them down to the edge of the sea.

The wind had come up, and the waves were rising. Lisa walked out ankle deep. She had reached back with the bat and prepared to hurl it when Derek Dzvirko realized what she was doing and came charging down to the water's edge.

"Give me that goddamn bat, Lisa," he shouted. "I have to give it back to the kid or I'll have to pay for it."

She glared at him, drew in her breath, and then hurled the bat across the beach at him. It fell in front of his toes in the sand.

Lisa turned back toward the sea, took Donny Semenec's brother's survival knife and flung in into the surging purple seas, then threw Marty's scuba knife behind it.

They heard a car motor dying on the parking lot at the far end of the boardwalk.

"Oh, shit," Lisa whispered. "They patrol out here at night."

"So?" Heather said. "So tell 'em we came out here to have an orgy."

They heard male footsteps approaching on the creaking boards. Dzvirko looked as if he was thinking about running. But they all stood still, turned toward the boardwalk, waiting.

A moment later, Kaufman and Marty appeared in the darkness, followed by Ali. Marty was carrying the sheath.

KAUFMAN WAS EXCITED. ON THE WAY BACK, HE HAD WORRIED THAT the others might not have waited at the beach. Coming down the steps, he looked around eagerly to make sure they were all still there. He ran out onto the sand and began barking orders.

"Where's the other shit? The knives and the bat? Where are they?"

"I got the bat," Dzvirko said. He showed him.

"Where's the knives?"

"I threw them in the ocean," Lisa said sullenly.

"You threw them in the ocean?" Kaufman asked. "You threw them *where* in the ocean?"

Lisa shrugged and looked down at her feet, refusing to answer or meet his gaze.

Donny snickered. "She's been about to go postal ever since you guys left. She thinks she's gonna get caught."

Lisa whirled on him. "I didn't do shit," she said. "Anybody gets caught, it will be you, asshole. You stabbed him first."

Kaufman was quiet, thoughtful. He looked around carefully at each of them. He began to speak, quietly at first with his head cocked, not looking at any of them.

"So. So you have been talking about getting caught. And who did what. Well, that's a good talk to have. You need to talk about that. What did you decide, by the way?"

He began to walk, moving from one to the other, looking them each hard in the face, beginning with Donny, who was closest.

"You. Dopehead. What do you think? Did you kill him?"

"No," Donny said, shaking his head nervously. "I mean, I stuck the dude, I admit that, everybody saw me do that, but I didn't actually kill him. He was still alive after I stopped sticking him. You saw him run."

Kaufman went to Dzvirko. "You?"

"You know I didn't kill him."

"You didn't? You didn't kill him? Well, who the fuck was it that helped me drown the son of a bitch?"

"He was dead. . . ."

"He was dead?"

"He was so far fucking gone," Dzvirko said, shaking his head, speaking to the sky, "he was so far gone, man. When I helped you pick him up, I wasn't picking him up to kill him. I wasn't . . ."

Dzvirko stopped speaking and stared at Kaufman. As he stared, his pudgy face began to shake like Jell-O and then to crumble, and then he began to cry. "I didn't kill him, man."

Kaufman went to where Lisa was standing with Heather and Ali. "Ladies?"

"We didn't do shit," Heather said.

Ali watched Kaufman warily and said nothing.

He walked to Marty and put his arm around his shoulder. "Now, Mr. Marty and I have already spoken, on the way back from retrieving Mr. Marty's sheath to his knife, which he left at the murder scene."

He paused and then said it again for effect.

"Murder scene. Murder. You do know that we murdered a guy tonight. Your friend. You do understand that we took his life. I just want to make sure everybody's up to speed on that."

He whipped around, grabbed Donny Semenec by a fistful of shirt, and lifted him off his feet. He shouted in his face, "You do have enough of a fucking brain in there to understand that you killed that motherfucker, don't you?"

Donny smirked.

"Damn straight," he said.

Kaufman dropped him and turned on the others. "Let me explain something to you people. I know you're just out here having your thrills and playing your games and shit. This goddamn smokehead over here behind me probably thinks he's still playing Mortal Kombat.

"But this ain't Mortal Kombat. This ain't a game. Your old buddy that you were all pissed off at and so on, well, he's lying in the ditch back there in Weston with his fuckin' eyeballs hanging out and sand crabs eating his guts."

A gasp escaped from Marty's lips. He put the back of his hand to his mouth and stared at the group in dismay, as if guilty of a gaffe.

Kaufman said, "Look, I don't intend to go down for this shit. And if anybody here takes me down, either on purpose or because of being stupid, then I'm gonna come find that person and kill his ass."

He turned toward Lisa. "Or her ass."

He faced them all. "Kill. I will kill you if you fuck me up. Now, people, we are going to sit down here, and we are going to work on our fucking alibi until I am satisfied with it."

They came forward sheepishly, one, then two, then all of them, and sat in a half-circle on the sand around Kaufman. He prodded them for ideas, and, reluctantly at first, they offered suggestions. After a while, when they had all caught on to the idea of the thing, the conversation grew more animated, even enthusiastic.

Kaufman said they would all have to deny having gone anywhere near Weston or having been with Bobby at all that evening. Lisa was the one who remembered that Marty had eaten lunch at Pizza Hut with Bobby the previous noon.

"So that will make Marty the last one who saw him," she said.

"Why me?" Marty asked.

Kaufman shook his head. "Because somebody might have seen you there, asshole, so you can't deny to the cops you went there with him, or you'll look like you're covering up."

"Why do I have to talk to the cops?"

No one spoke for a while. Kaufman stared at Marty in disbelief. Then Lisa spoke quietly.

"You were his best friend. So you'll be the number-one suspect."

Marty blinked at her.

"I was his best friend, so I'll be the suspect?"

"Yeah," Kaufman said.

"I don't get that. I mean, why does that make sense?"

"Take it from me," Kaufman said. "It just does."

They decided Marty should think of something to tell the police about what Bobby had said at lunch, something that might help explain what had happened to him.

Marty came up with the idea of saying Bobby had told him about a rendezvous he had planned for later in the day with a girl he had met recently—someone the rest of them wouldn't know.

Weston, where they had killed him, was on the rim of the outback, the area they called "out west," a land of scruffy farms and fishing camps where the people of the old Florida still lived—the red-necks. Marty would say Bobby had bragged about meeting a hillbilly girl from out west. He was going to meet her that night somewhere out near Weston. Marty would say he was worried because Bobby had mentioned that the hillbilly girl had some kind of connection with the Davie Boys.

The picture would be plain: Bobby met the hillbilly girl somewhere. They drove in her car to Weston to have sex. The Davie Boys caught wind of it and found them. The rest was obvious.

That took care of where Bobby was. Next they needed to think of something to say about where they had been. They were at South Beach Park. Obviously they wouldn't tell the cops they had come here, because they had thrown away the weapons here. But the name of the place gave Lisa an idea: Why not say they had gone to the other "South Beach"?

South Beach is an area of restored art deco buildings along an old

strip of boardwalk in South Miami Beach. Nightclubs, cafés, and gal-
leries attract a sophisticated adult crowd at night, but the area also
draws kids from the suburbs seeking exotica, some of whom come to
bait and harass the large gay and lesbian populace.

They all agreed they would say they had gone to Miami Beach's
South Beach area to walk the boardwalk. It was as indisputable a story
as saying you had gone to meet a hillbilly girl out west—as if you
had gone to the moon. Who would know?

By now they were all feeling a little better, except for Marty, who
was still uneasy that he was going to be a prime suspect.

"It seems to me, if I'm his best friend, I should be the last person
they think would go out and whack the dude."

"Yeah, well, that's what you'd think," Kaufman said, "but you're
not a cop, and you don't realize what sick bastards these guys are and
how they suspect you even more if you're like the most innocent-
seeming person in the world. It's like, the more innocent you are, the
more they want to fuck with you."

"Jeez," Marty said.

Kaufman wanted to know who would be the first person to miss
Bobby. Without a moment's hesitation, Marty said, "His dad."

"His dad?"

"Yeah," Marty said. "He really loves him."

Everyone looked at Marty, who stared at Kaufman and then
shrugged. "He gets up to cook his breakfast for him. Stuff like that."

"So will he call you?" Kaufman asked.

"Yeah, he might."

"Well, you have to be ready to chill him out. The longer you can
keep him from calling the cops, the better chance the 'gators will have
finished everything off out there."

"Yeah."

It was decided that Marty would call Bobby's house as soon as he
got home. It was now almost 3:30 in the morning. The Kent family—
Fred, Farah, and Bobby's sister, Laila, a college student home for the
summer, would be asleep, with the answering machine turned on.
Marty would leave a phony message for Bobby, something that would

give the impression Marty believed Bobby to be safely at home and snug in bed, too.

Lisa suggested, "Like maybe Bob told you to call him when you got in, so you're just calling him like everything's normal."

Marty agreed it would be a good idea. They all agreed that they had come up with a good plan. Even Kaufman seemed to have calmed down.

Marty said he was tired and needed to go home. Lisa came over and hugged him tight, rocking him slowly back and forth, bathing his forehead in slow soft kisses.

"Marty and me are going to go back together," she said. "Ali, you take the others back."

Ali shrugged.

In the parking lot, Derek Kaufman waited for Dzvirko, Donny, and Heather to cram into the back of the Mustang, and then he took the front passenger seat.

On the long drive back out to Weston to drop Kaufman off, none of them spoke. They put a tape of the Geto Boys on the stereo and cranked it up full blast. Roaring west on Sheridan down long empty lanes, they passed a joint and bobbed their heads in rhythm with the low growling beat of the music.

Lisa and Marty drove home alone. Lisa wanted to hug Marty and to pet him, but he was nervous, distracted.

"You don't think we're going to get caught for this shit?" he asked her.

"No," she said. "How are we going to get caught?"

"I don't know. That guy just got me nervous."

"He's fucked."

"Yeah."

He dropped her off at her mother's house, and then he went home.

Marty went to the phone in the kitchen, picked it up and dialed Bobby's house.

On the second ring, Fred Kent reached over to the bedside table next to his head and picked up the telephone. The machine had already picked up, so Fred waited for his own recorded greeting to end.

As soon as the greeting ended and before Fred could speak, Marty said, "Bobby, this is Marty Puccio. I called you. You asked me to call you when I got home."

"Hey, Marty," Fred said.

Marty hung up.

FRED LAY IN BED WITH HIS EYES OPEN. IT WAS 4:00 A.M. HE WAS groggy. The call had been strange. "This is Marty Puccio," Marty had said, giving his last name. Of course it was Marty Puccio. Who was it going to be, Marty Someone-Else?

"I called you."

So what? Fred rolled over. Who in the hell knew? Who knew what they were up to?

He couldn't sleep. He got up out of bed.

"This is Marty Puccio," he had said.

Why did he just hang up when Fred said hello to him? Fred went back to Bobby's room and checked.

Empty. The bed still neatly made.

So he hasn't been home all night. So this is some kind of crap that they're up to. Fred went back to bed, disgruntled, with a vague sense of unease lurking far at the back of his mind. He managed to get a little more sleep.

FRED KENT WOKE EARLY ON THURSDAY MORNING, JULY 15, 1993. The first thing he did, even before putting his clothes on, was go check to see if his son had come in.

Still gone. Never here. Up to something with that idiot down the street.

Fred decided to work from home that morning rather than go into his office. He would make phone calls to clients while he waited for

Bobby to show up. He would come in soon, and Fred would try to find out where he had been all night.

Bobby was so close. He had finished high school, in spite of some rocky roads along the way. He had one foot in a decent program at a community college. It wasn't everything Fred had hoped for his only son, but it wasn't failure, and it left the door open for successes later, when Bobby finally grew up.

If Fred could just guide him, coax him, trick him along somehow beyond perils like Ali Willis and the high school dropout Marty Puccio, then Bobby would emerge as a man worthy of respect, a success in America. It was a dream never far from Fred's mind.

He checked Bobby's room at 10:00 A.M., expecting to find him sprawled on the bed, passed out and hungover from the previous night's adventures. But the room was empty.

Fred Kent made more calls from his small home office at the opposite end of the house from Bobby's room. He went back at 11:00 A.M. and checked, then went back to his desk.

If Marty Puccio called at—whatever time it had been, early morning, before 5:00 A.M.—then Bobby was not with him at that time. Presumably, they had not been together for a while.

It was not like Bobby to stay away from home all night and then fail to show up the next morning. Something was wrong. Fred Kent pushed away from his desk with the sick feeling in the pit of his stomach that every parent knows, hates, and dreads. He was afraid for his son.

CHAPTER SEVEN

LISA WOKE UP AT ABOUT 10:00 A.M. WITHOUT STOPPING TO BATHE, SHE reached for clothes that lay dirty on the floor, pulled them on with quick grunting motions, shoved her hair back with one hand, then went straight to the phone and called Marty.

"You got your ma's car?" she asked

"Yeah."

"Come get me, baby. I need to be with you."

Ali, Heather, and Donny were sleeping curled together like dogs in the loft. Lisa climbed up the ladder far enough to stick her head over the ledge and told them to be sure to get out of the house before her mother returned. Then she hurried out front to wait for Marty.

By 11:00 A.M., they were both in Marty's room sitting on his bed. Lisa reached for him several times and tried to initiate lovemaking, but each time Marty pulled back quickly and turned away.

"What's the matter?" she asked.

He turned toward her, his face an alabaster mask, shiny with sweat, stony hard except for the silent working of his lips.

"We better not fucking get caught for this, Lisa," he said.

The front doorbell rang. Her arms shot forward to clutch him. The sudden movement shocked him, and he jumped to his feet.

"Jesus Christ," he said. "What was that?"

"It's the doorbell," she said. Her heart was pounding so hard that she could barely breathe.

"Oh, God," Marty said in a high whining whisper. Tears sprang to his eyes. "Oh, shit, Lisa. I am so fucking scared."

She stumped on her knees across the bed to him and tried again to grab him to her, but he wrenched away from her, so that she tipped clumsily over the edge and fell in a mound at his feet.

"Goddamn it, Lisa!" he said in a high hoarse whisper. "Get up! Get the fuck up."

The doorbell rang again, and this time there was pounding on the door. Marty was standing hunched forward, gasping for air. Lisa was on the floor, lifting herself on one stiff arm and looking up at him.

He straightened himself and walked to the front of the house. He looked out through the large window in the living room and saw nothing on the street. No police cars. No action. He put his eye to the peephole in the door and saw Fred Kent standing outside, a slight, dapper figure in neatly pressed chino trousers. Marty knew right away who it was, even though Fred was standing with his back to the door and his hands in his pockets.

Marty reached for the lock, but his hand was trembling so badly that he had to use both hands to get it undone. He pulled the door open halfway and looked out.

Fred Kent turned. The minute he saw Marty's face, he knew that something was badly wrong. His own heart came up in his throat.

"Marty," he said, "what is wrong? What's happened? Is Bobby here? What's the matter?"

Marty shook his head to answer that there was nothing wrong, but for a moment he could not make any words come.

"Marty," Fred said, beginning to lose patience, "is Bobby here with you? He didn't come home last night."

Lisa had come to Marty's back, out of view of the open crack in the door. She took his hand and squeezed it.

"He didn't come home last night?" Marty sputtered.

"No. When was the last time you saw him?"

"Oh, man," Marty said. "I knew it!"

Lisa squeezed his hand hard, sensing that he was about to go off the deep end.

"You knew what, Marty?" Fred demanded.

"I knew something would happen to Bobby. Last night he had a date with this country-looking girl. She might have been hooked up to a gang or something. Maybe a gang took him away, you know, and . . ."

Lisa shoved past Marty, pushing the door all the way open and putting herself between Marty and Fred. Her face was angry and tense. She looked up at Marty.

"You don't know what you're talking about, Marty," she said. "That's just a bunch of shit."

"Lisa!" Fred said. "Have you seen Bobby?"

Marty grabbed a fistful of Lisa's long greasy hair in one hand and grabbed her upper arm with the other hand. His face was dark with anger. He pushed her roughly back into the house and said, "Shut up, Lisa! Stay the fuck out of this."

Fred squinted his eyes and peered at Marty for a long silent moment. "Well," he said finally, his voice controlled and quiet. "I guess we should report this to the Hollywood police."

"I don't know. I don't . . . he could be, well, you know, you can't ever tell, but, uh, I wouldn't call them just now, like, not right away."

Fred stared at Marty. Marty was quaking.

"When would you call them?"

"Well not, uh . . . like, I would just wait, like, maybe for a couple days."

Fred turned on his heel and walked back down the block—the block his little boy had run down, skipped down, sailed down on his skateboard, flown down on his bicycle, roared down in his car, always to see "my friend."

Something was very wrong, disastrously wrong, and that idiot was involved. Fear and anger swept up over Fred like flame from the gut of the Earth. He marched straight into his house and called the police.

*   *   *

"OH, GOD, MARTY, WHAT IN THE FUCK IS THE MATTER WITH YOU?"
Lisa shrieked at him. "Why are you running your mouth with all this
shit?"

"Shut up!" he shouted. He slapped her hard across the face, then
drove her back through the house, cuffing her across the face and on
the sides of her head. "Just shut up, fat bitch!"

FRED KENT WAS PREPARED FOR SOME KIND OF RUNAROUND: THE
police would tell him his son had not been missing long enough or
something to that effect. To his surprise, the person on the other end
of the line sounded concerned, asked several detailed questions, and
then asked Fred if he would mind speaking to a patrol officer.

"No, not at all. Please. Send someone. And thank you very much
for your concern."

Fred immediately called Marty. "The police are coming to talk to
me about Bob, Marty. Would you mind coming down to see if you
can help?"

MARTY HUNG UP THE PHONE AND THEN COLLAPSED BACKWARD ONTO
the bed, so frightened that his teeth were literally chattering. "Oh,
God, Lisa, the asshole's already called the fucking cops. He wants me
to talk to them!"

Lisa was sullen.

"Of course he called the cops, Marty. You told him Bob was probably killed by a gang."

"I did not, goddamn it!"

Lisa sat down beside him, reached for his hand and then told him softly that he had to go down the street and show concern for his missing best friend.

AT 11:45 A.M., HOLLYWOOD PATROL OFFICER DEBRA RAMSEY PULLED up in a squad car outside the Kent house. Fred and Marty were waiting. They came out on the lawn with the officer to talk.

She was a slender, attractive brunette in her mid-thirties. Her eyes expressed a sad, world-weary toughness that Fred found reassuring.

"I'm very worried," he said to her, allowing himself to show more emotion than he had earlier in front of Marty.

Taking the cue, Marty said that he was terribly worried, too.

Fred told Ramsey the story Marty had told him about the country girl Bobby had met the day before.

Ramsey turned to Marty with a notepad in her hand. Staring down at the pad, she asked, "Where did she meet him?"

"At the Publix where we work. The deli. We both work there."

She wrote it down.

"Which Publix?"

"Dania."

She jotted.

"When?"

"Yesterday."

"Were you there?"

Marty hesitated.

She looked up. "Sir?"

"Yeah. I was there." He looked flustered. "We both worked. That day."

"Did you see this girl he met?"

He paused again.

She was watching his face now.

"Yeah," he said. "She came in. That's how we met her."

"You met her?"

"Well. We both did. She was there, you know." His heart was pounding. "So, yeah. But he was the one that went out with her."

"Yes, sir." At some point in the last few moments, the sadness had evaporated from her eyes. Her face was a stone mask.

"What did she look like?"

"What?" Marty asked.

"I said what did she look like?"

He shrugged. "I don't really remember."

She dropped her notepad to her side and looked at him without speaking. Marty shuffled and shrugged.

"I just don't . . . you know. A lot of people come in."

"Sir, you said she was a country girl. Just tell me what she looked like. How tall was she? The color of her hair. Was she pretty? What was she wearing? Did she say anything about her name or where she lived? Describe her the very best you can, sir."

"I don't remember."

"Sir?"

"I'm sorry. I don't remember what she looked like or anything. I just don't remember even what she looked like. Or anything."

Ramsey jotted down a service number on the back of a business card and handed it to Fred. "Please let me know if you learn anything more."

"What will you do?" Fred asked.

"I will make a report, and then we'll be in touch, or you can call us if you learn anything about where your son is."

WHEN ALI, DONNY, AND HEATHER ARRIVED AT ALI'S PARENTS' HOME on Parsons Circle that afternoon at about 3:00 P.M., Ali's mother was having a cigarette and coffee in front of the kitchen television.

They had driven straight from Lauderdale, smoking dope and listening to music the entire way. As they trooped past Virginia, barely glancing at her, Ali mumbled, "Hi, Mom." Then they disappeared into her room.

Virginia shrugged. "Well, what's the matter with those kids?" she thought.

No one emerged from the room for three hours. A little after 6:00 P.M., Ali came out and busied herself gathering a tray of food—sodas, sandwich materials, chips, cookies. She carried the tray back into her room without speaking to her mother.

Virginia drifted over by the door of her daughter's room and heard muffled voices inside. The television was on low, and the three of them were talking. She couldn't make out words, but she could tell that they were engaged in animated conversation.

Half an hour later, Ali emerged from the room and came to where her mother was sitting at the kitchen bar. Ali sat down on a high stool next to Virginia.

"Hi, honey," Virginia said. "What you up to?"

"Ma?"

"Yes, baby?"

"Is it a crime if you like witness a crime but you don't report it?"

Virginia shrugged. "What kind of a crime?"

"Murder," Ali said.

They looked at each other. Ali's expression was mildly curious but otherwise flat.

"Who witnessed this?" Virginia asked.

"It's just hypothetical," Ali said. "We're just discussing this in there, and we just wondered if it would be a crime if we had witnessed a murder and didn't report it."

Virginia mulled it over for a moment. "I presume it would," she said. "I don't know, but I would presume it would."

"O.K.," Ali said. She bounced off the stool and skipped back into her room.

Virginia shrugged. Wondering if they had found something better to watch on television than she had, she picked up the remote and channel-surfed for a while.

*   *   *

FRED AND FARAH KENT PASSED A SLEEPLESS NIGHT, EACH OF THEM rising alone several times, trying not to wake the other. At about four in the morning they met in the kitchen, held each other, and gave way to tears for the first time. Fred promised he would call the police again first thing Friday morning.

He called at 7:30 A.M. and asked for Officer Ramsey. Ramsey was not yet on duty, but the Hollywood dispatcher said he would send someone else. While Fred waited for the police to arrive, he called Marty Puccio and asked him to come down again.

The patrol car appeared and two male officers came to the door. Marty showed up a few minutes later. Unlike the Kents, he had slept well, and he was much more in command of himself than he had been the night before.

The policemen explained again that Ramsey was not yet on duty. They would ask her to call Fred when she came on. At the time, they regretted that they had no new information to report.

Fred was nodding to show that he understood. Farah stood just behind him, her eyes welling with tears.

Marty spoke up suddenly. "This really sucks," he said.

"Pardon me, sir?" one of the officers said.

"Well, I mean this guy is my best friend, and he's their son, and he's been missing for two days in a row now, and it doesn't look to me like you guys are doing jack shit!"

One of the officers moved a little closer to Marty and looked him up and down.

"And you are?"

Marty shouted at him, "I'm his best friend, goddamn it! And I want him found! Jesus! Is that too much to ask?"

The officers turned toward Fred. He met their gaze and said evenly, "He spoke to Officer Ramsey. That should be in her report."

One of the officers turned back to Marty. "What would you have us do that we're not doing, sir? If there is something you can think of that might help us find your friend, please tell us. All we want to do is find him."

Marty returned the officer's cool gaze. "I don't know. You're the fucking cop!"

The officer winced slightly, then turned back to the Kents and assured them they would hear from Ramsey when she came on duty. Then they left.

Fred said, "You were kind of rough talking with the police, Marty."

"Yeah," he said, "well, I'm getting sick of this shit. I'm sorry, but I want some action. I'm starting to get worried here."

DEREK DZVIRKO WENT TO THE DNA COMIC STORE THAT AFTERNOON and found an acquaintance with whom he sometimes played Mortal Kombat—a young man named Terry, whom he barely knew. He asked him if the two of them could go outside and sit on the grass in front of Pizza Hut for a while.

They sat cross-legged on a mound of carefully clipped turf with the busy midday shoppers whirling around them in the Embassy Lakes Mall, and bit by bit, as if joking at one moment, then earnestly spilling his guts the next, Derek recounted the entire story of the murder to this person he barely knew.

Once in a while, as Derek spoke, Terry offered monosyllabic interjections—Gross! Man! Fuck—but he was not otherwise shocked or astonished by what Derek told him.

When Derek had finished recounting it, the other man asked him what he was going to do.

"I don't know, man. I can't sleep or do shit. I'm real uptight, because I'm, like, you know, just worried, like I'm really worried they're going to find some shit out there that will give us away, and I'll like, you know, get caught. I'm really fucked, man. I can't stop thinking about it. I think like, maybe I should go back out there and make sure the body's still in the water where the 'gators will get it and, like, make sure we didn't drop something or leave something, you know?"

Terry eyed him for a while. "Well, man, you didn't kill the dude, did you?"

"Me? No! Hell no! I didn't have shit to do with it! But I was like, you know . . . there! So somebody could say I was like a witness or some shit, and maybe, I don't know, if you know about something like this that happened, maybe you're supposed to tell the cops or they might have some fucking law where they can get you in trouble, you know, like fine print or something, like say you were at the scene of an accident and you left without reporting it."

"Yeah," Terry said. "They had that in Driver's Ed."

"Yeah, I know. So. Shit. I don't know what to do."

"It's like you need an alibi, man. You need somebody who could say you were with them like that whole time, so you could say, shit, I wasn't nowhere with any of these other assholes that night."

Terry suggested they call Herb Williams, a smart kid they both knew. Derek had actually known Williams longer than Terry had.

They went to the pay phone outside the Pizza Hut. Terry placed the call. When Herbert Williams came on the phone, Terry handed the phone to Derek.

Derek explained that he had been a witness to a murder. He told Williams that he had become anxious about getting into trouble over it.

"Why don't you tell the police?" Williams asked.

Derek said a Mafia hit man was involved, and the hit man had vowed to unleash the vengeance of the Mafia on anybody who breathed a word to the authorities.

"I need to go somewhere for a while, man," Derek said. "What I really need is to catch an alibi from somebody, like, you know, get somebody to say he was with me that whole time."

"Say it to who?"

"Well, to the cops mainly, I guess."

"Yeah. I see what you mean. Well, I'll tell you what, man, I think it's going to be pretty hard to find anybody who would be willing to lie to the cops about a murder. I would think you would be better off telling your folks about it, just for some moral support.''

Derek thanked him for the advice and hung up. Terry stayed around for a few minutes and then drifted back to the comic store, having lost interest. Derek leaned against the wall of a video store with his hands in his pockets, staring aimlessly at the passing crowd. Herbert Williams's idea was something he hadn't really considered.

NAKED, BATHED IN SWEAT AFTER FRANTIC SEX, LISA AND MARTY LAY side by side on top of the bedclothes in his room, alone in the house in the late afternoon. They had smoked a lot of dope, and Marty seemed finally to have calmed down.

Marty whispered to the ceiling, almost to himself, ''Do you think they would say I was guilty of it?''

Lisa turned to face the side of his head. ''I guess. You stuck him in the heart, right? When he was on his back and you were sitting on top of him?''

''Well, no shit, Lisa,'' he said, turning his head sharply to face her. ''I had that fucking Mafia guy with a baseball bat in his hand telling me what to do every minute.''

She turned back toward the ceiling, thoughtful. ''Yeah, that's true. I guess they would say he did it.''

''No shit. I mean, he like bashed his brains out with the bat.''

''No shit,'' she said. She snickered. Then giggled.

Marty started giggling, too. Then they both laughed out loud.

''That was so gross,'' she said, trying to catch her breath.

''Yeah, I mean, he goes like''—he joined his hands and swung both arms in the air above him, as if making a golf swing—''*thwock!*''

''Oh, shit!'' Lisa said, gasping and laughing. ''That was so sick!''

They were both quiet for a while.

''Do you think I could get in trouble?'' she asked.

''For what?''

''Just for being there. Maybe I'm like a witness.''

He thought about it. "Well, they could say you were. Like a witness, you know. But that's no big deal."

She took him in her arms. "How do you feel?"

"If I don't get caught?"

"Yeah."

He turned, drew her to him, and kissed her deeply. "Shit, babe, I feel like a ton of bricks just got lifted off me, like I could fly."

She nodded. "We did it. We actually did it."

"Yeah."

"We killed a guy."

The phone rang, and both of them jumped. Marty snatched it up. It was Derek Kaufman. He wanted to know what was going on. Marty assured him everything was under control. He gave him the details of his talks with Fred Kent and the police.

Kaufman was satisfied that Marty was handling his end all right, but he was worried about the Palm Bay crowd. He asked Marty to call them and check them out. He suggested he and Marty might need to make a trip up there to chill them out. Marty agreed it was a good idea, and he said he would call them.

OFFICER RAMSEY CALLED FRED KENT LATE IN THE DAY AND TOLD him she had nothing new to report. Fred told her he had nothing new, either.

ALI, DONNY, AND HEATHER HAD BEEN LOCKED INSIDE ALI'S ROOM for more than twenty-four hours, since their arrival the previous afternoon. Ali popped out briefly Friday afternoon to gather some cold beers and salty snacks, which she took back into the room with her.

At about 9:00 A.M. Saturday, Virginia was clearing the dishes from her breakfast with her husband.

"Ma," Ali said, "what if you witnessed a crime, but you like called a hot line and reported it, but you didn't like give your name or anything, would that be legal?''

''I don't know what you mean, Ali. What kind of crime?''

''I told you!'' she said impatiently. ''A murder!''

''What are you kids up to?'' Virginia asked.

''Nothing! Just tell me, for Christ's sake!''

Virginia could see that Ali was just on the verge of one of her serious meltdowns—something Virginia would do almost anything to avoid.

In her most consoling voice, she asked, ''If you saw a murder, honey, and you just called a hot line and reported it, but you didn't give your name or anything? Would that be enough?''

''Would it?''

''Well, I don't know the law, but I don't think so. I think you would still have to say who you were. Why are you asking me these questions?''

''Ma!'' Ali said petulantly. ''Why wouldn't it count? You could still say you reported it.''

Her mother stared at her, trying to read what was going on beneath her daughter's face. ''Are you talking about a murder murder?''

Ali looked away and shrugged. ''I guess. A guy got killed.''

''Well, why would you just call a hot line?''

''I'm asking!''

Ali stamped her foot and flew off into her room. Heather was waiting, holding the telephone toward her.

''It's Marty,'' she said in an urgent whisper. ''He wants to talk to you.''

Marty told Ali that Derek Kaufman seemed to be nervous, worried that Ali, Heather, and Donny might do something stupid. He was talking about going up to Palm Bay.

''Did you check out your car?'' Marty asked.

''For what?''

''For evidence.''

''Like what?''

''I don't know.''

When Ali hung up, she was literally vibrating.

"That Kaufman guy is talking about coming up here to see us."

Donny sprang to his feet. "Oh, no," he said excitedly, "you got to keep that guy away from me. I definitely cannot handle seeing that guy. I don't want that guy near me."

Ali ordered the other two to get dressed and follow her. The three of them tromped out past Virginia. Ali led Donny and Heather through the garage to the circular driveway out front. She ordered them to help her inspect the Mustang.

When they had satisfied themselves there were no forgotten weapons or bloodstains that would give away the car, Donny turned to head back to Ali's bedroom, but Heather said, "They can tell from the tire tracks."

Ali ordered them into the car. She drove to a discount tire dealer and had all four of the relatively new tires on the car replaced. Then they drove home, stalked past Virginia, and disappeared into the bedroom again.

MARTY'S PARENTS AND BROTHER WERE AT HOME ON SATURDAY, AND it was awkward having Lisa there all day. He took her home in midafternoon. Maureen was off on her usual busy round of Saturday afternoon errands.

Lisa was unable to stay at home by herself. She walked the better part of a mile to the home of Claudia, the Pizza Hut waitress. Claudia had already heard that something big was being planned, but she didn't know yet it had actually happened.

She was at home with her parents in the large, expensive new golf-course home they had bought two years earlier. Lisa asked at the front door if Claudia could go somewhere with her "to talk." Claudia didn't want to leave her house, so she suggested they go to the screened Florida room in the back.

There, Claudia sat down on a canvas chaise while Lisa stalked around her nervously, sweating heavily in the sultry late-afternoon heat. Lisa spoke in an animated jabber, gesturing spastically with her arms.

"You're not going to believe this shit, Claudia. You are not fucking going to believe it. We killed Bobby."

Claudia blinked and watched, then said, "Pardon me?"

"We killed him. He's dead. We did it. We killed him. You should have seen it. Marty stuck him right in the heart. . . ."

Claudia said, "Lisa, what are you . . . ?"

"No, shit, listen," Lisa said, her breath coming shallow and fast. "Even that kid, Donny, that loser? You met him. He even stabbed him, right in the back of his fucking head."

"Lisa . . ."

"And, no, wait, listen, it was so weird! And this guy, Derek, who's like a hit man, Eileen told us about him, he like, he takes this baseball bat, when Bob's down on the ground, and Bob's like, he's gurgling, like a baby, and blood is just shooting up out of him, and his guts are like hanging out of him, and his eyes, his eyes are just, it's so sick, they're like popping out of his head, almost like hanging down on his cheekbone, and this guy . . ."

"Lisa, stop!"

"This guy, Derek, he takes a baseball bat, and he just swings it and just like about half caves in his fucking head."

Lisa stopped walking around. Her shoulders heaved while she worked to calm her breath. She stared at Claudia, her eyes huge in wonderment.

"You watched this?" Claudia asked.

"Yeah. I was right there. And Ali and Heather, we were all there. We saw it. Most of it. Heather . . . you met her, right?"

"I guess."

"She's so strange. She gets this totally blanked-out look, you know, like she's not even there, and she curls up in a little ball on the floor in the back of Ali's car, and she's just back there, hugging her knees and kind of rocking, like she's totally fried, but then, after, she just kind of shrugs and says, eh, fuck him, you know?"

Claudia looked down. She said nothing for a while. Then, in a small voice, she asked, "Lisa, are you really telling the truth?"

Lisa came closer to her, stooped over her, and said in a loud excited whisper, "Listen, Claudia, I'm real worried about how we left him out there. I mean, he's just out where anybody could see him. I can't stop thinking about it, about somebody, you know, like just walking up and finding him. We should have hid him better. We should have pushed him all the way into the canal, so the 'gators would get him or he'd at least fucking sink or something. That's why I came over."

Claudia looked up slowly. "What?"

Lisa knelt in front of her.

"Claudia, I have to go back out there. I need a ride. I need somebody to help me move it."

"It?"

"The body."

Claudia reached out with one arm and pushed for Lisa to get out of her way. Then she rose to her feet.

"You murdered Bobby Kent?"

Lisa rose to her feet and backed away from Claudia. Her face was suddenly rigid and angry. "I didn't say I murdered anybody. I was just there. And they killed him. I wouldn't really say they murdered him. He was, like, fighting back."

"He was?"

"Well, he was trying to get away." Lisa's face fell flaccid again, her eyes round. "He was begging Marty, you know, saying, 'Marty, I'm sorry, I'll do anything, just please don't kill me.' "

Lisa came closer to Claudia with something like a smile on her face. "When he said it, Marty went up to him and just whacked him in the heart with his diving knife. The whole thing was just so totally . . . totally . . . extreme."

Claudia walked away from her.

"Wait," Claudia said, shaking her head, "wait. You're way out of whack, Lisa. You want somebody to take you out there to move a body? I don't . . . anybody that's crazy enough to do that . . ."

"Well, fine, fine," Lisa said, "we won't move the body, then. I just want to make sure the tire tracks are gone."

"No way, Lisa. No way."

"Hey, come on!" Lisa said.

"No. No. Look, Lisa, I gotta go. I'm late for work. I'm supposed to be at Pizza Hut in half an hour."

Lisa was angry. "Well, screw you, Claudia. All's I wanted was a ride. I hope you have a problem someday so you can ask me to help. Shit. You don't have to act like it's a federal case or something because I asked you for a fucking ride." She turned brusquely to leave by the driveway door, then stopped and turned back.

"Claudia."

"What?"

"Keep your mouth shut about this."

"No shit, Lisa."

Claudia watched out the door to make sure she was gone. Her mother looked out from the door to the house. "Is that Lisa leaving?"

"Yeah."

"Is everything O.K.?"

"Yeah."

"What's going on?"

"Nothing."

"What are you up to?"

"Nothing." She shrugged and smiled sweetly. "I gotta go to work, Mom."

ALI CAME OUT OF HER ROOM WITH DONNY AND HEATHER AT HER heels. Donny and Heather, who had exchanged few words with Mrs. Slay during their residency in her home, stood sheepishly behind Ali at a distance, their eyes averted from Virginia.

Ali was petrified. She told her mother they had been witnesses to a murder in Lauderdale earlier in the week. They hadn't done anything wrong themselves, she said, but after talking it over nonstop for the previous two days, they had decided the police might be able to make something out of the fact that they had not reported the crime.

They could not report the crime, she said, because a Mafia hit man was involved, and he had threatened them with death if they betrayed him. Now Marty Puccio was possibly on his way to Palm Bay with the hit man.

"What do you want me to do?" Virginia asked.

"I need to move out of here," Ali said.

"To where?"

"To an apartment."

Virginia shook her head. "So that's what this is all about," she said. "All this business about a hit man. You want me to get you an apartment!"

"Ma!" Ali shrieked. "I want you to hide us! You got to hide us!"

In the background, Donny was nodding in animated agreement. Heather was expressionless.

"Just forget about it," Virginia said. "I'm not going to get you an apartment!

"But Marty is coming with the hit man!"

"Just forget about it. Just don't think about it. Put it out of your mind. I am not getting you an apartment."

Normally at this point, especially if she really had been trying to get her mother to buy her something, Ali might have gone into one of her plate-throwing curse-shrieking tantrums. But on this occasion she was merely defeated. Her arms fell to her sides; she stared at her mother in slump-shouldered bafflement; then she led the other two back into her room.

A moment later Donny emerged again, but he was only looking for food. Virginia watched while Donny—wordless, smirking, stumbling around the room like Dopey—gathered a tray of goodies and then disappeared back into Ali's room.

*   *   *

AT PIZZA HUT THAT EVENING, CLAUDIA WENT TO THE PAY PHONE BY the door during a slack period and called a special hot-line number for runaways.

"I know a teenager," she said, "and I don't know if she's just making up stories, but she says they killed a kid named Bobby Kent."

The hot-line number was operated by the regional 911 police dispatching operation. As Claudia spoke, the operator at the other end was entering the phone number and location of the pay phone on a report form and entering the name Bobby Kent into a database query.

After a few minutes of conversation, Claudia decided she had made a mistake and hung up. Half an hour later, two detectives appeared at the Pizza Hut. Both in their forties, tired and a little rumpled at the end of a long day, Detectives Ed Schubert and Jack Hoffman looked bored when they showed up at the cash register and asked the manager for Claudia.

A missing kid. A rumored murder. It could mean nothing.

Claudia was terrified. She told the detectives about her visit from Lisa but begged them not to tell Lisa she had called the police. They said they would do their best to protect her. They asked her for the names of the other people Lisa had said were there.

Claudia gave them Lisa's full name and told them where to find her. They already had Marty Puccio's name from the report Officer Debra Ramsey had filed.

They went first to see Lisa, because her house was nearest to them. It was about 11:00 P.M. when they arrived.

"We're trying to help find your friend Bobby Kent," Hoffman said.

"I don't know where he is," Lisa said at the door, sullen, not inviting them in.

They asked if she had heard anything. She said she had not. They asked if she had any hunches or guesses about where he might be.

"No. How do I know where he is?"

The two officers watched her face for a while before either of them spoke. Schubert looked at Hoffman, and Hoffman gave him a barely perceptible signal with his eyes.

"Miss Connelly," Schubert said, "we have received information to the effect that your friend Mr. Kent may have been murdered."

Lisa stared at them.

"Would you have any ideas about that, Miss Connelly?" Hoffman asked.

"No."

Her face was outwardly even, but the eyes had gone hard and furtive. "Well, who told you all this stuff?" she asked.

Hoffman's face, a rough jowly mask under curly salt-and-pepper hair, relaxed to an empty smile. "Oh, Miss Connelly, it was an anonymous call. And, of course, we wouldn't want to reveal that person's name, anyway, just as we wouldn't reveal your name, because we wouldn't want to expose anyone to danger." He allowed his face to harden slowly. "Would we?"

"What?"

They asked her a few more questions, thanked her for her assistance, then left.

It was quitting time. They looked at each other in the car, and both made shrugging gestures. Bullshit or not, quitting time or not, the next move was a visit to Mr. Marty Puccio.

LISA CALLED HIM THE INSTANT THE POLICE WERE OUT OF SIGHT, BUT he was outside with his dog. Ten minutes later, he called back.

"Oh, shit, Marty," she gasped into the phone, "somebody made an anonymous call to the cops. They were just here. They know about Bobby."

"What?" Marty hissed. "How in the fuck could that happen? You mean they found him?"

"No, I don't think so. I think they still don't know where he is. Somebody just told them that he got murdered."

"Murdered?" Marty said, shocked.

"Yeah. That's what they said."

"They used that word?"

"Yeah."

"Shit, Lisa. Did you talk to anybody?"

"No, I didn't fucking talk to anybody, Marty!"

She heard an adult voice muttering in the background, then heard Marty speaking away from the phone, "Be right there."

"Oh, man," he whispered into the phone. "They're here. I gotta go, Lisa."

Marty met them on the front lawn. They approached and stood close to him, faces in his face.

"We have received some information about a homicide, Mr. Puccio," Schubert said. "It may involve your friend who has been missing, Mr. Kent. Naturally, we don't want to bother Mr. Kent's parents with this at this point, until we have been able to develop some more conclusive information."

"Yeah," Marty said, bobbing his head in agreement. "Well, jeez, I mean, this is kind of rough. I've been worried about it. But you know, you keep hoping."

"Would you be willing to help us, Mr. Puccio?"

"Me? Oh, sure, of course, whatever I can do, yeah, of course. What can I do?"

Hoffman said, "Would you have an objection to giving us a sworn statement?"

"Me? No. Sure. Of course not. Yeah, if that will help. Will that help?"

"It might, sir. If you wouldn't mind stepping over here to the car. We'd like you to sit inside. Do you have any objection, sir, to being tape-recorded?"

"No. Not at all. I just want to, you know, like help you guys do whatever."

They put him in the backseat. Hoffman sat in the back, also, with the tape recorder on the seat between them. Schubert sat in the front, looking backward over the seat at Marty. Hoffman administered an oath to Marty, then asked him to sign a form. He turned on the tape recorder, asked Marty to state that he understood that he was under oath and that he was being tape-recorded.

Marty was calm, collected, and polite. He spoke with a tone of deep concern.

"We wanted to talk to you, Mr. Puccio," Hoffman began, "because we had information that you were among several people who were the last people to see Mr. Kent alive."

"Yes, sir. I think I was."

"Just for the record, how long have you known Mr. Kent?"

"Thirteen years, sir."

"Did you see much of each other?"

"Yes, sir," he said. His eyes began to redden. "We saw each other every day. About twelve hours a day. We were brothers."

"You were brothers?"

"We were like brothers."

Schubert leaned over the seat. "When did you last see him, Marty?"

Marty turned to face him. "It was after eleven last Wednesday night. Out in front of my house."

"Who all was there, Mr. Puccio?" Hoffman asked.

"Ali was there, this girl we knew, Ali Willis, from Palm Bay. And Lisa Connelly, my girlfriend. And Derek Dzvirko, who's Lisa's cousin. And then, uh, this kid Donny, and this girl Heather, who came with Ali from Palm Bay. They had come to pick us up, me and Lisa, to go to South Beach. Bob was still getting ready."

"He was gonna go out with you guys?" Schubert asked.

"No. He was getting ready for a date. He was going to go out with this hillbilly girl he had met. Him and me had worked that day, and then, later, he said, 'I'm going to go out with that girl I told you about earlier.'

"And then, we were walking to the car, and she came up. He had told me he had known her from a party, and I guess he ran into her again somewhere."

Hoffman asked what she looked like. Marty said he didn't remember, only that she had an accent and was a country girl.

He described in detail what Bobby had been wearing the last time he had seen him, when he had come out of his house briefly and talked to them just before they all left for South Beach.

Then, speaking in a flat, matter-of-fact tone, Hoffman said, "We have information that you saw him again after that point."

Without a pause, Marty said calmly, "Well, that information is false, sir."

Schubert said, "We also got some information that Bobby was stabbed by one of three guys who were in your car that night."

"No, sir."

Hoffman said, "Did you have anything to do with stabbing Bobby Kent or disposing of his body?"

"No way."

Schubert said, "Do you have any knowledge of who did?"

Speaking softly and earnestly, Marty said, "I think it's gang-related, and somebody from the Davie Boys might be in on it. There were always times he wouldn't tell me the whole stories about what he was up to. He wasn't one hundred percent honest with me all the time.

"But I took him for the friend he was. There were times he protected me in school. I was like ninety-five pounds, and he was like one hundred fifty pounds.

"He was a member of the Evil Nation," Marty said, ad-libbing. "I know that. He tagged it on my sidewalk."

When Marty stopped talking, the two detectives sat without speaking for a long while. He returned their gazes. They asked him what he did at South Beach. He said they walked the grove, met a couple of Lisa's friends, whose names he didn't remember and whom he could not describe. He told them about going back to Lisa's house, sneaking in, and sitting around talking until the wee hours.

Schubert asked him about the phone call he had made at 4:00 A.M. Thursday to Fred Kent.

"I called and told Bobby I couldn't really talk. When I discovered it was his father, my heart just about dropped into my stomach. I thought it would be rude to talk at that hour. They sound so much alike, him and his father. I have made that same mistake hundreds of times before. So I just hung up.''

No one spoke for a while. Then Schubert said, ''Well, Marty, what do you think has happened to Bob?''

Marty shook his head somberly. ''I think it's gang-related,'' he said. Then his face dropped, and his voice began to quaver. ''I hope to God, I pray to God he's not dead, because . . .''

He sobbed suddenly, then put the back of his hand to his mouth, and bit it for self-control. ''I just don't know how I'd live the rest of my life. The last two days have been very hard for me.''

Dry-eyed, the two detectives waited for him to regain his composure. Then Hoffman asked him about Ali.

''Wasn't she kind of upset with him?''

''She didn't like him anymore. She just wanted to be friends.''

Schubert leaned closer and spoke to Marty in a confidential hush. ''Wasn't Ali tied up in some kind of a prostitution ring at Cooper City High School?'' he asked.

''Yeah. I think so. I heard something about that.''

''Well, what did she say about that? What did Bob say?''

Marty thought it over and then shook his head. ''I think they just didn't want to talk about that.''

Hoffman said, ''They didn't want to talk about it? Who didn't?''

''Her and Bob, I guess.''

''You mean like, to each other? Or to you? It was too painful for them? Or what? Didn't Ali ever say anything to Lisa about it?''

''Yeah, she said she was just going out with guys on dates, but she wasn't doing anything sexual.''

''But they were paying her.''

''Yeah.''

''She wasn't doing anything sexual, but they were paying her.''

''Yeah.''

They asked who Donny was. They asked who Heather was. Marty said Donny was Ali's boyfriend but also Heather's.

''He was kind of on both girls,'' Marty said.

"He was?" Hoffman said.

"Yeah."

They asked him to describe the area of South Beach where they had spent the evening. Marty said he couldn't remember much about it.

"You can't describe it?"

"No."

Hoffman said, "Mr. Puccio, do you have any knowledge of Bobby Kent's death?"

"No," Marty said meekly.

"Were you present at the time he was killed?"

"No."

"Is there anything you'd like to add at this time?"

"No."

They turned off the tape recorder, thanked him, and left. On the way back to Hollywood police headquarters, the two detectives agreed that they had no body, so they had no murder. But at least they knew one thing for sure. Marty Puccio was a lying sack of shit.

ON SUNDAY MORNING WHEN CLAUDIA'S PARENTS CAME OUT OF THEIR house to go to church, Lisa was standing on the curb waiting for them. She was already sweaty at nine in the morning. She wore no makeup. Her lumpy red hair had not been washed in several days and clung to her head and neck like wet upholstery. She wore a baggy T-shirt and long baggy pea-green shorts over dirty tennis shoes. As soon as Claudia's parents began backing down the drive in their late-model Jaguar sedan, Lisa lurched forward, stomped heavily up to the car, and waited for them to roll down the windows.

They explained to her that Claudia had been called in to work early to set up for brunch. She grunted a kind of assent and then backed away from the car to let them leave. Then she walked off on her long hot walk through several golf-course communities to the Embassy Lakes Mall.

When she arrived at the Pizza Hut, Lisa's clothes were black with sweat, and her face was a blotchy map of anger. Claudia was standing behind a counter when Lisa found her.

"I can't talk right now, Lisa," she said.

Lisa reached over the counter, grabbed her hands, and pulled her to her. "Someone made an anonymous call," Lisa said.

"I don't know what you're talking about."

"The cops know about the whole thing. They know who was there. They know he got stabbed."

"Well, I didn't do it, Lisa," Claudia said, trying to pull free. Lisa released her and dropped her hands to her side.

Like a claw at her throat, fear suddenly seized Claudia. She was afraid Lisa was going to lift her hands up and point a gun at her.

"Lisa," she whispered, backing away slowly. "Please. Please don't hurt me, Lisa."

The weekend manager, a stocky, blond, middle-aged woman, walked up behind Claudia from the kitchen. "What's going on out here?" she asked.

Lisa looked up.

Claudia said, "I have to go," and fled to the back.

As she turned to leave, Lisa bellowed, "I know it was you, Claudia!"

LISA RUSHED HOME AND CALLED MARTY. HE CAME OVER IMMEDI-ately. Together they called Ali from Lisa's bedroom.

"Fucking Claudia called the cops," she said. "She told them all about it. They have everybody's names."

"They have my name?" Ali asked, gasping.

"I don't know if they know who you are, but they know about you. They came to see me. They tape-recorded Marty. They knew about how it went down and everything. We gotta get out of here, girl. We're coming up there. Marty says we need to find a way to get out of the state for a while."

Ali said, "Lisa, don't come up here if the cops are on you!"

"We got to, bitch!" Lisa bellowed.

Marty snatched the phone away from her. "Ali, we have to get the fuck out of here today. We're comin' up there. You got to hide us until we can figure out a way to go to New York or some place like that."

ALI HUNG UP THE PHONE AND RUSHED OUT INTO THE KITCHEN TO confront her mother. Donny and Heather followed her. While Ali implored her mother, Donny made exaggerated hand-wringing gestures in the background and kept saying over and over again, loudly but as if to himself, "I cannot be with those people. I am not going to be with those people. Please, please, I can't be with those people." Heather found an overstuffed armchair and curled up in it like a watchful cat.

"Mother, you are going to have to get us out of here," Ali said. "They're coming up here. The cops are after them for this murder. They're coming to our house."

"All right," Virginia Slay said, "if that's how it is, then I'll get you a motel room somewhere and you can go stay there for a while."

"But what are you going to tell them about where we are?" Ali asked.

Virginia shrugged. "I'll just tell them you went with a friend somewhere."

"They know what my car looks like," she said.

Virginia saw that Ali was starting to get hysterical.

"Look, I'll drive you to the motel. That way, your car won't be there. It will be here. I'll just tell them one of your friends picked you up in a black Bronco. So, if they look for something, they'll be looking for a black Bronco."

Donny was still stalking in the background, moaning about not wanting to "be with those people." Ali went to him, touched him on the neck, and said, "It's O.K., my ma is going to take us to a hotel."

He stopped, stared at her, then smiled sweetly. "Cool," he said.

*　　*　　*

LISA WAS AT HOME ALONE THAT EVENING WHEN HER MOTHER CAME IN.

The moment Maureen saw her, she said, "What's the matter with you, Lisa?"

Her clothes were dirty and wet with sweat, her face a ghoulish mask of melting makeup. She was standing in the center of the living room with her arms clutched in to her chest.

"Ma," she said. "I have to tell you about something."

Maureen sat on the sofa while Lisa stalked up and down the living room, gesticulating, speaking in hushed whispers at one moment, shouting the next, giggling, sobbing. Bit by bit it came out, jumbled beyond comprehension at first but then in an ever clearer, more unmistakable picture. When Maureen began to understand what her daughter was telling her, she managed to maintain an outer calm, but she could not stop the tears flowing from her eyes.

So this was where the dreams above her bed had taken her. Maureen's little girl, her unexpected blessing, the miracle baby, joy of her heart, comfort in her loneliness.

"What am I going to do, Ma?"

"Get in the car."

They drove straight to the home of Linda Bohnert, Maureen's sister and Derek Dzvirko's mother. It was 10:00 P.M. Linda was watching television. Derek was already in bed, as was Linda's husband, Richard.

"You'd better turn off the TV and come out in the kitchen and sit down," Maureen said. "I have some very bad news."

Lisa stood sullenly by the refrigerator. When Linda was seated, Maureen said, "Lisa and Derek were involved in the murder of Marty Puccio's friend Bobby Kent."

"I didn't murder him," Lisa whined.

"Shut up, Lisa," her mother said.

Linda was staring at Maureen. Between the eyes of the two women, a lifetime of sisterly knowing passed. Maureen barely tipped her head forward, and Linda knew that it was true. She sobbed, threw her face in her hands, then leaped up and ran to fetch her husband.

Richard, groggy from the early edge of a deep sleep, listened to only part of Maureen's explanation. He stood by the refrigerator with folded arms. Taped to the refrigerator just above his shoulder was a little bag of sand and a postcard that said, "Richard's Florida Beachfront Property"—an ironic reference to his hopes and dreams before Pan Am had folded and he had been forced into the lawn-mowing business.

As soon as he was sure he had caught the drift of what she was saying, Richard turned and went to Derek's room.

"Derek, get up!" he said. "Get in the kitchen! Right now!"

Derek shambled in, clad in boxer shorts and a blousy T-shirt, hair sticking up in all directions, eyes puffy from sleep and crying.

"Oh, shit, Lisa," he mumbled, mouth beginning to quiver loosely, "you musta told."

Richard Bohnert worked the two of them through the details of the story. When it was all told, he turned to Maureen.

"What are you going to do?"

"What are you going to do?" she asked.

He stared at her, then shrugged. He looked at Linda. "Call the cops."

Linda nodded yes, as if to say, "Of course."

"Ma!" Lisa bleated.

Linda and Richard gazed at Maureen.

"She's real scared about this guy she says is in the Mafia," Maureen said.

Richard was silent at first, as if stunned. Then he said, "Oh, give me a break, Maureen. This is some punk gangbanger."

"Ma!" Lisa shouted.

"Well, I told her she had to go to the cops, but I told her I would take her to a motel and let her figure things out a little better first."

"Figure things out?" Richard asked. "What's she gotta figure out, Maureen?"

"Ma! You promised!" Lisa said.

"Well, I'm just gonna take her to a motel for a night, and then we'll go ahead and contact the authorities."

Richard gazed at the two sisters. Finally Linda said, "O.K., Maureen. But we're calling the cops."

"Just like that?"

"Well," Linda shrugged. "I'll probably call Joe, first. See if he has a friend. You know."

Maureen nodded, understanding. They would take Derek to see Joe Scrima, their brother, owner of the garbage-hauling business where Maureen worked, patriarch of the clan as it had resettled in Florida. Joe Scrima was a man who knew his way around and had friends among the police. Months earlier, when Maureen had told Lisa she was going to send her family after Marty, Joe Scrima was the family she had been thinking of.

An hour later, after Maureen had left with Lisa, Joe Scrima listened patiently to the boy's tale and then quickly agreed the story needed to be told to the police. Immediately. He called a friend with the Broward County Sheriff's Department, who called Detective Frank Ilarraza. Ilarraza showed up at about midnight.

In his early forties, a homicide detective for five years, Frank Ilarraza was not exactly what any of them had expected. With a studious stoop, darkly handsome behind a large black mustache, Ilarraza spoke softly in a strong northeastern accent and came across less like a homicide cop than a professor.

Derek sobbed and told everything.

For an experienced homicide cop, Ilarraza was almost on the verge of being a little excited. The story had poured from the fat boy's lips. Ilarraza had listened carefully and taken detailed notes.

He knew that the Hollywood P.D. was working a missing person case on the kid Derek was talking about. He also knew two Hollywood detectives had developed information earlier that night indicating that it could have been a homicide.

But experience told Ilarraza there was absolutely no telling what this story really was all about. Kids got themselves into such incredible messes and then tried to lie their way out of them. It could be anything. Maybe none of it happened. Maybe some piece of it. He would just have to go to Weston and see if there was really a body there.

"Look, Derek, I need you to go out there with me and show me what you're talking about."

Derek shrugged and looked at his parents. The Bohnerts looked at each other.

"Why does he have to go out there with you?" Linda asked. "Is that safe?"

Ilarraza blinked. "Is it safe? Yeah, I would assume it would be safe. But I need him to come out and show me where the body is. Can you do that, son?"

Derek shrugged again and looked at his parents. He didn't want to go.

Richard said, "Derek, go with the officer. If you know where the boy's body is, go show him."

CHAPTER EIGHT

DEREK SAT NEXT TO ILARRAZA IN THE FRONT SEAT. WHILE THEY DROVE, Ilarraza phoned his partner, Chris Murray, and asked him to stay in touch in case there turned out to be something in the kid's story.

It just didn't seem likely, though. From what the kid had said, these weren't hard-core gang kids. They were little white middle-class, mall-rat wannabes, acting tough in front of each other, maybe. The malls were jammed with kids like this. They walked the walk and talked the talk when their parents' backs were turned. Some of them had drug problems and crappy lives, and sometimes one of them would get his hands on a gun and work up enough nerve to pop off a few rounds from a speeding car.

But that was a far cry from standing there face-to-face with one of your running buddies and beating his head in with a baseball bat. Or sticking a knife in his heart. Or sitting on top of him and slicing his throat open while he begged for mercy.

Those were hard-core killer things—things every homicide cop had seen, a window on a reality other people didn't even want to know existed, let alone look through, a black window with flame, screams, and slimy squirming on the other side.

On the other side of that brittle pane was the universe of evil, where killing is joy, torture is sex, and ruining a human life is the ultimate accomplishment.

Not too many mall rats are there yet. Maybe this kid got drunk or stoned and had something sexually scary happen to him, something he couldn't remember. Maybe it was all the kid's own hysterical fantasy. Maybe the whole point was he was trying to talk his parents out of grounding him for running up a long-distance phone bill. Frank Ilarraza was moving west slowly on South Post Oak Road. Derek seemed to be having trouble finding the spot, which was no big surprise. There probably was no spot. Now the kid would break down and start crying about whatever the real problem was—he thought he got a girl pregnant, or he thought he got a boy pregnant, whatever.

Then Derek pointed.

"Here."

Ilarraza pulled his unmarked car off on to the sandy shoulder and peered out into the gloom. He picked up a flashlight from the floor of the car and let himself out. He shone the light around in an arc along the scrubby canal banks and saw nothing.

"Stay in the car," he said.

He walked a few yards closer to the water. He thought he heard something—a high-pitched buzzing in the distance, perhaps a hundred yards farther west along the canal bank. It was a sound that could have been either mechanical or animal. He took a few steps in that direction, then trained his light toward it and began walking.

Fifteen yards up the canal bank from the police car it hit him, like a snake striking—the stench. He recognized it immediately. Even for a cop, even for a soldier or a doctor, no smell is so vile or assaultive as the stink of a corpse in full rot.

Flies. That was what was making the howling buzz in the distance. The closer he drew, the more ferocious the stench became. He threw his hand over his mouth. Now he could see the cloud of flies whirling up off the canal bank, jutting this way and that like a dancing demon.

And there he was. The dead boy. Half in the water and half out. Exactly the way the fat blubbering kid in the car had said he would be.

Ilarraza drew closer and stretched his neck forward against the bitter cloud of stench coming off the body like smoke. He could see Aero-Jam sneakers, blue jeans, a T-shirt—the uniform of a hard-body surfer. Bulging from the leg and armholes were fat doughy blobs of meat and flesh, gnawed by beasts. Spilling from the gut was a rope of intestine that trailed off into the greasy canal. The quick movement of feeding creatures blistered the surface of the water. The head was huge and white in the moonlight, eyes bulging crazily from their sockets.

So this was the boy they had killed. Someone's son. The joy of a mother's heart, song of a father's very soul. And they had done it the way the Dzvirko boy had said, hacking and crushing him while he watched his own destruction and pleaded for his life.

Ilarraza's light scanned slowly around and around the scene. His policeman's mind watched coolly, making an inventory, alert for danger, planning the next step. But another piece of him was looking, too, the part that wasn't a cop, wasn't a pro, didn't have procedures and duties to think about. The part that was only human looked. He saw that the mall rats had gone through to the other side. In spite of himself, he shuddered at the incredible, staggering, life-sucking horror of that.

ILARRAZA RETURNED TO HIS CAR.

"Did you find him?" Derek asked.

"Shut up."

He called Chris Murray, his partner. He told him what he had found. He said he was going to call the crime-scene people, and that he would call him right back.

Ilarraza moved his car closer to the body in order to watch the scene and keep it secure until the crime-scene people and the medical examiner could get there. A few minutes later, he called Murray again. He filled him in quickly on the Dzvirko interview. Then they were both quiet on the phone for a while. He gazed out the windshield toward the dark of the Everglades. The cell phone hissed softly in his ear, like a shell.

They both knew what this was. This was a big case.

IT WAS A BIG CASE BECAUSE IT WAS A BRUTAL, EVIL, HIDEOUS MURder that involved kids from the mall instead of kids from the ghetto. There would be soul-searching newspaper columns, editorials, and television news specials, all based on the same factor. They were white and middle-class. That and that alone meant the difference. It was a big case.

From this moment forward, it was their case. Other cops had developed bits and pieces of it. All of the police who had touched the case so far had done good work. No one had messed the thing up by violating anyone's rights. All of the information had been processed quickly and efficiently.

But Ilarraza and Murray had the body. It was lying in a stink of flies and rot a few yards away from the front bumper of Ilarraza's car. That made this their case. They owned the stench.

The challenge now was not unlike the one a diamond cutter would face if someone suddenly plunked down a huge raw stone on his worktable: The first cut would tell all. Depending on their first move, this case would break into either treasure or dust.

If they could break the case the right way at the beginning, then the suspects would fall down one after another like dominoes. If they broke it the wrong way, if they made the wrong choice on whom to go after first, then the suspects would line up against them, that is, they would get together, talk and plot, hire lawyers, and put on a united front.

Murray asked Ilarraza what he thought the first move should be. They needed to get Dzvirko under lock and key. A patrol unit would take care of that. But then what? They discussed the pros and cons of several choices. But it didn't take them long to focus on the same point.

The Mafia hit man.

Derek Dzvirko said they had hired a professional Mafia hit man. All the rest of them, Derek had said, were terrified of the hit man.

In his interview with Dzvirko, Ilarraza had asked him what it had cost them to hire a professional Mafia hit man, and Derek had realized for the first time, in answering the question, that they had never actually discussed price.

Derek had described to Ilarraza how the hit man had instructed the group to signal him by tapping on his bedroom window so as not to awaken the hit man's mother and father.

These two veteran middle-aged homicide cops were of the same mind: Ilarraza should stay here and help get the crime-scene investigation rolling. Murray should call for substantial backup and go get the Mafia hit man. Without having to spend a lot of time telling each other why, both men thought the hit man was the best place to strike first in order to split the case open.

As Murray began making calls to arrange the arrest, he allowed himself another thought, too: This should be good.

Dzvirko had provided a general description of the house where the hit man lived—good enough to pinpoint the place, once they were actually in the vicinity. Murray had two other things to take into consideration. One was the effectiveness of the arrest itself—nabbing the suspect without exposing police officers or citizens to harm.

The other was drama. As long as they had to arrest this person anyway, they might as well do it in a way that would serve to get his attention.

According to Dzvirko's description of the location, there was some kind of forest or palm grove in the back. It was far enough out west that it might back up on a stretch of undeveloped sawgrass. So it was reasonable to assume they might have to chase somebody through some brambles and some briars.

*   *   *

WHEN KAUFMAN'S STEPFATHER, RONALD ESPOSITO, PEERED THROUGH the front-door peephole at 4:00 A.M., he saw Broward County sheriff's officer John Palmer holding up his badge.

"We have an arrest warrant," Palmer said loudly through the door. "Open the door immediately."

Esposito opened the door.

"For Derek?" he asked. Then the lights came on. Esposito blinked and ducked his head, shocked by the searing glare of spotlights trained all along the front and sides of the house. When he was able to focus through the glare, he muttered, "Man alive!"

Poised like machines at ten-yard intervals all the way across the front of the house, German shepherd police dogs sat at attention, each next to its handler. Noses twitching eagerly; every dog stared straight at Ronald Esposito's face. Whatever this was about, it was obviously not one of Derek's routine run-ins with authorities over skipping school or shoplifting.

"Where is Derek Kaufman?" Palmer asked.

In a barely audible voice, Esposito said, "In his bedroom. Asleep."

Joan Esposito had appeared behind him in a housecoat. He turned to her.

"Is he in bed?"

She shrugged to show she didn't really know. "What is it?"

Palmer and four other officers stepped into the house and told Esposito to take them to Derek Kaufman right away. Esposito scuttled off through the rambling hallways. The officers followed close behind him with their guns drawn. When Esposito opened the door to Derek's room at the back of the house, one of the officers put a hand on his shoulder and shoved him smoothly but firmly out of the way. Then two of the officers stepped smartly into the room with their guns pointed at Derek's face.

Palmer stepped in after them and shouted at Derek to get out of bed. Derek opened one eye lazily. He focused on the guns, then shot from the bed as if in response to an electrical shock. Palsied with fear, eyes reeling, he stared at Palmer. His mouth worked wildly, soundlessly.

They handcuffed him behind his back, then ran him at a trot back through the house and out the front door. On the front porch, they yanked him to a stop. An officer reached forward, put a hand on top of his head, and tipped his head backward so that he was staring straight out at the dogs.

"Oh, shit," he muttered. "Oh, shit, oh, shit, oh, shit."

They put him in a patrol car, notified him that he was being arrested on a warrant for murder, notified him of his right not to answer questions until an attorney was present, and warned him that anything he did say might be used as evidence against him.

Then they turned on the tape recorder.

The detectives watched without showing that they were watching. It was a key moment in their work. There were other such moments in other callings—a priest's deathbed prayer, a banker's foreclosure, a gambler's winning hand—when a person's work provides a window straight into the innermost stuff of another human soul.

For cops, this was it. Not chasing the crook. Not testifying against him in court. But this: Here on the car seat with the Miranda warning out of the way and the tape machine punched on. What was he going to show them?

Derek Kaufman was six feet three inches tall, 235 pounds, with his hair cut in a screw-you buzz with a rattail all the way down his neck and "CMF" tattooed on his right arm. Based on looks, he could be the meanest son of a bitch in the jailhouse.

"We have already taken detailed statements from other people who were involved in the murder of Bobby Kent," Palmer said. "We know about your involvement. We want you to tell us about it."

The other detectives looked, trying not to show they were looking, because showing him they were interested might spoil the mood, and anyway, their interest—their real interest—was none of his business. It wasn't even about the crime. It was what he had.

Kaufman turned from one face to another, his face rigid, eyes opaque. He looked up and saw his mother standing off at a distance on the lawn with his stepfather. He looked back at Palmer. His face twitched, then shook, then crumbled. He made a small cry, then collapsed in convulsive sobs.

"Oh, God, oh, God."

The detectives watched silently. The Mafia hit man was exactly what Ilarraza and Murray had guessed he would be. A punk. He didn't have shit. Good. They had struck the stone in precisely the right spot.

Palmer moved in, started talking to him, bringing him down, getting him under control. The trick was to make him feel this was all just business, all pretty normal, the kind of scrape a fellow gets into now and then, the sort of thing that needs to be sorted out. It wouldn't do any good for the suspect simply to implode beneath the horror of his own act, and that was always an option. People like this seldom if ever have the spine to live up to what they have done. If the young man went crazy on them, they wouldn't get the kind of roll out of him they would need in order to knock the rest of the suspects over quickly.

Palmer was quiet, emotionally flat, matter-of-fact, as if filling out a report on a fender-bender. He asked how it had started. Kaufman, biting the air for composure, couldn't get himself together at first. When he began to answer the questions—started telling the story— that helped. So he kept telling.

He told the police how the group had contacted him, how they had told him about this friend of theirs who had raped a girl, how they had talked about killing him in revenge. As soon as he started rolling with the story, Kaufman began to get himself back under control, and as soon as he started regaining control, he began spinning the story to his own advantage:

He had never believed they were really going to kill anybody. He would never have gone along with a thing like that. Now he and Detective Palmer were trying to get this case taken care of, trying to sort out what had happened and why.

Ringing them, in the brittle white glare of the spotlights, were the dogs, panting at their masters' sides.

Palmer listened quietly through most of the story, through all of the telephone conversations and meetings, to the ride to Weston, the ruse used to lure Bobby Kent, the moment when Donny stabbed him in the back of the neck, when Marty shoved a knife deep in his heart. He told how Marty got on top of Bobby when he was down:

"He was jabbing him in the neck, you know?"

"Yeah. Kind of jabbing him?"

"Yeah. And then he tried to cut his neck like this." Kaufman made a sawing motion over his lap.

"Yeah. Kind of sawing on him?"

"Yeah. He cut his neck open like that, like sawing."

Palmer looked up. He seemed bored, worn out perhaps by all the detail, all the note taking. "Umm. One of the other suspects who has provided a statement said that you hit him with a baseball bat."

So much for the bullshit. Time to cinch this bastard up.

"So," Palmer said, "was that when you're talking about, when he was down, or what?"

"Yeah," Kaufman said, nodding, "he was on his back. I mean, Marty had already cut his throat and stuff. And I'm standing right by his body and stuff like that, and I had seen him choking, and his head was kind of up, and he's kind of like moving his head around, so I just put the baseball bat up, I don't know, maybe a quarter of the way from the leg and just let it go, hit him in the head."

"O.K.," Palmer said, scratching notes. "So you hit him in the head."

"Yeah, but I mean, I didn't want it to sound like I did a full swing, just like up a little by my leg, and hit him in the head, and he fell unconscious."

"Uh-huh," Palmer said, as if not very interested. "So he was making sounds prior to hitting him?"

"Right, and then when I hit him he was quiet, and I wanted to, well, I guess to put him out of his misery, like I said."

"Yeah."

"Yeah. I wasn't trying to kill him. I was trying to make him unconscious."

Palmer looked back over his notes. He rewound the tape recorder and punched play to make sure he had a good recording. He checked the notes again to see if he had missed anything. Then he looked out through the open door of the car and nodded to the deputies who had been waiting to transport the prisoner.

PALE HANDS OF DAWN WERE SLIDING INTO THE OCEAN SKY WHEN the deputies hauled Kaufman away. Palmer sat in the car and put together a conference call. They had the full details of the crime and the names of everyone involved, as provided by Dzvirko and now confirmed in detail by Kaufman, with supporting details from Claudia, the Pizza Hut waitress. In their attempts at justifying their own behavior, both of the young men had fully incriminated themselves.

But neither Kaufman nor Dzvirko seemed to be at the center of the story. Even allowing for their transparent lies about their own roles, neither of them was able to provide certain key elements.

It wasn't necessarily a matter of motive. Motive was more important in movies and on TV than in real police cases. With people like this, there often was no clear-cut motive. If they were capable of thinking up a motive, they might be capable of thinking up a life.

More important than motive was knowing the patterns, how they had come together, how long ahead of time they had begun to plan, how they had done it, what each person's role had been, and what kind of corroborative evidence the police would need to seek in order to hand the state a case that would stick. It was important to know who had been a ringleader and who had followed along for the fun.

The people at the center of the story, based on what the police had heard so far, seemed to be Bobby Kent, his best friend, Marty Puccio, who had stabbed him in the heart while he begged for mercy, and the girl, Lisa Connelly.

Dzvirko and Kaufman said in their statements that it was Lisa who was the shotgun. She had said, ''I want that fucker dead tonight.''

All of the suspects seemed to believe that the fantasizing punk, Kaufman, was really a Mafia hit man. The fact that the hit man had caved in and spilled his guts should help bring the rest of them along.

But the Palm Bay part of the group was still out of range. Because neither Dzvirko nor Kaufman knew any of their last names, they were going to be harder to find. The ideal thing, before going after Puccio and Connelly, would be to have the Palm Bay crowd locked down and on tape.

MARTY CALLED LISA, AND MAUREEN TOLD HIM THAT SHE WAS GONE, not reachable. He hung up quickly. He knew exactly what her tone meant.

In a panic, he called Kaufman several times, but no one answered at his house. His parents were in Miami, arranging legal counsel.

Soon after the group met Kaufman, he had given them a phone number for Tom Lemke, a sixteen-year-old who was one of his merry stereo-stealing band. Kaufman had identified him as a mob lieutenant. Marty still had Lemke's number. Perhaps the Mafia would be able to help him get out of the state.

Marty called a very bewildered Tom Lemke and said he realized that Kaufman had gone underground but that things were getting too hot for him. He told Lemke he needed cash and transportation out of the state. Lemke said he wouldn't mind having those things himself.

Lemke gave Marty a beeper number and told him to check back. Marty asked Lemke what part of town he lived in, and Lemke told him. As soon as Marty was off the phone, Lemke set about trying to find Derek. Eventually he reached Derek's parents, who told him that Derek was in jail for murder.

Lemke called the jail and left a message for Derek. Jail officials had been given instructions to let Kaufman make all the calls he wanted to make, in hopes that those calls would lead to the arrest of additional suspects, so it was not long before Derek was able to call Lemke back from his cell.

Once Derek had laid out the bare bones of his situation, Lemke said, ''Some dude named Marty wants me to give him some money and give him a ride to another state or some shit like that, man.''

"Well, don't do that, man."

"No?"

"No, no way, man. You don't want to get involved in this shit. This is some serious shit. Just tell Marty it's over, I'm in jail, they know everything, he should just turn himself in."

After a long silence, Lemke said, "You killed a guy?"

After an even longer pause, Kaufman said, "I guess so."

Moments after hanging up from Kaufman, Lemke's beeper started going off. He didn't recognize the call-back number. When he called, Marty answered.

"Where are you?" Lemke asked.

"I'm just down the street from you, at the Winn-Dixie. You know where that's at?"

"Yeah."

Lemke told him he might have some news, but he said he had to get off the phone. Marty gave him his pager number and told him to beep him when he was ready to talk.

Lemke hung up and went outside to the front lawn where he found his father. He told him that Derek Kaufman was in jail for murder and that one of the kids who was in on it with him was down the street at the Winn-Dixie, beeping him.

His father pointed toward the house. They both walked back inside, took seats in the living room, and went over it again.

When Lemke's father felt that he more or less understood what his son was telling him, he told him to call the boy back immediately and tell him what Derek had said.

Lemke did as his father had instructed. He beeped Marty. When Marty called back, Lemke told him everything Derek had said.

"Christ!" Marty said, his voice trembling, eyes moist. "I thought guys in the Mafia were supposed to be so fucking tough!"

"Yeah," Lemke said. He had no idea what Marty was talking about. "Who's in the Mafia?"

"Derek."

"Derek's not in the fucking Mafia."

"He's not?"

"Nah. He wanted to be in the Davie Boys, but he was too chicken. Anyway, he says you should turn yourself in."

"Well, shit," Marty said, "if I turn myself in, they'll probably put me in jail!"

Just out of earshot over Lemke's shoulder, his father asked in a hoarse whisper what they were talking about. Lemke cradled the phone to his shoulder and said, "He's afraid they'll take him to jail."

Shaking his head in disgust, the father said, "Tell him you'll write to him."

"Hey, man," Lemke said, "I'll write to you."

The father snatched the phone out of his son's hands and hung it up smartly. A short time later, Tom Lemke was on the phone to the police, telling them everything he knew.

DEREK DZVIRKO'S PARENTS HAD ASKED MAUREEN CONNELLY TO take their daughter, Michelle, seventeen, home with her so that the girl would not be present when the police arrived to interrogate her older brother. When Maureen got back to her house with Lisa, there were several messages from Broward County sheriff's detective Chris Murray waiting on the answering machine.

Maureen told Lisa they would have to decide what to do right away. Lisa still wanted to go to a motel, and Maureen agreed. But she said, "Tomorrow, first thing, you're definitely turning yourself in."

They drove to a Days Inn on Federal Highway, toward the beach side of Lauderdale. On the way there, Maureen reminded Lisa that she was going to have to turn herself in the next day.

"But, Ma, I didn't murder anybody."

"Well, somebody did."

"Not *murder* him."

"Well, kill him, then. He's dead, right?"

Lisa became hysterical.

"Ma, if I turn myself in, they'll arrest me."

"We're going to call Jeff," Maureen said.

Jeffery Smith had represented Maureen's brother several times and other members of the family occasionally in a variety of matters, some criminal. A successful Lauderdale criminal attorney in his mid-forties, Smith had gone into semiretirement a few years earlier after a bad car wreck. Now he spent most of his time on a large boat in the Florida Keys, coming back to Lauderdale a few days each month to visit his law office and tend to personal business.

The possibility that Smith might agree to come out of retirement to help Lisa and Derek Dzvirko meant nothing to Lisa, under the circumstances.

"I need to be with Marty!" she sobbed. "If they arrest me, I won't be able to be with him."

In the backseat, Michelle had heard all she wanted to hear. She clamped a set of headphones over her ears and turned on her tape player.

Lisa got worse, more out of control. She insisted she had to be with Marty. "If I stay here by myself, he might do something stupid, and the hit man might get him."

"Look, Lisa," Maureen said, "forget it with the hit man thing. Richard is right; it's just some dumb kid you all fell for."

"But I want Marty!"

"All you want to do is shack up with him 'cause I'm getting you a motel room."

"Ma!" she shrieked. "I want Marty!"

At the motel, Maureen left the two girls in the car and went in to register. She gave the clerk her card, said she was renting the room for her daughter, and then gave Michelle Dzvirko's name. Once she had the key, she drove to the parking space in front of the room, and she and the two girls went inside.

Inside the room, Lisa exploded into a full-blown, shrieking and shaking, lamp-throwing, chair-kicking tantrum, screaming over and over again, "I want Marty! I want Marty!"

Maureen told her she was going to take Michelle, go buy some food and something to drink, and come back in half an hour or so.

The instant Maureen was out of the room, Lisa snapped out of it and sat down to work the telephone.

She found Marty at the Hollywood Y. The person who answered the phone called him out of the weight room. Marty was breathing hard when he came to the phone.

"How are you doin', baby?" she asked him.

"What do you want, Lisa?"

She could hear him breathing. She told him she was at the Days Inn and she wanted him to come be with her. He asked who else was there. She said they could be alone. He said his brother had dropped him off, and he didn't have transportation. His voice was weak, on the edge of trembling.

"What's the matter, Marty?"

He told her what Derek Kaufman's friend had said, that Derek was not a Mafia hit man, that he wasn't even really in the Davie Boys, that he was in jail, spilling his guts to the cops and telling Marty he should do the same thing.

Lisa launched into a long excited monologue about what they would do—spend the night together at the motel, then the next day get some money, leave the state.

She didn't provide any details of how they would do it or why leaving the state would help. They both assumed they could get money somewhere if they were really desperate. They both assumed an escape from Florida would carry them beyond the reach of their crisis. And it made Marty feel better to hear her talk.

"How can I get to where you are?" he asked.

Her heart filled. "I'll have my mom come get you," she said.

Maureen put up a fight. She had planned to leave Lisa's cousin with her for company or possibly stay herself. But when Maureen saw that Lisa intended to throw another tantrum, she relented. Forty-five minutes later she returned with Marty, clad in a tight-fitting white tank top and shiny black shorts.

When Lisa and Marty saw each other, they rushed into each other's arms and began to embrace with such passion that Maureen was embarrassed and left with Michelle.

"But remember, Lisa," she said on the way out, "tomorrow you're turning yourself in."

AFTER VIRGINIA SLAY HAD INSTALLED ALI AND HER FRIENDS IN A nice motel in Palm Bay, Ali called Brian Rupp, the Oakland Park detective who had been videotaped having oral sex with a teenage prostitute. Rupp, who was on suspension but still on the force, would be fired the following month. When she called, he was at home with his family, watching television.

She and Rupp had maintained contact even after his involvement in the arrest of her friends. Ali had served as one of his better informants, providing him with names of many of the other girls in the prostitution ring. She also had given him gifts, and she had been a guest on his boat.

At one point, when she sent him a baseball cap and shirt, with a note saying, "Thank You," Rupp's partner, Jay Santalucia, told him, "You need to get rid of that stuff, because if your wife ever finds it you're worse than Bobbitt."

Rupp was the first person she thought to turn to when she contemplated dealing with the official adult world.

She told Rupp that she and her friends were involved in a missing person case. He asked a few questions, and Ali conceded it was really a missing dead person case. She told him about the Mafia hit man and said that she and her friends were confused.

Rupp asked her where she was, and she gave him the phone number for her hotel room. He hung up and called Santalucia.

Both men were off duty. Santalucia said he thought the story was worth making a call or two. Rupp explained he was trying to make a family day of it and asked Santalucia to make the calls.

Ali had given Rupp Bobby Kent's phone number. Santalucia called the number, and Fred Kent answered on the first ring.

"Is Bobby there?" Santalucia asked.

Fred Kent knew he didn't recognize the voice and that the voice belonged to a man more mature than Bobby and his friends. Something faintly authoritative in the man's manner made Fred suddenly terribly afraid.

"No, he is not. He has been missing for a long time. Who is this?"

Santalucia paused. "This is Detective Jay Santalucia, Oakland Park Police Department."

"Yes? Why are you calling and asking for Bob? Don't you know he's missing?"

"No. I didn't. Have you actually filed a missing person report on him?"

Fred was confused. Why would a policeman not know that?

"Yes, of course. Four days ago. Or three, I can't remember. The last time we saw him was Wednesday night."

"I see."

"But why are you calling? Has something happened that you know about? I'm the father. We're going through hell here."

"No, sir. I'm just trying to develop some information we had been given about a missing person. I was just checking it out."

"What information?"

"Just that he was missing, sir. We really don't have . . . we don't really know anything."

"But you said you didn't know he was missing."

"Sir, I was just being careful who I was talking to. I didn't know who I was talking to, that's all. Can you tell me who you've been dealing with on it then?"

Fred gave him the name of Hollywood patrol officer Debra Ramsey. Santalucia got off the phone as quickly as he could.

Convinced that bad news was hovering not far away, Fred Kent went to the kitchen and embraced his wife tensely.

Santalucia called Ramsey, who referred him to Broward County detective Frank Ilarraza.

"Yeah," Ilarraza said on the phone. "Dead. Definitely. Killed him with a baseball bat. Knives. Drowned him."

"No shit."

"Yeah."

"And Ali Willis was in on it?"

"What's her name? All I got is Ali. From Palm Bay?"

"Yeah. Ali Willis. No shit."

"No shit, man. We got us some very naughty boys and girls here. We've been looking for this Palm Bay group. We need to notify the victim's parents, but we wanted to nab as many of the suspects as we could first."

"Sure."

"Can you get her for us?"

Santalucia paused.

"Ali Willis?"

"Yeah."

"Yeah," he said. "We can get her for you."

"How about the rest of her gang?"

"Yeah. Sure. We'll get 'em all."

Santalucia called Rupp. Rupp called Ali at the motel and told her she had to go to police headquarters and turn herself in.

She cried. She said that she was afraid. At one point she began to grow angry and said she hadn't done anything wrong.

Rupp told her to forget it. She was involved in a murder. You can't be involved in a murder and not have done something wrong. Even a very small role. Wrong. Bad. You definitely have to turn yourself in. He told her it wasn't like the prostitution thing. The authorities had let her off on that one—even treated her as something of a celebrity—because she was young, and the prostitution thing was something that older bad guys had done to her.

Murder was different. You have to turn yourself in.

"Will you go with me?"

"Definitely."

In a very small voice, she said, "O.K."

THE HOLLYWOOD POLICE PATROL CAR THAT PULLED UP IN FRONT OF the Kent home in the predawn darkness did not have its flashing beacons turned on, and the officers who rang the doorbell spoke softly, but the neighbors woke up anyway.

Farah Kent's white-hot scream broke the shell of night, pierced the hearts of all who heard it. Then the terrible, low, racking sob of the father. The high keening shriek of the sister. The neighbors sat up in their beds, heard these songs of grief, and rushed outdoors to give comfort, but the front door of the Kent household was already closed.

The police came out of the house and drove away. The Kents had locked their pain inside their house. They were in there with it, kneeling alone in their home in the Promised Land, holding the grief as if it were a living, writhing thing, waiting to see what it would do to them.

The neighbors, standing outside listening to the muffled wails, could do nothing, so they went inside their own homes, and closed their own doors.

MAUREEN CALLED LISA EARLY MONDAY MORNING AT THE MOTEL AND told her that she was coming to pick her up. Jeff Smith had agreed to meet them at his office on Federal Highway, near the county courts building in Lauderdale. Normally he would have driven back down to his boat in Key West that morning.

Marty, next to Lisa in the bed, was not awake yet. The night before they had gotten high and talked about getting enough money to get out of Florida. She looked at him, sleeping there, and her heart surged.

Maureen said she would be there in twenty minutes, that Lisa was to be dressed and ready to go, that Marty was not invited.

"Why?"

"Jeff will represent you and maybe your cousin. That's it."

Lisa started to object. Maureen told her to shut up. Sullenly, Lisa slammed down the phone, lifted herself from the bed, and began slowly pulling on her wrinkled shorts and sweat-stained T-shirt.

When Marty woke, Lisa explained she was leaving with her mother. He grunted, rolled over, and went back to sleep.

*   *   *

A SMALL ELEVATOR CARRIED LISA, MAUREEN, AND JOE SCRIMA UP TO a narrow hallway that made two sharp turns before bringing them to Jeff Smith's office. Inside the door was a tiny waiting area, more of a decompression chamber so the legal assistants could get a good look at visitors before allowing them into the inner sanctum.

In a sprawling room on the other side of the door four legal assistants worked at desks scattered in camps of filing cabinets and boxes. Stacks of files and loose paperwork drifting down to the floor like flying buttresses held each desk in place. The walls displayed a random mixture of diplomas, Xeroxed cartoons, and bounced checks held up by Scotch tape.

Jeff Smith's office was a narrow slot off the back wall, even messier than the main room. There was barely enough space for Lisa, Joe Scrima, and Maureen in front of his big desk, piled high with papers, plastic figurines lampooning judges and lawyers, spent plastic coffee cups, and well-scuffed phone books.

Smith, a rangy middle-aged man with a slight stoop and a humorous cast to his eyes, sat behind the desk with his feet up, chin on folded hands, and stared out the small window while he heard Lisa recite her version of what had happened.

When it was over, Smith turned and looked Lisa in the eye but was silent.

Scrima said, "So what do you think she should do?"

Smith shrugged. "Turn herself in to the cops."

Lisa looked up suddenly, balking. She looked at her mother, who looked away.

"Well, O.K., but if I have to turn myself in, I'm posting bond right away. I need to see Marty."

Scrima and Maureen looked at Smith.

He shook his head no.

"What?" Lisa said.

Maureen said, "We can probably raise it, Jeff."

"No," Smith said. "No. Folks. Listen. Listen to me. Lisa has to turn herself in. There will be no bond."

"Why not?" Lisa asked. "I can post bond if I want to. If I have the money."

"No, you can't post bond, Lisa. They won't set a bond. They won't let you out on bond. This is a murder case. You might bond out later, but for now, you're not going to be able to."

"Which means what?" she asked.

Smith was nonplussed. "What do you mean?"

"So what's going to happen? If I can't bond out, where will I go?"

There was a long silence.

"To jail, Lisa."

Lisa stared at her mother, then at Scrima. Her eyes began to redden and pucker, then thick tears spilled down her cheek. Voice trembling but sullen, she said, "Well, like, for how long?"

Smith shrugged. "A while, Lisa. These are very serious charges. You admit your part in this murder."

"What?" she said loudly. "I did not! I didn't have shit to do with it! Not the murder. I helped get him out there, is all."

"And you got your mother's gun the day before."

"Well, don't tell them that."

Smith shrugged. "Lisa, one way or the other, you're involved in a murder."

"Jesus!" she shouted at her mother. "What kind of a lawyer is he? I thought lawyers were supposed to get you out of trouble. He's trying to get me in trouble. I wasn't involved in the goddamned murder!"

Smith stood up. He was a tall man and could be imposing.

"Lisa, take it from me. You're involved."

"Who says?"

"The law says."

"What law?"

He looked to Maureen for help.

"Shut up, baby," she said. "Listen to Jeff."

"You shut up," Lisa shouted. "I didn't kill him. I didn't touch the son of a bitch. How can the law say I killed him? What law? You mean, like the cops?"

Smith sat back down.

"I am going to send you some books in the jail that I want you to read," he said quietly.

"What books?"

"Law books. Or books about the law. Do you know where laws come from?"

"Not really."

"Well, you need to understand some things. For now, the main thing you need to understand, Lisa, is that this is a death penalty state. You need to be very careful from here on out what you say and do. You could be executed for this."

Lisa stared angrily down at her lap.

Smith turned to Scrima. "If she cooperates, if we get in early, like today or tomorrow at the latest before they already have everybody else locked up, I might be able to cut her a deal."

Scrima nodded.

"But she'll have to cooperate."

Scrima nodded.

"It sounds to me like the one they're going to want is Marty," Smith said.

At the sound of his name, Lisa turned her face up and bleated, "I need to be with Marty!"

The adults were silent. Finally Maureen said, "You're not gonna be with Marty, Lisa."

"I need Marty! I need him!"

Smith turned and stared out the window.

"Please can I beep him?" Lisa asked.

Smith shook his head. "Oh, I don't know if that's such a good idea. Everything you do now, Lisa, it can be used against you."

Lisa balled her fists and squeezed her face into a purple ball.

Maureen said, "Let her beep him."

Five minutes later, when Marty called back, it was from the cell phone in his mother's car.

"Where are you, Marty?" Lisa asked between sobs.

"I'm on my way to turn myself in, Lisa. It's over."

Maureen and Scrima had to pry the receiver from her hands.

"He's gone," Maureen said. "He hung up. He's gone."

Lisa sank back down on her chair, threw her head back, then pitched forward and sobbed convulsively.

He was her lover. He was God.

MOST PROSECUTORS IN BIG URBAN DISTRICTS WOULD BE OUT OF BUSI-ness if they insisted on prosecuting only clean cases—that is, cases where the police have done good work, no glaring mistakes have been committed, the evidence has all been gathered in a responsible way that meets constitutional tests. District attorneys get accustomed to messy cases dumped in their laps—ones that might have been good but have been screwed up by the police or somebody else, and the D.A. has to make the best of them anyway. A career prosecutor can't afford to be a prima donna.

But here it was, right in front of him. Seven defendants, and not one serious screwup by the cops. Unbelievable. The police investigators had done a great job. It was enough to make you believe it might have been a good idea after all to make cops go to college.

Tim Donnelly sat hunched over a metal desk in a crowded room on the sixth floor of the Broward County Courthouse. Piled around him was a chaotic jumble of computer cables writhing over torn file boxes like serpents in the jungle, moldy coffee mugs overturned on the floor, lawbooks stacked against the wall. But none of the chaos and mess was visible to Tim Donnelly at the moment, because he was staring at the files, all seven of them, and the more closely he combed them, the better they looked—the neater, the tighter, the cleaner. A rocket ship.

Of the seven defendants, five had made taped statements to the police in which they incriminated themselves. Two had not confessed—Heather Swallers and Marty Puccio—but Puccio had made a long taped statement to the police a few days before the victim was found, and in that statement Puccio had basically hanged himself by being stupid.

It was an incredibly vicious crime. The mood of the defendants, from what Donnelly could see in their statements, was some kind of cross between arrogance and stupidity, as if they either didn't give a damn what anyone thought of what they had done, or—an even more chilling possibility—they had hacked this kid apart, crushed in his head with a bat, and dragged him still alive into the swamp to be eaten by the 'gators, without really understanding that they had done something seriously wrong.

He looked at the files and a shiver went through him. Donnelly had grown up in Nebraska, finished law school in 1981, served as a U.S. Marine Corps judge advocate, gone back to get a master's in litigation, and been an urban D.A. in Florida since 1987. He was as tough as the next guy.

But this. It was as if these kids didn't get it. And not just them. All the parents had hired expensive lawyers, and Donnelly could tell from the calls he was already getting that the lawyers were under a lot of pressure from their clients.

These parents wanted the kids off. Off. They wanted the kids to walk. They didn't understand why Donnelly was being such a hard case about it. He kept hearing phrases like "just kids," "stupid kids," "wrong place at the wrong time," "running with the wrong crowd."

Running with the wrong crowd? They *were* the wrong crowd.

Lisa Connelly's lawyer, Jeff Smith, in particular kept calling, angling for a deal. The day Lisa was arrested, Smith was successful in wangling an informal offer from the day duty officer in the State Attorney's Office. The minute Donnelly got his hands on the file, he made sure that the offer was withdrawn. But the fact that Smith had even been able to get that close was troubling. Donnelly didn't want to cut a deal with anybody.

He pushed back from the desk, rubbed his eyes with the backs of his fists, and indulged himself in a long groaning yawn.

Why would he cut a deal with Lisa Connelly? She helped organize the whole thing. Or Puccio, for God's sake—Kent's best friend, who stuck him in the heart when he was pleading for help? Or Kaufman, who crushed his face with a bat, or Semenec, who stabbed first, or even Willis, who had lured him out on the sand with sex the night before so that Lisa could sneak up behind him and blow his brains out—why on earth would anyone offer any of those five anything but the death penalty?

Swallers and Dzvirko were another story. They were involved in a brutal murder; they had done nothing to separate themselves from it; and they needed to pay some kind of serious price for that; but you could construct a case to say they were not intentionally at the center of it. Those two conceivably could argue they were only along for the ride, and that would put Donnelly in a weaker position if he tried to get a jury to convict them on a death-penalty charge.

The others: to hell with them. There was no reason to give any of them a break on any part of it . . . except for one thing.

They had one thing going for them.

They were white kids. White middle-class kids. Kids whose families would come to court in nice clothes. Kids whose parents had hired good lawyers.

And if Tim Donnelly had learned one thing in his years of prosecuting killers before Florida juries, it was this: All of the tough talk about cracking down on crime could dry up in an instant if the jury started feeling sorry for the defendant. In this case, the fastest way for that to happen would be for the jury to see these kids as the nice white kids from the nice white families who lived next door.

These brutal, soulless murderers could go free if their lawyers were smart enough and lucky enough to get the jurors to feel sorry for them. It was the dark little secret that kept cops and prosecutors awake at night: American jurors, for all their huffing and puffing about crime, could be fantastically forgiving.

People with their own brats at home—their own kids wearing

baggy pants, nose rings and perpetual expressions of sullen vacant-ness—could look at a defendant and say to themselves, "There but for the grace of God goes my son."

Next thing you know, the little monster is walking off down the street popping his fingers and rolling along, loose again.

Donnelly had to make sure that didn't happen.

In the meantime, Jeff Smith kept calling, looking for another deal for Lisa Connelly. So far Donnelly had been putting him off, but Smith was smart, very smart, and the instant he sensed that Donnelly was diddling him, Smith would go up the ladder.

There was peril in that direction. Donnelly had to worry Smith would be able to pull some string Donnelly couldn't see. The word could come down. Give it up. Give them a deal. Put this one away.

It was especially worrisome that some of the girls in the case had been involved in the whole mess in Oakland Park—the teenage pros-titution ring, the bad bust, the cops there who were in the process of being busted now themselves.

There was no telling how that might affect things. For Donnelly, the smartest thing was to put his head down, bull ahead, make the best cases he could and ignore all of the political what-ifs.

But he had to worry. Even the smallest amount of outside interfer-ence could cause certain things to happen.

He stacked the files on the desk in front of him, shaped the pile with the flats of his hands.

They would be tried separately. The defense lawyers would insist on that. The nature of the accusation—that they had conspired to-gether—meant each lawyer would want to show that his individual client was not really a member of the group. They would be hoping that in lying to save his own skin, each defendant would spill some more of the beans.

The traditional way would be to pit them against each other now, get them to blab by offering them deals, hope to get a solid conviction on a couple of them by letting the rest get away with slaps on the wrist.

Donnelly reached for another file, marked "Broward County Sheriff's Department, Crime Scene.'' He pulled out the photographs of Bobby Kent's body again.

He wasn't going to do it that way. These cases were too good. In fact, they were almost perfect.

The defendants were too evil. So what if they were white middle-class suburban kids? If what *they* did was not horribly wrong, and if it didn't make people angry enough to see them harshly punished—then maybe *nothing* was wrong. Maybe there was no wrong. Or right.

So he would do it the hard way. No deals. No bullshit. He would take them all down.

But there was a momentum that had to happen. He had to make the biggest cases first, while the witnesses were fresh. He needed to win early on Puccio—the best friend who stabbed his pleading buddy in the heart. Then Connelly. Then the others, ba-bam, ba-bing, one after the other.

There couldn't be any slip-ups or losses. Then the thing might unwind. The only thing those lawyers would need was a little bit of wriggle-room in which to make the juries feel sorry for their clients.

If one of them succeeded in making him stumble, Donnelly conceivably could lose the whole deal. If the lawyer for one of the weak cases moved for a speedy trial; if Jeff Smith found some way to make an end run around him and cut a deal; if any one of a number of things happened the wrong way, then all of these beautiful criminal cases could wind up ruined. White kids on parade.

MARTY SWAGGERED OUT INTO THE SMALL OPEN AREA WHERE PRISoners were allowed to congregate in the afternoon. Two months into his jail time, he was already taking on the look—hard eyes, paper-white skin, brutally defined muscles, blue-black hand-carved tattoos down his arms and legs. He nodded hello to Ken Calamusa, a big man from New Jersey with a long, curly country-singer haircut.

Calamusa, in his late twenties, had been in and out of reform schools and prisons most of his life. He was awaiting trial on a charge of eluding an officer. Back where he grew up, he was famous for that—making the cops run to catch him. People called him Marathon Man.

"You want me to cut your hair?" Marty asked him.

Calamusa shrugged. "Sure. Why not?"

He sat down on the bench next to a long metal table, with his back to Marty.

Mutual haircutting was a common pastime. It was one of the few activities during which prisoners were allowed access to scissors. The tips of the scissors had been ground off and rounded so that they couldn't be used as stabbing weapons, but the blades were still sharp enough to slice flesh.

A bored guard stood off at a distance, supposedly watching them, actually watching an afternoon soap opera on a television set bolted to an overhead rack. Several dozen other prisoners were packed into the small room, cutting each other's hair, gambling, arguing, doing insult routines on each other. Marty and Calamusa had to speak up to be heard.

"Don't fuck up my hair," Calamusa said.

"Oh, monsieur!" Marty crooned in a falsetto, "Meester Marty weel nevair fuck up your hair!"

Calamusa shook his head.

"Hey, man," Marty said, "don't be shakin' your head like that! I might cut you."

"Yeah, you cut me, asshole, and you know what'll happen next."

Marty snipped away at the ends for a while in silence.

"I can't believe I'm letting you cut my hair, man," Calamusa said, "and you're in here for murder. I shouldn't trust you behind me."

Marty ran his hand up through the hair on the back of Calamusa's head. "Why shouldn't you trust me?" he asked sweetly. "Bobby did."

Calamusa half turned. "You're sick, man."

Marty smirked and shrugged one shoulder forward. "He was my very best friend, since we were little boys together," he said.

Calamusa turned and faced him, pushed the scissors away with one hand.

"I don't believe you killed him, man. You're too much of a wuss."

Marty slipped down onto the bench next to him, leaned forward so that his face was inches from Calamusa's. Grinning and licking his lips, he said, "Fuck you, man. I killed that fucker. You want to hear how I done that fucker?"

Calamusa winced. "Hey, man, I heard all this shit from you a hundred times; I don't get no fuckin' thrill out of hearing this shit from you."

"Donny stuck him in the back first," Marty said in a throaty whisper, "and then, when Bobby turned around, I stuck my knife right into his fuckin' stomach, man, all the way up to the handle, and that hot blood squirted out all over my hand."

"Shut up, man."

Marty rose and came around behind him, stooped over him, hovering, breathing deeply as he spoke. Marty was sexually aroused.

"Bobby turned and ran, but we went after him, me and Derek Kaufman. I caught up to him and tackled him, and when he was on the ground, I got on him.

"I took the knife like this," he said, showing it with the scissors blade splayed open, "and I was like going back and forth on the fucker's throat, sawing on him, and there was all kind of blood gushing out, and Kaufman or somebody says you can't kill him quick like that, so I took the knife"—he lifted the scissors in the air over Calamusa to show—"and I started doing like this in his chest."

Marty whacked the knife up and down spasmodically in the air, stopping it each time a hairbreadth from Calamusa's neck. When he paused finally, Calamusa wriggled out from below him and stood up.

"Hey, fucker!" Calamusa shouted. "Don't be stabbin' at me with no fuckin' scissors, fucker!"

Marty smiled up at him.

"Hey, asshole!" Calamusa shouted at the guard. "Are you the fuckin' guard or what? You don't see this shit this guy's doin'? This guy is fuckin' crazy."

"Who you callin' asshole?" the guard muttered. Before Calamusa could answer, the guard had returned his gaze to the soap opera.

JEFF SMITH HAD COME TO THE JAIL TO PREPARE LISA FOR A SERIES of procedural hearings that were coming up. He sat across a small wooden table from her in the attorney's conference room and sighed. It was not going well. It never went well.

He had been meeting every day, sometimes for several hours, with the other attorneys hired to represent members of the group. Together, these lawyers probably comprised 90 percent of the top-notch legal talent in Broward County.

It was already clear that Donnelly intended to paint Lisa as the ringleader. That made Smith the unofficial team leader for the attorneys. Since the state was going to come after his client the hardest, he had to make sure she was under control and well prepared before the hearings ever started.

The other lawyers, most of whom he had known for years, wanted him to reassure them Lisa wouldn't blurt out something in court that would screw up the complex strategies they were all trying to build.

The lawyers would argue a number of things and try to pull the case in any of several directions, but they were more or less agreed that their best hope lay in getting the jurors to feel sorry for their clients. Poor misunderstood kids, confused, at sea in a wicked world, betrayed by a brutal society that had never cared properly for them. Now they have made this one mistake. A terrible mistake, but are we therefore to destroy these young lives?

These could be your own children, ladies and gentlemen of the jury. Go home and take a look. Notice a few nose rings? Baseball caps on backward? Hmm?

Poor little white kids.

That was the strategy. But that strategy required that Lisa not start running her mouth in court in a way that would make her look mean, scary, or evil.

At the moment, Lisa was sitting across from him at a scarred wooden table in the small prisoner conference room wearing a jail-house smock, no makeup, and her worst, puffy-eyed, sullen expression.

"I just don't understand why I'm still in here, Jeff," she said, not meeting his eye. "I mean, my ma keeps telling me how much it costs to hire you, like they gotta take out a mortgage on the house and shit, 'cause you're such a big-deal lawyer."

"Yes," he said. "Your mother does have to pay me. I don't work for free when I can help it."

"Well, why am I in here? How come I'm not out on bond?"

"No one is out on bond."

"I see people gettin' out of here every day on bond, Jeff."

He sighed. "Look, Lisa, you are in here on a capital murder charge."

"So what?" she shouted at him suddenly. "So what? I mean, I've been in here three months, for Christ's sake. I've done the jail thing. So what's the point in just keeping me here?"

Smith got up from his chair and walked to the small mesh-covered window. Outside was a limited view of a row of tidily maintained Dumpsters.

"Lisa," he said, "I worry that you still don't seem to understand the seriousness of the charge against you. It's capital murder. It just doesn't get any more serious than that."

"Christ, what kind of a fuckin' lawyer are you?" she bellowed at him. "Don't you even get it yet? Whose fucking side are you on? I didn't fucking murder anybody, Jeff! All's I did, I helped plan some stuff, so big fucking deal."

"The gun . . ."

"So what?" she screamed. "Shut up about the gun! They didn't use the gun! He wasn't shot! They cut him and beat his head in with the bat. I didn't do shit, Jeff. It's not fair."

She stood up. At five months, her pregnancy was just beginning to show on her large frame and girth. There were tears streaming down her cheeks.

Smith said a few more words and then found a way to end it. On his way to the car, he thought that he was going to have to find a way to explain things to her. He had to bring her to an understanding of her situation. He was overwhelmed by two conflicting feelings. He felt terrible pity for her, pregnant and alone in such a horrible place and situation. And he felt horror.

" 'I've done the jail thing,' " he muttered to himself as he slid behind the wheel. " 'I've done the fucking jail thing.' Good God Almighty."

CHAPTER NINE

IN NOVEMBER, ALL SEVEN DEFENDANTS WERE BROUGHT TO COURT FOR A preliminary hearing. They sat handcuffed together in two rows in the jury box, with Broward County sheriff's deputies standing behind them as guards. At the door to the courtroom, a bailiff examined spectators with a metal-detecting wand, but generally the security in the room was light and there was a sense of relaxed informality among the armed law-enforcement people in the room.

To the practiced eyes of the cops on duty that day, this group was no threat.

Half a dozen of the defendants' family members joined two print reporters and two local television crews in the spectator section. Except for the media and a couple of veteran trial watchers, who ducked in and out quickly to see what was going on, there were no spectators.

The lawyers were all out of the room for a long time, meeting with the judge in his chambers. The reporters at the back began trading media gossip—which station was rumored to be on the market, which sections of the local newspaper were being revamped.

The bailiffs and the regular deputies guarding the prisoners drifted into the same sort of aimless chat back and forth—who was being assigned where, who had taken the test for crime-scene technician.

Lisa, chained to the other women in the upper row, leaned forward and whispered to Marty, "If it's a boy, I'm gonna name him Marty."

Marty turned and gave her a half grin. "Will you send me a picture?"

"Yeah."

Heather, who was at the end of the row, separated from Lisa by Ali, said, "Are they gonna let you out to have it?"

Lisa turned toward her, glowering.

"Shut up, bitch. You're nothing but a fucking snitch. You cut a deal with them, we all know that."

Heather's face flushed, but she said nothing.

Ali examined Heather as if seeing her for the first time. "Is that true, Heather?"

Marty snickered and turned up toward them. "Christ, you don't even know that yet, Ali? What kind of lawyer have you got? Shit, her and Dumbo here"—he nodded toward Derek Dzvirko—"are snitching on all of us to save their own asses, or we wouldn't even be here today."

Dzvirko glowered at Marty but said nothing.

Derek Kaufman hissed at Dzvirko, "You sorry-ass snitch motherfucker. I know all about what you're doin'. You're gonna regret this shit."

Lisa stooped forward and said loudly to Kaufman, "Leave him the fuck alone, asshole. Haven't you done enough to screw up his life?"

"Listen, you dumb fucking bitch," Kaufman said, "you don't seem to understand that your fat cousin here is the main snitch that's screwing us, more than Heather is."

"Hey, man," Donny Semenec said hoarsely, "I didn't do shit. I don't even know what the fuck I'm doin' here, man. I didn't do shit."

Marty laughed bitterly. "You stabbed him, dude. What do you call that?"

Suddenly the seven became aware that the room around them had fallen silent. The deputies and bailiffs were staring at them coolly. The media people in the back had stopped talking to each other and were gazing at the defendants.

One of the reporters looked across the aisle to where the family members were sitting. A couple of the family members returned his gaze with uncomfortable smiles.

He turned back to his colleagues. "Jesus," he muttered. "It's like an *Our Gang* comedy up there. Like 'Who tattled'?"

When they realized they were the objects of stares, the seven fell silent and slipped down lower in their chairs. Every few moments, one or another of them would look up at the people watching them and then look away quickly.

JEFF SMITH AND THE OTHER LAWYERS CONTINUED MEETING AS A group, mainly because they were all struggling to come up with any viable defense theory. In one meeting, Smith asked the others, "How did this happen? How could kids like this do such a thing? But, even more to the point, how could they do it and not seem to have even a drop of remorse?"

"It's worse than no remorse, Jeff," one of the other lawyers said. "It's like they admit all of it, but they don't understand . . ."

He trailed off, unable to complete his sentence.

"They admit it," Smith said, "but they don't understand why everybody's making such a federal case out of it."

"Yeah!" another lawyer shouted. "My guy admits he stabbed the guy, but he keeps telling me he didn't do anything wrong."

"No, no, they didn't do anything wrong," Smith agreed. "I keep getting that. In fact, goddamn Lisa, she keeps telling me how mean Bobby was and all this shit, and I really get the feeling she thinks they did something good."

"These are mainstream kids," another lawyer said. "My client comes from a nice family. Fairly well off. Nice neighborhood. Great schools. Took him to church, took him to lessons. Bought him a car. You know, in today's world, the way things are, you just don't get many more chances than these kids have had. It really doesn't get a whole lot better for most people than they've had it."

They stared at each other in disbelief and bafflement—a room full of tough, big-city, middle-aged criminal lawyers who had seen it all. Or thought they had. Until this.

IN NOVEMBER 1993, ALMOST FIVE MONTHS AFTER THE MURDER, Judge Charles M. Greene called all of the lawyers in and issued them a stern warning: He was sick of the delays so far, and he was going to speed it up.

Judge Greene—an ex-fighter pilot, former prosecutor, handsome product of Union College in Schenectady, thirty-seven years old— was quick-witted and usually fun to talk to away from court. But he was not a man to be pushed. Beneath the intelligent surface lurked a certain military steeliness, an occasional temper. When Judge Greene talked about his court, his rules, and his personal expectations, smart lawyers tried to stay on his good side.

Judge Greene didn't really care who went first. But he did want the lawyers to know the trials would begin when he said they would begin—on time—and he intended to proceed from one trial to the next until they were all done.

The lawyers were polite and contrite. They promised to help move things along. Judge Greene asked them for a date that would represent the very soonest they could be ready, and they all agreed on February 1994. That would give them a total of seven months between the crime and the trial in which to prepare their defense.

Of course, the problem was that there was very little defense they could prepare. And that fact alone made delays all the more valuable. The main plan for the defense in cases like these is always delay.

When the state basically has the goods on someone, that person's best hope is to delay the trial until some of the goods go stale—that is, until memories begin to fade, witnesses move off or get hard to find, evidence gets misplaced.

In the end, the joke would be on Judge Greene. In spite of all their promises and long faces, the defense would find ways to delay the trial more than three dozen times, putting off the start of deliberations until September 1994—a total of a year and two months in which the state's case would be allowed to yellow and wither in Tim Donnelly's cheap cardboard file boxes.

In the meantime, however, just in case the good magistrate might somehow find a way to make good on his threats and put them into court sooner, Jeff Smith thought it might be time for Plan B.

SMITH, THE OTHER LAWYERS, THEIR ASSISTANTS AND SECRETARIES, already had devoted lots of time to the pursuit of useful legal precedents, and the search had produced nothing of real value. The Broward County Sheriff's Department had done such a clean, efficient job of pulling the case and the evidence together that there just were not very many really promising cracks to pry.

Tim Donnelly was doing very little to tip his own hand, but the few moves he did make, in terms of taking depositions or seeking subpoenas for evidence, all tended to point toward Lisa Connelly, Smith's client, as the chief architect.

Even though the establishment of a motive for the murder was not necessarily important in legal terms, it was potentially important for the jury. A strong clear motive would help the state win convictions if the state could show jurors in an informal way what on earth might have motivated these young people to do what they had done.

With the trial only a few months off, it was increasingly clear the state would use Lisa to set up the motive. Donnelly would argue that her sexual obsession with Marty—in particular, her jealousy of Marty's closeness with Bobby—was the primal source of the evil that eventually enveloped them all.

What Donnelly probably had in mind was a straight no-nonsense approach: It was sex. It was jealousy. It was evil. Don't get hoodooed by the lawyers. Look at Lisa. You can see it on her face—and in her belly.

Smith's concern was to serve his own client. Toward that end, he

already had sent Derek Dzvirko to another lawyer, in case there might
be any kind of conflict of interest in his representation of both Lisa
and Derek.

But if Jeff Smith could somehow neutralize Lisa as the prime
mover, he might wind up doing them all a big favor. If Lisa didn't
work as the linchpin of Connelly's no-nonsense approach, then everybody else might have some wriggle-room.

But putting any kind of real dent in the case against Lisa was going
to require some very innovative work, to say nothing of grasping for
straws. Lisa, meanwhile, continued to be her own worst enemy, always responding with sullenness, anger, and creepy self-righteousness
whenever anyone challenged her on anything.

After scouring the legal frontiers, Smith had come up with something. He didn't claim it was golden. It was just the best he could do.

"Urban psychosis," Smith told the other lawyers.

After a deadly silence, one of them said, "Jeff, why don't you tell
us about urban psychosis."

The August 1993 issue of *Trial* magazine had included a report on
a Milwaukee case in which the lawyer had been successful with a
theory of what he called "urban psychosis" in the defense of an
impoverished African-American girl who had murdered a friend for a
leather coat.

"The theory is that these kids are totally numbed out by the violence and the immorality of the world around them."

"Yeah?"

"So they can't distinguish between right and wrong."

They stared at him.

"But they're not nuts," one of them said.

"No. But they can't really be held responsible for what they do."

There was a long painful silence in the room. Finally someone
muttered quietly, "Jeez, Jeff."

Smith shrugged. "That's as good as it's gonna get, gentlemen."

After another wordless pause, another of them said, "O.K., Jeff.
Run it up the flagpole."

They filed out of the room quietly.

On the way out, someone muttered "Jeez" again.

AT THE FIRST HEARING AT WHICH THERE WERE MEDIA PEOPLE IN THE room, Smith informed Judge Greene that he might want to subpoena experts in a new area of the law known as "urban psychosis."

Judge Greene turned and stared off at the wall for a long moment, as if gathering his thoughts.

"What kind of psychosis, sir?"

"Urban psychosis."

The reporters in the back, who had been looking a bit heavy about the eyelids up until then, opened their eyes and notebooks wide.

"I may not be familiar with that concept, Mr. Smith," the judge said. "Would you enlighten me? Is it something you think applies to your client's case in particular?"

"I think it may be very appropriate in this case," Smith said.

"And it is?"

Smith explained that these young people had been exposed from birth to a cultural bombardment of violence and amorality. Everything they saw, heard, and felt from early childhood—movies, video games, news clips of people getting shot and blown up, images of high city officials having sex with hookers—the whole sorry, deadly, numbing sluice washed over them until it created a sense of normality around evil.

"And the result of this is what?" Judge Greene asked.

Smith drew himself up, assumed his most somberly urgent expression, and said, "They lose the ability to distinguish between good and evil.

"Herd mentality is how I look at it," he said. "My client wanted to be accepted. She didn't want anybody to say she was a nerd.

"And she was unable to differentiate between right and wrong because of the pervasive presence of violence in her life."

The Florida newspapers were full of it the next morning. There was even mention of it on the national news. The first few stories were fairly wide-eyed and uncritical, merely conveying the news that a new theory of the law might be propounded in the Fort Lauderdale case.

But it didn't take long for the tone of the coverage to shift toward skepticism and, from there, to downright ridicule. One reporter found legal experts who were willing to explain some of the background of this whole genre of defense argument.

Arguments like these—battered wife, abused child, victim of oppression—all grew from an area of defense theory associated with post-traumatic stress disorder, much of which grew out of the period after the Vietnam War.

The argument then was that Vietnam vets who had committed serious crimes, even murder, were not responsible for their actions because they were victims of a mentally disabling disease caused by the extreme stress of the war. It was a kind of social/political diagnosis: A psychiatrist might not deem them crazy enough to meet the legal test for a plea of innocence by reason of insanity, but a jury might nevertheless be persuaded to spare them, out of sympathy for what they had suffered.

Whatever the merits may have been originally, post-traumatic stress arguments had been stretched to the limits in recent years, and they had taken an especially tough beating in South Florida. In one particular case, which seemed quite close to what Jeff Smith was arguing, a lawyer had claimed that his client's act of murder was brought on by a syndrome he called "television intoxification."

The jury on that one voted twelve thumbs down.

But even the experts who seemed able to discuss these other theories and arguments with straight faces grew openly derisive when reporters asked them about "urban psychosis" in the Bobby Kent case.

One expert pointed out to a reporter that it might be tricky establishing city life itself as a murder defense, since so many people live in cities. That would make for an awful lot of people walking around with a license to kill.

Several of the experts observed that even if one bought into urban psychosis as a defense, the kids in the Kent case weren't urban. The theory itself was introduced in a case that involved extreme poverty, racism, and an environment of horrific crime in an urban wasteland.

The Lauderdale kids didn't live in that environment. They lived in neighborhoods that were suburban and privileged. They had grown up in the kind of houses and neighborhoods middle-class people all over the world strive to attain.

John Monahan, a law professor at the University of Virginia and a psychologist, said, "Terminal boredom is not a defense."

Monahan suggested perhaps their defense could be altered somewhat to a plea of "suburban psychosis," associated, he suggested, with "a pathological fear of lawn mowers."

After the article quoting Monahan appeared in the Fort Lauderdale *Sun-Sentinel,* the urban psychosis theory was never publicly mentioned by the lawyers again.

The media, however, continued the hunt for sociological explanations. In October 1993, the *Miami Herald*'s Sunday magazine, *Tropic,* published a comprehensive story about the case, well reported and edited by reporters Scott Higham and April Witt, with a powerful foreword written by *Tropic* editor Tom Shroder. In it, Shroder struggled with the question of motivation and cause.

"You read this story trying desperately to believe that the kids who committed this crime are freaks, aberrations," Shroder wrote. "But in the end that delusion is denied you.

"In the end, the place these sad children lived is too obviously a place of our own making, a toxic waste dump of our collective failings as a society."

In newsrooms all over Florida, editors were throwing their fists in the air and shouting, "These kids just couldn't *do* this! I want to know why!"

Their reporters obediently dug up experts—all of them therapists and social scientists, nary a priest or a rabbi in the lot—to say why white kids from the mall would murder one of their own friends with knives and baseball bats.

Charles Patrick Ewing, a psychologist and law professor at the State

University of New York at Buffalo, said in a *Miami Herald* story, "Adolescents are peer group animals. They tend to be much more involved in peer group relations on a daily basis than adults or younger children are.

"They are much more concerned about what their peers think of them than adults are," Ewing said.

Ewing also mentioned economics and class as causes of teen homicide.

"I see it increasingly with working-class and lower-middle-class kids," he said. "They are underemployed, uneducated.

"They really don't have any hope. They may be working delivering pizza today. But what are they going to be doing next year? Or five years from now? They are not looking toward the future. The future for them is this afternoon."

The lawyers had started the ball rolling with the urban psychosis stuff—quickly abandoned when the media ridiculed it. Now the media were mining the same vein, coming up with social and economic reasons why the kids did it and why, by implication, it really wasn't entirely their fault.

The lawyers welcomed the media's help. These cases were going to be tough. The object was clear: Get the jurors to feel sorry for the defendants. But doing it—that would be the biblical passing of the camel through the needle's eye.

Urban psychosis was obviously too in-the-face. Educated middle-class jurors would laugh. Average folks would snicker. Poor and minority jurors might even get mad.

But somewhere in the journalistic treatment of the case, there seemed to be a tiny window of opportunity. True, they were products of the middle class; they grew up in nice houses; they attended some of the best public schools tax money could buy. And after they dropped out of school, their parents bought them cars and clothes and seemed unperturbed when they didn't even manage to hold down the menial jobs for which they were qualified.

True, they seemed to have operated as prostitutes and God-knows-what out of their parents' comfortable homes. But most of that stuff could be kept out. There were all kinds of rules of evidence the lawyers could use.

The lawyers could work with the Patrick Ewing argument: Sure, these kids were products of the post–World War II American middle and working classes in one of the most comfortable and affluent societies in the history of the planet. But what had their country done for them lately?

Corporate downsizing. Airline executives having to mow lawns for a living. Kids reduced to hawking pizza in a football stadium just because they didn't finish high school.

It was tough. Discouraging. You had to feel really sorry for these kids. No wonder they murdered somebody with a baseball bat.

Well, it might take some fine-tuning, especially after they got a look at the juries. But it wasn't as if they had to get these kids off, either.

Basically, when you got right down to it, the state had them nailed, absolutely dead to rights. The lawyers rarely saw cases in which the defendants had left themselves so little wriggle-room.

The fact was, it would be a great legal victory to get any one of them out of court with less than a capital murder conviction. The trick at this point was to save their lives.

And Smith, in particular, believed it could be done. His client, of course, was a girl, and that helped a lot. It was always difficult for jurors to vote for the big one against any female, especially a young female.

But that gave the others a better shot, as well. If they just got the right juries, if they worked hard at the poor-little-white-kids theme, if luck was with them, they could save the lives of these defendants and maybe even get some of them off pretty lightly, in spite of the gunboat cases Tim Donnelly had lined up against them.

*   *   *

ON A LATE TUESDAY AFTERNOON IN THE SUMMER OF 1994, ONE OF
Jeff Smith's legal assistants shepherded Lisa's family—her mother,
her uncle, and other members of the clan—across the big center room,
navigating the stacks of files and other obstacles on the floor, and
showed them into Jeff's office. It took a bit of arranging to find chairs
for all of them.

Jeff waited until they were all seated, then leaned back in his chair
and held up both palms, smiling.

"You all doing all right?"

Most of them nodded and smiled back at him. The uncle seemed
a little distant, Jeff thought. Maybe just tired after a long day in the
garbage business.

"I wanted to let you know where we stand at this point," Jeff said.
"We have filed forty-four motions for delay in this matter, and Judge
Greene let us all know by telephone yesterday that there aren't going
to be any more delays granted."

The uncle leaned forward, red-faced. "Good!" he blurted.

Jeff sized him up for a moment. "You like that, eh? You're eager
to get on with it."

"I sure am."

"Well, someday you'll have to share with me why you feel that
way. Right now, I need to get some business out on the table.

"As I believe you know, I was effectively offered a deal at the
very beginning of all this, even though Mr. Donnelly now claims it
wasn't his deal, and I was the only lawyer in the case who was able
to discuss a deal."

"We don't want a deal," the uncle muttered.

Smith stared at him in silence for a while.

"You don't want a deal. O.K. Well, that's fine, because you're not
going to get one. Donnelly isn't offering anything, not one iota, except
he says we can plead guilty to capital murder and throw ourselves on
the mercy of the court for the punishment phase."

Maureen sniggered, then shook her head in disgust. "Fat chance,"
she said, half under her breath.

Smith folded his hands on the desk and nodded. "Fat chance," he said quietly. "Fat chance. Look. Let me say what I have to say here, and then you all tell me what it is you think you need to say."

They stared back at him sullenly.

"The lawyers for the other kids and I have been meeting a lot, trying on different ideas for size. We thought about the urban psychosis thing, and we've kind of decided that's a little too rad."

"Why?" the uncle asked.

"Well, I'll get to that. O.K.? We're not abandoning that thought process entirely. We just think we may need to soften it a little—"

"Soften it?" the uncle snarled. "Jesus. Here this kid is being charged with murder, the damn D.A. is going on TV and calling her a cold-blooded murderer, and half the media in the country are calling her a killer, and you want to soften it?"

Smith could feel his face reddening. "Look, you understand why they're calling these kids murderers, right? They murdered somebody."

"Hey, now that's it," Maureen said loudly, rising to her feet and slapping the top of her chair back with one hand. "He's supposed to be her damn lawyer, and he's calling her a murderer, too."

"Just sit down, Maureen," Smith snapped. "All right? Because, look, I came out of retirement to help you with this case, and I have poured untold hours into it that you sure as hell haven't paid for, and I don't need this aggravation. The least you can do is give me the courtesy of hearing out what I have to say, and then you can share your feelings with me."

She sat back down slowly, with a baleful eye on him.

Smith exhaled heavily, got himself back under control, then rose to his feet. "Lisa is charged with cap murder," he said quietly. "The death penalty is a possibility. The electric chair. The state is making her out to be the ringleader.

"Now, there's something you need to know about all this 'urban psychosis' crap. The state of Florida does not allow any form of diminished capacity as a murder defense."

"What's that?" the uncle asked.

"I'm about to tell you. Diminished capacity is urban psychosis, post-traumatic stress disorder, any of these defenses that come shy of a nut defense. That is, you're not going to go for a full insanity defense, because you don't think you can prove it, so you try one of these other things to attempt to show your client is sane but can't think right and therefore shouldn't be held accountable.''

"Yeah?" Maureen said.

"You can't do that."

"You can't?"

"Not in Florida."

"Well, that's not fair, is it?" she asked.

He bit his lip and looked them all in the eye, one after another. "Now, I can't offer diminished capacity as a formal defense and get her off on those grounds. But the reality is, and the state knows this, no jury in Florida wants to send that little white girl to the chair. So I can talk about things like diminished capacity, and even if it won't fly as a formal legal theory of defense, it will be enough to give the jury the excuse it needs to let her off of cap murder, whether it's technically kosher or not.''

"So she goes free," the uncle said.

"No," Smith said, nodding emphatically and waving with one palm. "No, she doesn't go free. That's not an option. The state will offer a lesser-included charge of murder two, murder in the second degree, which is jail time, and it's between twelve and a half and seventeen years; probably like fifteen years is what she would actually serve. So the jury will knock it down to that, but they won't let her off.''

They were silent.

"Now, Donnelly is one thing. He's pretty hardcase about this, and the bad news for us is that this thing is in the papers and on TV so much, so that makes it pretty hard for a guy like Donnelly to back down.

"But Donnelly's not the boss. And the people I hang with are the boss. They know that this is probably a murder two case. Donnelly could get lucky, he could draw to a hanging jury, but the chances of that are kind of iffy. Plus, this kind of case just eats a huge hole in their budget, it eats up all kinds of time and energy, it makes Fort Lauderdale look like shit, and it's better to have it go away sooner rather than later.''

''So what's your point, Jeff?'' Maureen asked.

''The point is, I think if I go in to Donnelly's superiors right now and offer them a plea to murder two, we can save Lisa from the chair for sure, and we can probably get a guarantee of short years.''

''How short?'' Maureen asked.

''Heather Swallers is getting a fifteen-year guarantee for cooperating. I would hope to do that well or a little better.''

Smith sat back down. No one spoke. He looked at them. They looked back.

Finally Maureen said, ''I can't believe this shit.''

''What shit is that, Maureen?'' Smith asked.

''I can't believe you're ready to send my little girl . . .''

She stopped, unable to go on. Suddenly she began to sob. The other members of the family all leaned toward her and comforted her.

The uncle bellowed: ''You're supposed to be her lawyer, Jeff!''

''I'm not her fairy godmother!'' Smith said. ''I don't know what to tell you people. I guess you want to hear some kind of fairy tale. But Lisa was involved, very involved, in a very brutal killing, and I am not going to sit here and tell you that she is going to walk away. . . . What? What is it you want to hear? Do you honestly believe Lisa can just walk from this?''

Maureen blew her nose, then straightened herself and folded her hands primly on the lap of her loose-fitting blue jeans. ''Jeff, I'm sorry, but we have been talking amongst ourselves, and we have been forced to decide that you just are not the fighter we need for Lisa right now. It's not personal. I hope you understand we have to do what we have to do for our Lisa.''

''Which is?''

''We have found us another lawyer.''

Smith tried to think how he was going to take this. On the one hand, it meant he could go back to his boat in Key West, do some fishing, and not have to spend any more time talking to these people.

On the other hand, he had come back to Lauderdale and had devoted incredible hours of work to helping them. He was the one lawyer who had gotten anywhere—one single inch—with the state.

By calling in every chit and personal connection he had out there in the local legal community, by fighting in the trenches for delays, by searching the law for a far-out theory that might sway the jury, and by knowing how to cut to the practical realities—juries don't like to send white girls to the chair—he felt that he had brought Lisa within range of a favorable outcome, which to him meant anything less than the chair, especially if it meant a jail term of less than the max.

In addition to that, it always looks bad for a lawyer to get dumped by the client this close to the court date, in such a highly publicized case. If he wanted to, Smith would be justified in getting very angry about this.

"Who you talking to?" he asked.

"Kayo Morgan," the uncle said.

"Kayo Morgan," Smith said. "Kayo Morgan? Kayo Morgan."

He knew he had come across somebody recently with a name like Kayo or Bulldog or Fang or something like that.

All of a sudden it hit him.

"The guy who's been on *Court TV* this week!" Smith shouted. "The guy with the ponytail and the blue jeans! Is that who you mean?"

They nodded yes.

"You saw him on *Court TV*. That's how you found him?"

They nodded yes.

"And what does he say?"

"He says she's innocent," Maureen said.

"Innocent? Innocent! He used that word? He says she's innocent? She admits . . . she has made statements to the police that she orchestrated the baseball bat and knife murder of her boyfriend's best friend. And she's innocent? Innocent of what? The Chicago fire?"

"She didn't do a damn thing," Maureen said. "She never should have been put in jail, and she ain't gonna serve a day after her trial, if I have anything to do about it.''

The uncle said, "Kayo's a fighter, and you're not.''

Smith gazed out the window for a while, cloaking himself in composure.

"I understand," he said quietly. "I respect your decision. Tell Mr. Morgan I will do whatever I can to cooperate with him. I believe this ends our business with each other.''

When the legal assistant had ushered the last of them out, Smith muttered to himself, "Totally, completely, fucking unbelievable!''

AS IT TURNED OUT, THE KEY TRIAL WAS THE FIRST, AND IT WAS NOT Lisa's. The first to stand was Marty. His trial, which opened September 12, 1994, set the weave for the other trials. His lawyers were Thomas E. Cazel of Fort Lauderdale, one of the winningest criminal lawyers in South Florida, and Kenneth Duckworth of Hialeah, whose practice was more civil than criminal but who was nevertheless an experienced litigator.

The jury was mainly middle-aged and was made up of six white men, a Hispanic man, an African-American man, one white woman, and three Hispanic women.

The courtroom was smallish and dingy and wouldn't have held a large crowd, but none appeared anyway. Outside in the corridor a mob shuffled loudly up and down the cavernous passage, carrying on the daily commerce of criminal justice in a typical American city. A gaggle of local press looked in and out, keeping track of this and several other stories that day.

Several of the reporters and television film crew members, male and female, were dressed in their customary shorts and T-shirts: They were mainly interested in whether or not they would be affected by a new dress code someone was trying to promulgate for the courthouse.

The dress-code idea seemed like a long shot. Half of the people in the hallway looked as if they had come to court in their PJs. Normally, where dress is concerned, the press is held to a lower, not higher, standard than the general public. But as a half-dozen reporters gathered in the front row before the opening of the Puccio trial, the dress-code issue at least gave them something interesting to talk about.

At the two polar ends of the public seating area sat Bobby Kent's parents, Farah and Fred, and Marty's parents, Martin and Veronica. All four fixed their eyes straight ahead at the judge's bench so their eyes would not meet.

Two bailiffs brought Marty into the room in handcuffs. Marty flinched and his mother winced when the bailiffs leaned behind him to unlock the cuffs. Then Marty smiled coolly to his mother to say he was all right. Her eyes welled with tears. Her husband put his arm around her and hugged her.

Fred and Farah Kent stared unblinking at Marty. Fred's face was a mask. Farah's dark eyes were ablaze with hatred.

On the surface, Marty looked younger and milder by far than he had at the time of his arrest. His hair was cut short and looked very red against the sheet-white jailhouse pallor of his skin. He wore a pale-blue V-neck sweater over a white shirt, with a dark tie cinched against his neck. The collar of the shirt, loaned by his father, was a size too big, which made it crumple around his neck in a winsomely boyish way.

On closer inspection and beneath the ill-fitting clothes, he looked even more pumped-up than he had back when he was doing steroids with Bobby and pumping iron at the Y. As soon as he turned his gaze away from his mother, his face fell slack, eyes dead, lips numb. The overall effect was eerie, as if he were a choirboy from Hell.

Tim Donnelly, when he came forward to open the case, smiled toward the men and women waiting apprehensively in the jury box. It was a decent, plain, middle-western kind of a smile that implied no attempt at being buddy-buddy. Not a tall man but barrel-chested and broad-shouldered, he rolled a little on his heels as he walked, fists turning at his thighs. He looked like the kind of man you would listen to, in part because you wouldn't want to get him mad.

He looked each juror in the eye before he began. He folded his hands at his chest. He explained quietly what he was about to do. He was about to tell the story of Bobby Kent's murder, as the state believed it had happened. He explained that later on he and his witnesses would present evidence to prove that the state's version was the right one. Then he began.

"A young twenty-year-old man, Bobby Kent, is missing. He has been missing for four days."

Donnelly turned, walked away from them a few yards to give them some breathing room, then turned back to face them.

"His parents last saw him on Wednesday night. On the following Sunday evening, Detective Frank Ilarraza follows the directions he has received from the missing boy's friend Derek Dzvirko to a lonely spot in the western extreme of the county, under twin peaks of sand on the edge of the Everglades.

"Floating there facedown in the khaki-colored water is the missing young man."

The jurors were rapt, as if watching the first moments of open-heart surgery.

"Dr. Daniel Selove, the medical examiner, arrived and removed the body from the water. He saw that the young man had been stabbed in the neck twice, in the right shoulder three times, his throat had been slit twice, and he had been stabbed in the left chest with a seven-inch deep wound into the chest cavity.

"There was a deep penetrating stab wound in the abdomen. Two lacerations of the scalp. Two vertebrae had been fractured."

Donnelly held his hands up in front of his face as if warding off knife thrusts. "There were defensive stab wounds to the hands and arms."

Donnelly dropped his arms and approached the jury. "Eventually the Broward County Grand Jury indicted seven individuals in the death of Bobby Kent.

"We are going to show," he said, "that the people who did this to Bobby Kent were not strangers. You will see, in fact, that the conspirators in his death were Bobby Kent's closest and dearest friends."

He backed away again and allowed that thought to settle on the jury for a moment. Then he pointed to Marty.

"Bobby Kent and Marty Puccio were not just friends but best friends. They met in the third grade, and they had been inseparable ever since.

"We will show that, deep down, beneath the surface of this friendship, Mr. Puccio harbored jealousies and hatred of Bobby Kent. He accused him of picking on him, abusing him, embarrassing him in front of other people.

"In early 1993, Mr. Puccio met and began dating Lisa Connelly, who introduced him to several of her friends. Alice Willis and Lisa Connelly had been friends as children. Ali, as she was called by her friends, now lived in Palm Bay, several hours north of Fort Lauderdale.

"Ali and Bobby dated, but that relationship ended in May 1993. At about that time, Lisa also discovered that she did not like the way Bobby treated Marty. Or Alice."

Donnelly went to the jury box and put both hands on the rail. "On July 13, 1993, a Tuesday, Alice Willis, Heather Swallers, and Donald Semenec drove to Lisa's house in Ali's new red Mustang five-point-o with T-tops. The whole group later drove to the home of Derek Kaufman, who lived on an estate at the western end of Broward County.

"Derek Kaufman was the twenty-year-old self-proclaimed leader of a group called CMF—the Crazy Motherfuckers."

None of the jurors looked even mildly shocked by the word. For the first time, a few of them did pry their eyes off Donnelly and shoot Marty flat gazes.

Donnelly explained how the first attempt had failed because Lisa couldn't pull the trigger. He told the jury how both Lisa and Marty had become angry and frustrated, vowing that Bobby had to be killed right away.

Donnelly walked the jury through all the idiotic humdrum events of the following day—trips to the comic book store, people sneaking in and out of Maureen Connelly's back window. He described the borrowing of the baseball bat.

"At eleven-thirty P.M., Mr. Puccio was waiting in his garage, dressed in black pants, a white T-shirt, a black trench coat, and red bandanna.

"When the friends gathered that night, Mr. Puccio brought the plan up first. He wanted Bobby dead. He showed the group the diver's knife he had brought along for the job. Lisa said he needed to die. Derek Kaufman, who didn't know him, said, 'Let's do it. Someone like that needs to die.' "

Standing rigidly at the jury-box bar, Donnelly described the drive to Weston, everything in detail, who rode in what car, the stop to buy Donny something to drink. He explained how, once there, Ali had lured Bobby down to the water's edge. He explained the code-word phrase, in which Heather asked if there were any alligators in the water.

"At that moment, Donny sneaks up behind Bobby and stabs him in the neck."

Donnelly threw his hand suddenly to his neck and stumbled backward, away from the jurors. " 'Oh my God! I'm bleeding!'

"And he turns to Marty, his best friend. 'Marty!' But Marty says no words in return. Instead"—Donnelly drew his hand back to show the thrust—"Marty stabs him in the stomach!"

Donnelly stalked back toward the jurors. " 'No! Help me, Marty! I'm sorry, Marty! I'm sorry!' "

He described how Kaufman, Semenec, and Puccio chased Bobby across the sand. He described Ali turning on the headlights and seeing the three young men standing over their fallen prey.

"At that point, Heather can hear Bobby Kent moaning. She can see Derek Kaufman take up the bat. Then the lights go off. She hears, 'Thud!' And then there is no more moaning."

At this point, a few of the jurors could no longer maintain their masks of equanimity. They shook their heads and frowned in what may have been disgust, terror, or some of both.

"Then, in the darkness, Heather hears Derek Kaufman say, 'Somebody help me! We got to take his body and get rid of it.'

"Derek Kaufman lifts him by the arms, Dzvirko by the trousers.

They take him to the bank. Dzvirko hears a wheezing sound in his throat, drops him, and runs to the car.''

Donnelly described the drive to the beach, the burying and unburying of weapons, the planning of the alibi. He told the jurors about Marty's phony call to Fred Kent, to make it look as if he believed Bobby was still at home. He told about Ali, Lisa, and Marty going back to erase tire tracks.

Donnelly explained how Lisa had blabbed the story to Claudia Arbelaez, and Claudia had called the police. He described Marty's long voluntary sworn statement to the police in which he told a series of self-serving lies.

Donnelly quoted Marty's statement to the police. '' 'I think it's gang-related,' he said. 'I hope to God, I pray to God he's not dead, because I just don't know how I'd live the rest of my life. The last two days have been hard for me.'

"It is the next night," Donnelly said, "after Marty has given his statement, that Derek Dzvirko meets Detective Ilarraza and shows him the body.''

He described the next day, the abortive hiding out in motel rooms, the feeble plots of escape, the eventual surrender. He told the jury that Marty had bragged about the murders in prison and that they would hear from the people to whom he had boasted.

Donnelly explained that Heather had been given a reduced sentence of seven to fifteen years in prison in return for her cooperation and a plea of guilty to second-degree murder and conspiracy to commit first-degree murder. Dzvirko, for the same plea bargain, would get seven to twenty years.

Donnelly thanked the jury and returned to his table. Judge Greene announced a pause for lunch.

OF THE TWO LAWYERS AT MARTY'S TABLE, TOM CAZEL WAS CLEARLY the stronger criminal litigator. But it was Ken Duckworth who opened.

In his late fifties, in a boxy tweed suit over creaky cowboy boots, with oily gray hair stuck to his temples, he was a less than prepossessing presence in the courtroom. But what he had to say was even less impressive.

Duckworth started out by referring several times to the "alleged conspiracy" in an almost comically sneering tone. He agreed that his client, Mr. Puccio, might have said something to the effect of "I wish he were dead," but then Duckworth asked: "How many times have any of us said that?"

The jurors looked down, as if counting on their fingers and coming up with zero.

Duckworth went through some of the details of the killing, especially the point at which Derek Dzvirko said he saw Donny Semenec stab Bobby in the neck "with a knife."

Duckworth said that, where Dzvirko's sworn testimony related to Marty Puccio, what Dzvirko actually had said was that he saw Marty "hit Bobby Kent with something."

Duckworth repeated it. "Something!"

Not specifically a knife. So Marty might theoretically have struck Bobby in the abdomen with something harmless. Even if Dzvirko swore he saw Marty thrust something into the area where Bobby later was found to have been deeply stabbed, the state would not be able to prove, Duckworth suggested, that it was Marty's stabbing motion that did it.

Duckworth referred several times to the murder as "this unfortunate tragic incident." He pointed out that one of the state's main witnesses, Swallers, was a "drug user."

He said Marty would admit that he lied to the police after the murder but did so entirely because of his fear of Kaufman, whom he believed to be a hired killer.

In the end, Duckworth said, Marty was a confused kid who had made some poor choices, exercised bad judgment, and allowed himself to fall in with the wrong companions.

"But you cannot convict him by mere guilt by association," Duckworth concluded.

For the rest of that day, a succession of police witnesses appeared, establishing the time chain, introducing photographs, explaining who had confessed to what, when, and where. The reporters began slipping out shortly after the lunch break, and by midafternoon none was left.

THEY WERE ALL BACK THE NEXT MORNING, HOWEVER, FOR THE TES-timony of Heather Swallers. Paler and chubbier than she had been before jail, Heather was now nineteen years old and had already lost what girlish prettiness had been left before her arrest. She sat round-shouldered in the dock and answered questions in a flat somnolent drone. She told where they had gone in the cars, who had driven, who had ridden with whom. To all questions of distance and time, she struggled for a response and then said "about fifteen minutes."

Then she told the story of Bobby Kent's death.

"I was a few feet away. I saw a hand raised back behind me with a knife, and then Donny Semenec stabbed Bobby in the neck.

"Bobby leaned forward, with his hand on the back of his neck. I ran to the car."

"Which car?" Donnelly asked.

"I ran to Ali's Mustang."

"When?"

"As soon as I seen Bobby Kent lean forward and say, 'Oh, fuck!' I ran to the car."

"Did you hear anything?"

"I heard Bobby Kent say a couple of times, 'Marty, I'm sorry.' I was sitting in the car with my hands over my ears. I kept hearing him say he was sorry. I was looking out of the backseat.

"Two minutes later, Ali got in the car, in the front, and turned the lights on. I said, 'Let's go to the beach, Ali. They said everybody's supposed to meet at the beach.' I was trying to see if I could get her to leave.

"The car moved a few feet, but then Derek Kaufman yelled, 'Shut the fucking car off.' Kaufman and Marty and Donny were all out there standing around Bobby. He was on the ground."

Heather's voice grew softer, flatter. The jurors all tipped forward on their seats, squinting to hear.

"Derek Dzvirko came to the car and got in," she said. "And then about two seconds later he got back out."

"Where was Bobby?" Donnelly asked.

"He was lying by Ali's car. You could hear him moaning. He was about four feet away."

"He was moaning?"

"Yeah. You could hear him. He was, kind of like gurgling. You could hear gurgling, too, like his blood coming out. I saw him on the ground."

"And then?"

"Derek Kaufman brought the bat. He was holding it, like, down. I turned my head. Then, uh, I didn't hear him like moaning or anything anymore. I heard Derek Kaufman say, 'Somebody needs to get out here and help me carry the body.' "

Donnelly walked back to his table and leafed through some notes, giving Heather's testimony time to register on the jury.

"And, uh, Miss Swallers, where was Lisa Connelly during all this?"

Heather shrugged. "Lisa was just standing next to Marty Puccio's car, like hyperventilating, like she couldn't breathe."

"What happened next?"

"Donny Semenec got in the car with us and said he wanted a cigarette. And then, so, uh, we left and went to the beach."

She described events at the beach, sitting around talking about this and that, not really much said about the murder. She described Lisa going out of control briefly because she thought she could smell blood in Marty's mother's car, and she said that Ali had gone off on a crying jag at one point.

On cross-examination, Tom Cazel asked her about her drug problems, and she admitted without hesitation that she had used lots of drugs and been addicted to crack cocaine. Beyond that, the defense made almost no effort to shake her on any of her factual testimony.

When she had finished testifying, the judge called the lawyers to the bench to discuss a question about the next witness, Derek Dzvirko. Duckworth motioned for Marty to come up to the bench so that he could hear what was being said. But Marty shrugged and stayed where he was, slouched behind the defense table.

DEREK DZVIRKO TOOK THE STAND IN LATE AFTERNOON. TALL, chubby, his dark hair cropped close, wearing white pants and a black shirt buttoned to the neck, he looked less like a nitwit than he had at the comic book store and more like a thug. He affected a surly insouciance, as if he were testifying for the state under duress but wanted everyone back in the Broward County jail to know he was cool.

"We were all in the same room at Lisa's house, and Ali said, 'I have a problem. We gotta kill Bob.' I was, like, O.K., whatever.

"We discussed rat poison, a knife, shooting him, a drive-by. You know, things you see in the movies. The conversation lasted about an hour."

He described the same long catalog of meaningless detail Heather had testified to—aimless trips here and there, sneaking in and out of Maureen Connelly's house.

Finally he came to the killing. He told how Bobby had pleaded for mercy. Then, in describing how Marty had stabbed Bobby in the gut, Dzvirko went out of his way to say, "I didn't see what he had in his hand at the time."

He told of Kaufman screaming at them to help chase Bobby down. He said he jumped in Ali's car, hoping to get away.

"When I reached over and turned the ignition on and the headlights, Bobby Kent was on his back. Derek Kaufman was kind of standing over him, and Donny Semenec was crouched down, like looking at him. Kaufman started yelling to turn the car off.

"Derek Kaufman's hand goes up with the bat, and the lights go off, and then I heard a crack.

"Then Derek Kaufman is yelling for someone to come help and

finish it. 'We have to finish it!' He yelled for me to come up, and I pretended I didn't hear him. He told me to come help him, and I'm, like, scared. So somebody handed me a pair of gloves.

"Derek says, 'We got to move him out of sight and get his wallet so they can't I.D. him.' I took my shirt off, because I didn't want to get blood on it. I took him by the pants cuffs.

"But I dropped him. When I dropped him, he was making a wheezing sound, and his shirt was all covered with blood."

He told of the drive to the beach, how Heather had asked for pot, and how, after she had smoked some, she had said, "I don't feel bad for what happened. I just blanked."

When the defense team's turn came, Dzvirko relaxed visibly. He was a state's witness. He should have been worried about what the defendant's attorneys would do to discredit him.

But he was suddenly at ease when Duckworth rose to cross-examine him, and Cazel and Duckworth were relaxed and friendly, too. Duckworth steered him straight to some key areas of his testimony, especially the curiously voluntary statement about not having seen a knife in Marty's hand.

Clearly something was up. The defense had stressed in its opening remarks that Dzvirko would make this statement. He had indeed blurted it out unbidden when Donnelly was leading him through his direct testimony. Now in cross-examination he was cheerfully giving it an even more detailed rendition.

Donnelly, at his table, was fighting to keep himself under control, but one hand reached over, picked up a sheet of blank lined notepaper and crushed it into a very small, very dense ball.

It was a deal. Some kind of jailhouse scam. Dzvirko had done his deal with the state, had bargained and received murder two and a limit of twenty years—fairly easy treatment, in a death penalty state, for someone who had procured the bat, helped lure the victim to the scene, and then helped sling the still-breathing body into the sluice by the pants cuffs.

But something had happened. Donnelly might never know what. Dzvirko was locked up in the Broward County jail with the rest of them, and even though reasonable steps had been taken to protect him, you just never knew. All of a sudden Dzvirko wanted to help Marty, and it was possible he was doing it to save his own life in jail.

The trouble was, Donnelly had come to court with a bulletproof case, and now this fat punk from the comic book store was trying to put a hole in it.

Was it a hole big enough for Marty Puccio to wriggle through to freedom? Probably not. What was the defense going to say Marty did have in his hand when he stabbed Marty in the gut? A banana?

The danger, however, was that it might be just the sliver of doubt the jury would need in order to justify rolling Marty down from capital murder to murder two.

And that could be bad news. Of the lot of them, Marty was easily the most evil—his perfidy was the easiest to demonstrate to a jury—because Bobby had been his best friend since childhood. Bobby had begged him for forgiveness, for life itself, and Marty's answer had been a ripping stab in the gut. It was Marty's betrayal that had all the newspaper columnists in Florida misquoting Shakespeare.

If Marty could wriggle out of the death penalty, then some or all of the rest of them might prove hard to convict.

Donnelly also had to keep some political wind in his sails. So far his superiors had been supportive and had given him a green light all the way. But if this one walked, then the pressure might build to do deals with the rest of them.

Donnelly didn't know why Dzvirko was trying to roll over on him. He didn't have time to find out. What he had was a fifteen-minute recess. Fortunately for Tim Donnelly, he had a very good memory for paper.

A TV reporter started to come through the gate to ask for an interview, but Donnelly kept his back to him and waved him away. He bolted for the door at the back of the courtroom, trotted down long narrow corridors and up several flights of steel staircase to his office.

He flew into the room. He said nothing to the other people working there, and from the look on his face, they knew better than to speak.

He pulled boxes out from beneath his desk, tore into one, shoved it aside, opened another, yanked out a file, riffed through it quickly, came to a page, paper-clipped it, and then walked briskly back out of the room and down the hall. He hurried down the staircase at a trot and was back in court in time to give the reporter his interview after all.

When Judge Greene reconvened, Dzvirko was back on the stand, and Donnelly had him on redirect. Donnelly walked up to him without looking in his face. He put the file folder down on a railing right in front of Dzvirko. Donnelly hadn't said a word yet, but he was angry, and Dzvirko knew it.

''Mr. Dzvirko, you gave a statement on February seventeenth, 1994, if you would care to refer to it?''

Dzvirko looked off into the middle distance, trying hard to be cool, as if he couldn't be bothered, but it was obvious that he was nervous.

''And then, also, I am going to refer you here to your deposition to Mr. Duckworth on April eighteenth, 1994, page ninety-two, line ten. In both of these statements, you stated under oath that you saw a knife in Mr. Puccio's hand.''

Dzvirko was silent.

''Did you see a knife in his hand, sir?''

Dzvirko dropped his head. He shook his head as if something was wrong. He labored, as if trying to remember.

''Would you care to refer to these statements, Mr. Dzvirko?''

He lifted his head and shrugged insolently. He frowned at Donnelly. He was trying to look browbeaten, as if Donnelly were forcing him to say something against his will.

''Did you see a knife?''

He barely bobbed his head yes.

The judge said, ''Answer the question out loud.''

''Yes,'' he mumbled.

''What?'' Donnelly asked sharply.

''Yes.''

''You did see a knife in Marty Puccio's hand?''

"Yes."

Dzvirko looked to the jurors, hanging his head pitifully. Most of them stared back at him with disgust in their eyes.

Whatever he had been trying to pull, whatever the defense was trying, it hadn't worked. Dzvirko had merely helped cement the impression that they were all lying scum.

THE NEXT ORDER OF BUSINESS WAS A HEARING ON THE HOLLYWOOD Police Department's tape recording of Marty's statement to them after the murder. After a complicated set of arguments, the judge ruled Donnelly could play the tape for the jury.

Then the judge heard arguments in another hearing on evidentiary photographs. Under the direction of Sergeant Robert Haarer of the Broward County Sheriff's Department, the sheriff's crime-scene unit had assembled an array of photographs that were very sharp, very clear, and very unnerving. They included tight-focus full-on shots of Bobby's maggot-infested head, for example. The pictures would have a major effect on the jury. Donnelly wasn't ready to introduce them yet, but he needed to make sure he had permission to bring them in later.

Judge Greene had already ruled in a prior hearing that crime-scene photographs in general would be admitted. He asked Donnelly, however, to come forward and show him specifically which photos he wanted the jury to see.

Donnelly carried an armload of glossy prints up to the bench, and Cazel and Duckworth stepped up behind him. Duckworth motioned for Marty to join them, but again Marty turned his face away, ignoring the invitation.

Duckworth walked back to the defense table and leaned over him. "You need to stand up there with us," he whispered hoarsely. "If you don't, it looks to the jury like you don't care."

Marty stared at him with numb disdain, his eyes flat and reptilian. Then he rose, very slowly, and followed the lawyers to the bench.

The jurors probably had not been able to hear what was said, but few of them missed a syllable of Marty's body language.

A series of police witnesses appeared—their testimony dry and procedural. The jurors were beginning to droop. The flickering of the lights overhead, the dull drumming of the ventilation system, the endless scraping hubbub outside in the hall, and the sheer dullness of the testimony had conspired to lull the jurors into a near trance when Dr. Daniel Selove took the stand.

He was the medical examiner. In his mid-thirties, dressed in a funereal black suit, with his sandy hair parted in the center, Dr. Selove seemed at first the element that would finally push the jury over the edge into full-fledged coma.

But, as Selove spoke in his soft croaky voice, Donnelly began distributing the photographs to the jurors.

"I saw the deceased lying down in a state of decomposition."

Donnelly passed around the picture showing Bobby's body on its face in the muck, bloated and black with rot. The room became even more quiet, the jurors even more still.

"How did you determine that the body was decomposing?"

"The skin on the back had a black, orange-brown color and was very swollen, and there were maggots on the back," he said.

Donnelly passed a close-up of the maggots. The color drained visibly from the faces of several jurors.

Selove described rolling the body over and finding the intestines protruding from the abdomen, for which Donnelly provided a graphic photograph. While Selove spoke, Donnelly passed out pictures of the stab wound to the heart and the two separate slices across the throat.

Selove explained how he had gauged the length of time the body had been lying where he found it according to the life cycle of the maggots. It takes twenty-four hours for the eggs laid by flies to hatch into maggots, he explained, and then there was the fact that some of the individual maggots he found were not brand-new but older. He explained how to tell the difference.

Donnelly distributed pictures to illustrate.

The next step involved the use of a doll made of gray knitted material, like the cloth monkeys given to small children, except that this doll was life-size and looked eerily like a floppy corpse.

Donnelly sat the cloth corpse-doll slouching in a wooden chair facing the jury. A few yards away, Marty's own posture behind the defense table was a spooky echo of the doll's.

Donnelly began asking Selove to tell him again where each of the knife wounds had been inflicted. As Selove ticked them off, Donnelly inserted a long knitting needle in the location of each wound.

One needle in the back of the neck, another in the right shoulder, and another, and another, and another, until there were five needles sticking out of the doll's back.

One needle in the scalp on the right side of the head. A needle in the front right biceps. A needle in the thumb. A needle in the upper left chest, deep to the heart. A needle in the right abdomen, almost all the way through the body. Two needles in the throat.

The gray doll sat lifeless in the chair facing the jury with long steel knitting needles protruding from it like quills. Its soft floppy silence was a hideous scream.

"Dr. Selove," Donnelly said in a flat, matter-of-fact tone, "as I look at the photograph I have in my hand, it seems to me that I see many of what appear to be cuts or wounds on the body and places where there is tissue missing that we haven't accounted for with the needles."

He showed Selove the photo he was referring to and then passed it to the jury.

Marty was at the defense table, just falling into a doze.

"Those," Selove said, "are the result of crab and other animal activity."

The jurors looked up from the picture to Marty just in time to see his heavy lids closing.

Cazel cross-examined. He worked patiently but closely on the medical examiner, worrying through his testimony in detail. Over the course of the next hour, Cazel succeeded in getting Selove to make a number of admissions concerning the angles at which various wounds might have been inflicted, the types of motions that would have been necessary to inflict certain wounds, and the relative positions attacker and victim would have had to occupy. In several areas of minute detail, Cazel forced Selove to agree with him on small points Selove didn't seem to want to concede.

The jurors were paying scant attention. Staring into the middle distance, they looked sapped and hollow-eyed. The floppy doll still sat before them with long shiny aluminum knitting needles stuck into it. Every once in a while, one of the jurors stole a glance at Marty, who was asleep.

Nevertheless, Cazel seemed to be patiently building a structure that might conceivably be put to good use later on. There were, after all, some problems with the state's case—problems a good lawyer might be able to work with.

There was no physical evidence linking Marty with the crime. No fingerprints had been found on weapons or at the scene; there was no fiber or other trace evidence; there was no cellular evidence, from hair, blood, or other body parts.

The state had some very detailed accusations against Marty, but so far the accusations had all come from Swallers and Dzvirko—conspirators who had traded their cooperation for deals. Later in the trial, a couple of jailhouse snitches would testify against him, but it shouldn't be hard to punch holes in the credibility of people like that.

The other defendants could not be compelled to testify against Marty, because doing so would force them, in effect, to testify against themselves in violation their constitutional protections.

The only good, detailed, and believable evidence from an eyewitness describing Marty's role in the murder came from the long blubbering taped confession Derek Kaufman had made to the police in their squad car in front of his stepfather's house the night the body was found.

The transcript of that confession could not be introduced under the rules of evidence in Florida, however, because it was the word of a co-conspirator. A conspirator's statement could be introduced only if the state had been able to independently corroborate everything in it from other sources and evidence. Judge Greene had already ruled in a preliminary hearing that the Kaufman statement was effectively un-corroborated and therefore could not be shown to the jury.

That ruling left Cazel a sliver of maneuvering room. In the absence of physical evidence or a strong eyewitness statement, Cazel might be able to weave together something useful from the tiny concessions Selove had been forced to grant him.

CHAPTER TEN

OVER THE NEXT SEVERAL DAYS, THE JURY HEARD MORE POLICE EVIDENCE, listened to bits and pieces of the story from some of the young people who were not involved in the murder but knew about it, and heard from two of the people to whom Marty had bragged of the killing in jail.

Donnelly played the tape of Marty lying to the Hollywood police. He twice played the part in which Marty said Bobby was "like a brother."

Toward the end of the week, Donnelly put one of Derek Kaufman's boy-hoodlum pals on the stand. Sneering, with rings in his nose and ears, the boy told a long rambling story about how Kaufman had come to him for guns to use in the murder, and how later Marty had called him, looking for Kaufman. In the course of the phone conversation, the boy said, Marty confessed to the main details of the murder, which the boy repeated.

Cazel took him on cross-examination. He got him to list his own most recent offenses, arrests, and other run-ins with the authorities. The boy was sullen and disrespectful. By the time Cazel sat down, the boy had been reduced to a surly hump of unpleasantness, and none of the jurors looked impressed.

Donnelly sat idly drumming a pencil on his table. He was whispering instructions to an assistant when Judge Greene asked if there would be redirect. Donnelly waved no.

Duckworth asked if he could take the witness back for something. The judge looked at Donnelly, and Donnelly shrugged.

Duckworth came forward, creaky in his cowboy boots, and said, "You say Marty Puccio told you this story about how he was in on the murder and so on, but you're the only one he told this to."

The boy shrugged.

Donnelly did not change his posture, leaning toward the assistant, but he put a finger up slowly for her to be quiet.

Duckworth said, "So you don't know of anyone else who would substantiate what you said he told you."

Donnelly went rigid, waiting, counting beats.

"Right," the boy said.

"Nothing more, Your Honor," Duckworth said. He started for his seat but pulled up short, startled when Donnelly leaped to his feet.

"Your Honor," Donnelly said quickly, "the state has opened the door to the Kaufman statement."

Judge Greene began to shake his head dubiously.

Duckworth stalked to the bench, shouting, "Oh, come on! That's ridiculous, Your Honor!"

Cazel, looking very grave, was on his feet and at the bench in seconds, stepping in front of Duckworth to cut him off.

"We need time to brief this, Your Honor."

Judge Greene adjourned the trial for an hour.

Donnelly's keen ear had caught Duckworth in a very serious tactical error. There had been no reason to ask the punk witness anything about what other witnesses might or might not be able to substantiate of the story he claimed Marty had told him on the telephone. How on earth would the punk know?

But when Donnelly came back into court after the hour-long recess, he argued forcefully that Duckworth had used the punk's responses to convey to the jury the impression that there was no other witness who could substantiate the punk's version of things.

"And there is such a witness and such evidence," Donnelly said. "The tape-recorded statement of Kaufman."

Cazel argued that the law was clear: Kaufman's statement was uncorroborated, according to Judge Greene's own ruling, and therefore the jury was not supposed to hear it. He said that Donnelly was using a legal technicality to trick his way around the clear intent of the rules of evidence.

Donnelly said, "The statement will not be presented as probative, Your Honor, but to refute the defense's implication that no such evidence exists."

Greene recessed court for the rest of day and studied the question overnight. The next day he ruled that Donnelly was correct: The defense had opened the door to the Kaufman statement by asking the punk the wrong question.

Donnelly presented the jury with almost all of the Kaufman statement—a detailed and completely damning description of the murder, putting Marty right at the center of events.

At the end of the seventh day of trial, the defense announced it would put Marty on the stand the following day.

Marty didn't have to testify, since he was the accused. Given Marty's sullen attitude at the defense table so far, most of the reporters had assumed the defense would keep him as far away from the witness stand as possible. For one thing, unless Marty had a very good story and a firm grip on his lip, Donnelly would rip him up on cross.

The next morning before the bailiffs opened the doors to the courtroom, a sizable crowd of press had gathered and an even larger contingent of the public, so that when the doors finally were unlocked, people had to rush in and scrabble for seats.

Marty took the stand in a crisp white sweater, brown tie, and brown trousers. His hair had grown out a bit since the first day of trial, but his skin was as stony-white as ever.

Cazel asked him about his family life.

"Well, my parents, we didn't really see too much of each other, sort of a hi-bye basis, that sort of thing," he said. His voice was soft, trying to be nice.

He told about his childhood. "When I was a kid I tagged along with my older brother a lot. He was my hero, him and professional surfers.

"I was eight years old when Kent moved on my block."

"Did you like him?"

"At first he seemed like a nice kid, but then he started bullying other kids in the neighborhood, trying to pick on them. Once I found out he was a bully, I didn't want to hang out with him. But then after, I transferred to South Broward High School, and I didn't know anyone but him there. So, like in ninth grade, I started walking lunch with him.

"In the ninth grade, he started slowly picking on me. In the ninth grade he was a hundred forty-five pounds and I was about ninety pounds. We were both fourteen."

Marty told a long disjointed story about how "Kent" used to get his Doberman to attack him. At least twice a week, he said, he limped home on torn and bloodied ankles. He went from that to an explanation of how the surfers at the beach liked and respected him but did not respect Bobby.

He told of meeting Lisa for the first time on the beach, then of lifting weights with Bobby at the Y.

"Kent was using steroids at that time," Marty said in a very disapproving tone.

"What effect do you think that may have had on him?"

Donnelly looked up, as if thinking about objecting. The judge watched. Donnelly shrugged and went back to taking notes.

Marty said quickly, "It made his normal rages a lot worse. He was hitting me a lot. He fractured my nose once."

Marty turned toward the jury. "I was deathly afraid of him every day," he said.

The male jurors all looked away, avoiding Marty's eyes.

"Did you make any attempt to get away from him?"

"I begged my parents to move. But I was too ashamed to tell them what was happening. I left when I was sixteen for about four months and stayed with my aunt in upstate New York, but I couldn't take being away from my parents, so I moved back.''

When Marty finally reached the moment of the murder itself, the people in the courtroom perked up.

He said that his impression of the agenda for the evening that night had been that they were going to do some drag racing. He had worn his brother's Vietnam trench coat and the bandanna because that was how he often dressed. He had strapped a diving knife to his ankle, he said, because Bobby wanted him to. Bobby knew they were going ''out west'' to race the cars, and there was sometimes dangerous gang activity in that area.

Once at the murder scene, Heather had joined Ali and Bobby down by the water where they were discussing crocodiles. Marty and Lisa were up by the cars, engaged in a serious conversation about Lisa's pregnancy.

All of a sudden, Donny Semenec stabbed Bobby in the back of the neck. At that point, in one of his rages, Bobby turned on Marty.

''He hunched over, looking at me, and he yelled, 'You mother-fucker, I'll kill you.' I was really scared. He was in a rage, like an injured lion.

''He came walking toward me. At that time, I had the knife in the elastic of my pants. I swung at him. I'm sure I probably hit him, like in the hand or the arm or something. Then I started running to my car.

''He came running that way, too, but Derek Kaufman and Donny Semenec were chasing him. I got in my car and hid my head and locked the doors. I had my head down. About two minutes later, Lisa and Derek Dzvirko got in the car, yelling, 'Take off! Take off!' So I did.''

''You had always been afraid of Bobby, of what he might do to you?''

''Oh, yeah. He was, like, if I got caught lying to him, he would beat me up bad. If I ran out of gas or got a flat tire, I would get two black eyes and a swollen nose. Lisa saw him beat me up once because

I had these brownies and there were ants on them. She calls me up on the phone and says, 'Why do you take that?' And I said, well I forgive and forget mostly. But at times I was angry with him and even hated him.''

Cazel asked Marty why he didn't report the murder.

"When we were at the beach, Derek Kaufman told me he was like a gang leader, like a Mafia hit man, like a godfather, and he said, 'If my name gets mentioned, you and your family are dead.' ''

Marty explained everything he did after the murder—calling Fred Kent, the false statement he gave to police, hiding out at the motel, trying to arrange an escape—as the result of his fear of Kaufman. He provided explanations of the witnesses against him from the jail: They were snitches, trying to cut deals for themselves by lying.

Judge Greene broke for lunch. Marty would be Donnelly's witness after the break.

DONNELLY WAS DAPPER IN A GRAY DOUBLE-BREASTED VENTLESS SUIT and black loafers. He stood a few feet away from Marty, staring at him. He spoke in a clear but very controlled voice.

"When the police placed you under oath and taped your statement, you lied, right?''

"Yes, I did.''

"When you're under oath and you're afraid, you lie.''

"If I feel my life's in danger.''

"You're under oath today. And you are charged with first-degree murder today. Are you lying today?''

"No.''

"Did you use steroids?''

"No.''

"How often did he sic his dog on you?''

"It happened a lot.''

"How many times?''

"About one hundred.''

"And you continued to be friends?"

"He would promise me that it would never happen again."

"If you wanted to walk away from Bobby Kent you could have."

"If I had somewhere to go."

"You went to New York once."

"I wanted to be with my family."

"In this hi-bye relationship, right?"

"Right."

"Did Bobby tell you to bring a knife?"

"He said, 'Yeah, bring something on you like a pipe or knives.' "

"Were you prepared to use the knife?"

"No. If trouble had gone down, I would have handed it to him."

"Did you hand the knife to Bobby when he got stabbed in the back of the neck?"

"He started coming at me."

"Did you hand the knife to Bobby when he got stabbed in the back of the neck?"

"No."

"When you got to the scene, you talked to Lisa about her pregnancy?"

"Right."

"You saw Donny Semenec and Heather Swallers walk down to the water with Bob?"

"Right."

"Were you still back by the car?"

"At that time, yeah."

"And then you saw Donny Semenec stab Bobby Kent?"

"Not at that time. We heard joking and laughing, and I walked down there."

"Then you saw Donny Semenec stab Bobby Kent in the neck."

"I saw it out of the corner of my eye."

"How far away were you from Bobby Kent?"

"Three or four feet."

"And he turned to you and said, 'You motherfucker, I'll kill you'?"

"Right."

"Did he threaten Donny Semenec?"

"Donny Semenec had ran."

"Oh, he was gone? Well, when you saw Donny Semenec stabbing Bob, did you try to warn him?"

"Like I said, I saw it out of the corner of my eye."

"When you saw Donny Semenec stabbing Bobby, did you try to warn Bobby?"

"No."

"After Bobby was stabbed, did you say, 'Bobby, are you all right'?"

"No."

"Did you try to help him?"

"No."

"Could you see he was bleeding?"

"No."

"You didn't ask if he was all right?"

"When he was in one of his rages, I usually didn't say anything."

"Did you try to tell Bobby, 'Donny Semenec just stabbed you'?"

"It all happened in a couple seconds."

"At no time did you offer to help Bobby?"

"No."

"You were his brother."

"No, he was not my brother."

"Isn't that what you told the Hollywood Police Department?"

"I said he was like a brother."

"This man who was like a brother, you never offered help to him?"

"No."

Donnelly dragged him in and out of it for half an hour, asking some questions three and four times before Marty would give a simple yes or no answer. As it progressed, Marty grew more angry and sullen. Donnelly kept himself exactly on course. He wasn't being brutal with the witness, but he wasn't trying to be especially nice, either.

"You were so afraid of Mr. Kaufman that you agreed to stick to the alibi?"

"Yes."

"You were so afraid of Mr. Kaufman that you lied under oath?"

"Yes."

"You were so afraid of Mr. Kaufman that you lied to Mr. Kent?"

"Yes."

Donnelly walked to the State's table and switched on the tape recorder. It was already cued to play the part Donnelly wanted the jury to hear for a third time: In a voice dripping with fake sincerity, Marty said, "We saw each other every day. About twelve hours a day. We were brothers."

"You were brothers?" Detective Schubert asked on the tape.

"We were like brothers."

"When did you last see him, Marty?"

"It was after eleven last Wednesday night. Out in front of my house."

Donnelly switched it off.

"So that was a lie?" Donnelly asked.

"Which part?"

"Was the whole thing a lie?"

"Yes."

Donnelly's face flushed red. He switched the tape recorder back on.

Marty's voice said, "I hope to God he's not dead, because I just don't know how I'd live the rest of my life."

Donnelly switched it off. With his back to Marty, he said, "So was that a lie?"

"That was part of trying to make it look real."

Donnelly wheeled on him and shouted, "I asked you if it was a lie!"

"Yes."

Donnelly turned away from him and said to the judge, "I have no further questions."

*　　*　　*

283

AT 10:00 A.M. ON THE EIGHTH DAY OF TRIAL, TIMOTHY DONNELLY rose to present the state's closing argument. In a dark suit, white wing collar, red tie, and oxblood loafers, thick hair barely curling on the back of his neck, he was bent forward slightly as he approached the jury, fists swinging pugnaciously at his sides.

"This case has presented some unique questions regarding responsibility," he said to the jurors. "It's easy to get side-tracked. There has been a lot of media in here, in and out of the room, but you've been the only people who were here throughout.

"There are some weighty questions in this case. How could a friend kill a friend of thirteen years?

"This, however, is not the forum for those issues. Those may be the issues with the media, with community leaders, the psychologists, but that is not our focus."

Donnelly explained the all-important rule of "principals"—the thing Jeff Smith never had succeeded in getting Lisa to understand, the one thing none of them seemed to get. According to the rule of principals, you don't have to strike a single blow yourself in order to be guilty of a murder. You just have to be someone who helped make it happen.

"In a nutshell, it's this," he said: "All for one, and one for all."

He moved away from the jury box a few feet, and every juror's eyes followed him.

"It depends on three things. One, did he know what was going to happen? Two, did he intend to help by participating actively or by sharing in a benefit? And three, did he actually do something?"

Donnelly recited all of the evidence and testimony that had been introduced to prove each of these three points. Then he explained the elements of murder in the first degree: 1) Bobby Kent was dead, 2) Marty Puccio helped kill him, and 3) it was premeditated.

He explained premeditation as what went on in the period between the decision to kill Bobby and the murder itself.

He recited all of Bobby's wounds, each of the needles sticking out of the doll, to show that there had been no element of accident in his death.

When he had finished with those elements, Donnelly seemed to have come to the end of the prepared portion of his closing argument. He put his notes back on his table and took a moment to compose himself.

Still looking down at the table, he said softly, "To be friends or not to be friends?"

He looked up at the jury. Moving toward them, he asked, "Does anybody know, after his testimony yesterday?

"Marty said he wanted to get away from Bobby Kent. But they lifted weights together every day. He followed Bobby to different jobs. On the day Bobby Kent was murdered, they had lunch together.

"When he testifies, there is no expression on his face."

Donnelly moved off to the center of the room, speaking almost to himself, "No remorse. No remorse."

He turned back toward them. "You know, one of the most interesting things I thought in his testimony? He calls him 'Kent.' He never once referred to him as Bobby. It was always 'Kent.'

"He's more concerned with himself. Let me ask you, what is the purpose of all this abuse he tells us he suffered at Bobby's hand? What does that have to do with why Bobby was killed, if he didn't kill Bobby?

"What is the argument here? Is this Battered Buddy Syndrome? He's beating me up all the time, so I have to kill him?

"The first time Mr. Puccio ever fights back, he takes the knife out of his pants and stabs Bobby after Bobby has already just been stabbed by Mr. Semenec. How many times did he say Bobby had sicced his dog on him? A hundred? Beat him up? He never fought back. Not once. Until now. On this one occasion he takes out a knife.

"The defense now shifts. Now it's no longer the Battered Buddy Syndrome. It's self-defense. Bobby was in a rage."

Marty sat at the defense table staring angry daggers at Donnelly, his jaw twitching and fists clenched. Donnelly saw it, turned, and moved toward him, facing him from a few feet away.

"Dr. Selove said the wounds inflicted on Bobby, even the first few, were almost paralyzing. He must have been reeling, barely able to stand. And this man here before you, Marty Puccio, who had been best friends with Bobby Kent since childhood, his first reaction is to pull out a knife and swing at him?''

Cazel looked nervously down the table at Marty, who was obviously only barely able to restrain an impulse to sneer at Donnelly. Duckworth, sitting on the other side of Marty, barely touched his arm with one hand.

''Do you know what I think about what Mr. Puccio has had to say to you here, ladies and gentlemen?''

Staring into Marty's eyes, Donnelly said, ''It's ludicrous. Ludicrous! His defense isn't just flawed or wrong or misleading. It's absolutely completely ludicrous!''

They stared into each other's eyes for a long moment. Then Donnelly straightened, turned to the judge, and said, ''That's all.''

Cazel spoke to the jury for an hour and a half, during which he labored hard to build something out of the few small concessions he had been able to wrest from the medical examiner. His thesis was complex and included Marty's acting out of many different motivations, anger and fear chief among them, but his main message was that Marty might not have been the author of the fatal stab wounds.

He was careful, polite, painstaking. The jury was politely attentive.

Finally it was Donnelly's turn to rebut and close the trial. He complimented Cazel, giving him an A for effort.

''But that's not what this case is about,'' he said.

''By listening to the witnesses in this case, we can tell what this case is really about.''

He walked over, gripped the rail, and leaned close to the jurors.

''Life is cheap!'' he said. ''We've got no-fault insurance. No-fault divorce. And now they want no-fault murder.

''This is what it's about: I don't want to accept responsibility for my actions. I don't care what I did. I don't care if I murdered my best friend. I will not accept any responsibility for it or pay any price for what I have done. That's what this case is about.

''Perhaps Lisa Connelly is the casting director for this loosely knit group. Perhaps Mr. Kaufman is the choreographer. But the evidence is clear that at some point Mr. Puccio joins the conspiracy. He is a participant in it, and he in fact delivered some of the fatal wounds to Bobby Kent.

"Everybody in this case, when the action starts, they all end up in the car, trying to run."

Puccio's whole defense, Donnelly told the jury, was based on fear.

"Fear. Fear of what? Was it fear that drove Mr. Puccio to lie to Bobby Kent's family? To lie to his friends, to the police, to you? Fear of what? Of Mr. Kent and Mr. Kaufman? Or fear that he had just committed an atrocious crime, had just committed an awful murder and dumped the body in the Everglades, and now it's fear of being caught!"

The jurors' eyes were glued to Donnelly.

"Life in this case is cheap," he said again. "Responsibility is lacking. But we—you and I—we have our responsibilities, and I ask you to live up to your responsibilities in this case.

"Mr. Puccio is guilty. He is guilty of murder in the first degree. He is guilty of conspiracy to commit murder in the second degree."

EVENTUALLY, IN THEIR SEPARATE TRIALS, EACH OF THE FIVE WHO pleaded not guilty were found guilty. The trials took almost a year. In each trial, a different set of defense lawyers tried basically the same strategy Cazel and Duckworth had used unsuccessfully in the first trial—blaming others in the group, arguing their client was an innocent bystander. In Lisa Connelly's trial, Kayo Morgan accused everyone in sight of wrongdoing, including the judge and the prosecutor. Morgan put on a display of courtroom pyrotechnics that kept him on the TV news every evening of her trial, but Lisa's jury, like all the rest, voted her down the minute the jury room door closed.

To be sure, in Lisa's case the jury wound up where Jeff Smith had said it would—letting her off on the first-degree death-penalty charge and convicting her instead only of the second-degree murder charge. The jury's finding reflected Smith's long experience of Florida juries—that they may talk tough on crime, but they don't like to impose stiff sentences, especially not the electric chair, on females of their own race or social class.

Smith had believed he could get Lisa off with the conspiracy conviction on a deal with no trial and no crushing legal expenses to break the family. Morgan got her to the same place with a long, loud trial.

But Judge Greene had a little surprise for Morgan at the end of Lisa's trial. Exercising a little-used prerogative of Florida judges, Judge Greene went far beyond the normal sentencing guidelines for second-degree murder conspiracy—normally a maximum of twenty-two years in prison—and sentenced Lisa Connelly to life in prison without possibility of parole.

She had given birth by then to her child, a girl named Megan, whom she gave to her grandfather to raise. She is allowed to see the baby once a month for thirty minutes. She is now taking parenting classes in jail.

Heather Swallers and Derek Dzvirko pleaded guilty to second-degree murder and conspiracy. Heather was sentenced to seven years in prison. Derek, who took too long to say yes when Donnelly asked if he had seen a knife in Marty's hand, drew eleven years—four extra years for taking too long.

Ali Willis was found guilty of second-degree murder and conspiracy and was sentenced to forty years. Donny Semenec was found guilty of second-degree murder and conspiracy and was sentenced to life in prison.

Derek Kaufman was found guilty of first-degree murder and conspiracy to commit second-degree murder and was sentenced to life in prison.

In September 1994, after the jury in Marty's trial had found him guilty of first-degree murder and conspiracy, the jurors voted in the punishment phase of the trial to recommend to Judge Greene that he send Marty to the electric chair.

Judge Greene waited to make his decision on the death penalty until after all of the other trials had concluded.

Late in the summer of 1995, Judge Greene called all of the principals in the Puccio case to court to hear his decision. During the hour and a half it took him to read the reasons for his verdict, Veronica Puccio and a circle of friends stood in the corridor outside the courtroom in a circle, heads bowed, holding hands and praying for Marty's life.

The sentence was death.

AT EACH OF THEIR SENTENCINGS, THE SAME SCENE WAS REPEATED: In the dark hurly burly of the corridor outside Judge Greene's courtroom, in the middle of a crowd of people rushing to and from other trials in other courtrooms, the adult relatives of the defendants gathered and spoke to the small cluster of media representatives covering the Kent case.

In almost every case, they shrieked that the sentences were unfair. "He wasn't the only one," Marty Puccio's grandmother cried.

"She's innocent," one of Lisa Connelly's relatives said. "She made a mistake, that's all."

Ali Willis's stepfather said, "She was a dumb kid who was in the wrong place at the wrong time."

They did not say this:

My child is a murderer. I am sick with shame. When I think of what my child did to another human being, I want to die myself.

No one said that. Not one person.